HOW THE
WEATHER
WORKS

Exploring how wind behaves

Making raindrops form

Using a barometer

Making the most efficient use of sunlight

Using the heat energy of the sun

HOW THE
WEATHER
WORKS

Michael Allaby

Experimenting with the Coriolis effect

Testing angular
momentum

Examining clouds

Reader's
Digest

The Reader's Digest Association, Inc.
Pleasantville, New York • Montreal

A READER'S DIGEST BOOK
Designed and edited by
Dorling Kindersley Limited, London

Project Editor Stephanie Jackson
Senior Art Editors Spencer Holbrook,
Amanda Lunn
Editor Nicholas Turpin
Designers Sam Grimmer,
Elaine Monaghan, Helen Diplock
DTP Designer Simon Albrow
Production Meryl Silbert, Catherine Toque
Managing Editor Josephine Buchanan
Managing Art Editor Lynne Brown

Consultants Jack Challoner,
Brian Cosgrove, Philip Eden

The acknowledgments and credits
that appear on page 192 are hereby made a
part of this copyright page.

Library of Congress Cataloging in Publication Data

Allaby, Michael.
    How the weather works / Michael Allaby.
        p.   cm.
    Includes index.
    ISBN 0-7621-0234-9
    1. Weather—Popular works. 2. Meteorology—Popular works.
    3. Weather—Experiments—Popular works. I. Title.
    QC981.2.A45 1995
    551.5'078—dc20   94-43156

Printed in Singapore
5 4 3 2 1   03 02 01 00 99

Contents

The Science of Weather

Weather Basics

Climates

The Weather Machine

Cloud Atlas

Weather Forecasting

INTRODUCTION

A HUGE BLACK CLOUD appears on the horizon, moving slowly toward you. You can hear distant rumbles of thunder, then you see the lightning fork between the cloud and the ground. A thunderstorm is approaching. What causes thunderstorms? How do clouds form, and why do only some kinds of clouds bring rain? What are lightning and thunder? Why does the wind blow? In this book you will find answers to these questions and many more. You will read about how air and water produce weather, why weather is different in different places, and how to build your own weather station and make your own forecasts.

People have always been interested in the weather. Farmers need to know when they should sow and harvest their crops, sailors whether it is safe to go to sea. For most of history the reasons for clouds, rain, wind, and storms remained a mystery—mainly because people could see only what was happening locally. They had no way of gathering information about weather conditions over a wide area, so they could not detect general patterns.

Our understanding of the weather has grown from observations of what happens, attempts to explain why it happens, and experiments to test

the explanations. This is how scientists learn about the world, and *How the Weather Works* will help you learn in the same way. The book invites you to make your own observations of the weather where you live. It explains how the weather is formed and shows you, in simple steps, how to demonstrate these processes for yourself. The global "weather machine" is extremely large, but different parts of it can easily be examined on a small scale. The experiments in this book are designed for all the family and can be performed in or near your own home, using ordinary household items or equipment made from them. The few instruments you need but cannot make can be bought easily and cheaply.

Today, satellites transmit data that enables scientists to watch weather systems develop and move. Weather forecasters also rely on detailed measurements made at weather stations all over the world. These forecasts can help save lives by providing advance warning of dangerous conditions, allowing people to prepare for storms, floods, hurricanes, and tornadoes. Your home weather station could join this network. Then you can help professional forecasters and the many people who depend on knowing how the weather works.

The home laboratory

YOU CAN LEARN A LOT about the weather with your senses, but you can discover even more by carrying out some of the experiments in this book. Keep a small collection of everyday items at hand to use as "ingredients"—but always be sure to ask before using anything from around the house. Most of the experiments can be carried out on a table, a windowsill, or even outdoors, and if you do not have the exact ingredients listed, chances are that you can improvise with something similar. On these pages you can see some of the more common ingredients you will come across in this book.

Mixers and measurers

In any scientific field, it is vital that all measurements are accurate. Most scientists use the International System (SI) for measures, with meters for length, kilograms for mass, and seconds for time. The book uses both English and SI measurements (often rounded for easy use).

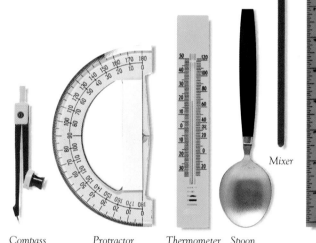

Compass   Protractor   Thermometer   Spoon   Ruler

Mixer

Electrical items

Always be very careful when you are using anything electrical in an experiment, and ask an adult to give you a hand. If you are required to use two electrical items in one experiment—two desk lamps, for instance—be sure that they are exactly the same (including the strength of the light bulbs).

Equipment

You can almost guarantee that a pen, pencil, or scissors will be needed for just about every experiment that you will do. Be particularly careful when you are using scissors, and ask an adult to help with any tricky cutting jobs. There are many other types of equipment that might come in handy for this book, such as a hole punch, felt-tip pens, ballpoint pens, and a white pencil or crayon.

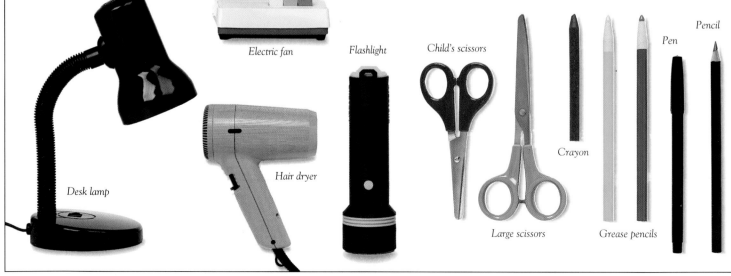

Electric fan

Flashlight

Child's scissors

Pencil

Pen

Crayon

Desk lamp

Hair dryer

Large scissors

Grease pencils

Materials

Many experiments in this book require some basic materials—paper, card, tape, or modeling clay, for example. If you cannot find any of these items around the house, all are readily available and cheap to buy. Be careful when you are use push-pins and toothpicks—they can be quite sharp.

Push-pins

Rubber bands

Wooden sticks

Tape

String   Glue   Modeling clay   Toothpicks   Drinking straws

Aluminum foil   Plastic wrap   Notepaper   Colored papers   Poster board and cardboard

Useful items

All sorts of items from around the house may prove handy for your laboratory. Mirrors, magnifying glasses, balls, and candles can all be used in one way or another. Ice trays will be needed for making ice. Be careful about using food containers; always ask permission first.

Tennis ball

Food coloring

Large and small balloons

Ping-pong ball

Paintbrush

Dishwashing gloves

Candles

Saucer

Matches   Dropper   Magnifying glass

Small notepad

Mirror

Plastic bottle

Baking dish

Plastic container

Large glass jar

Glass beaker

Pitcher

Jar with lid

Plant mister

Glass bowl

Observing the weather

WHEN YOU DECIDE that today will be fine or it will rain, or when you shiver and think it feels cold enough for snow, you are observing present weather conditions and predicting how they will develop. We know from experience the difference between a sky that brings fine weather or one that brings rain, and how cold it feels just before snow starts to fall. Everything we know about the weather is based on observations people have made for thousands of years. Scientists and meteorologists must find explanations, but the observations come first. The more detailed your observations, the more useful they will be; try keeping a weather diary. If the day is warm, it helps to know exactly how warm so you can compare one warm day with another. If it is windy, it helps to know how strongly the wind is blowing and its direction.

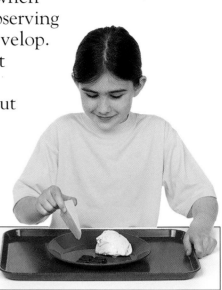

How fast do the leaves blow away— and where do they go?

How hot is it?

You can tell how warm the weather is by watching how it affects certain foods. Choose a hot, sunny day. Place three types of food on a tray to act as a heat gauge: something hard (chocolate), something firm (cheese), and something soft (ice cream). Which one melts first? Is it hot enough to melt all three?

The wind-chill factor

When the air is still, the exposed parts of your body—such as your face—are covered by a very thin layer of air warmed by body heat. If it is windy, that layer can be blown away, and your body must produce more heat to replace it. If the wind removes the warm air faster than it can be replaced, you will feel cold. This effect is called wind chill. The actual air temperature does not change, but wind chill makes it feel colder. The table below tells you how much cooler it will feel on a cold day. First, find out the air temperature and wind speed (pp.58–59). Then find the temperature along the top line, move your finger down the column until it is opposite the wind speed in the left- or right-hand column of the chart, and read out the temperature you will feel due to wind chill.

Where does the wind blow?
You can tell the direction and the approximate strength of the wind very easily. Gather a small handful of grass clippings or small leaves, and find an open space well clear of trees, shrubs, and buildings. Throw the leaves or clippings as high as you can into the air. Which way do they fly? The answer to this question will tell you the direction of the wind. How far did the leaves or clippings travel before falling to the ground? Were they carried away altogether so that they disappeared? The stronger the wind, the farther it will carry them.

WIND SPEED	°F (°C)	°F (°C)	°F (°C)	°F (°C)	°F (°C)	
Calm	35 (2)	30 (–1)	25 (–4)	20 (–6)	15 (–9)	
5 mph (8 km/h)	32 (0)	27 (–3)	22 (–6)	16 (–9)	11 (–12)	
10 mph (16 km/h)	22 (–5)	16 (–9)	10 (–12)	3 (–16)	–3 (–19)	
15 mph (24 km/h)	16 (–9)	9 (–13)	2 (–17)	–5 (–21)	–11 (–24)	
20 mph (32 km/h)	12 (–11)	4 (–16)	–3 (–19)	–10 (–23)	–17 (–27)	
25 mph (40 km/h)	8 (–13)	1 (–17)	–7 (–22)	–15 (–26)	–22 (–30)	
30 mph (48 km/h	6 (–14)	–2 (–19)	–10 (–23)	–18 (–28)	–25 (–32)	
35 mph (56 km/h)	4 (–15)	–4 (–20)	–12 (–24)	–20 (–29)	–27 (–33)	
40 mph (64 km/h)	3 (–16)	–5 (–21)	–13 (–25)	–21 (–30)	–29 (–34)	
45 mph (72 km/h)	2 (–17)	–6 (–21)	–14 (–26)	–22 (–30)	–30 (–35)	

Observing the weather safely

Most of the time, the weather is perfectly safe for you to observe, as long as you dress appropriately. However, sometimes weather conditions can be dangerous. The chart below can help you know what to do.

WEATHER	WHAT TO DO
Sunshine	Never look at the sun, and use suncream on sunny days.
Rain	Use an umbrella, or wear a raincoat—you will lose heat if you get wet.
Cold	Dress warmly, and wear a hat—most of your body heat is lost through your head.
Hail	Wear a hat—large hailstones can cause bruises.
Thunderstorm	Stay indoors, but if you are outside keep away from trees and tall objects.
Snowstorm	Swirling snow and poor visibility make you lose orientation. Stay indoors.
Tornado	Stay indoors on the lowest floor of the building, and keep away from windows. Stay with adults.
Hurricane	Follow the instructions for tornadoes.

Weather watch

It helps to be able to see how weather is behaving in the distance, so that you can work out how it will affect your local weather. You can use binoculars to examine distant landmarks. If you know the distance to the farthest thing you can see clearly, then you know the visibility. The movement of smoke from chimneys indicates the wind direction. Binoculars will also help you study clouds and their formation. Remember never to use your binoculars to look at the sun.

Your binoculars do not need to be very powerful to show visiblity or cloud detail

Wind cheater
Sometimes you need protection from the wind. On cold days, check the wind-chill chart below and dress accordingly. On warmer days, a jacket and scarf should keep you warm, and lotion and lip salve will prevent chapped skin and lips.

Gloves will keep your hands warm

Snowfighter
Keep warm and dry when you are out in the snow. If the snowfall becomes very heavy and windswept — like a blizzard—come inside as soon as you can.

Wrap up in a scarf to keep the wind out

°F (°C)	°F (°C)	°F (°C)	°F (°C)	°F (°C)	°F (°C)	WIND SPEED
10 (−12)	5 (−15)	0 (−18)	−5 (−21)	−10 (−23)	−15 (−26)	Calm
6 (−14)	0 (−18)	−5 (−21)	−10 (−23)	−15 (−26)	−21 (−29)	5 mph (8 km/h)
−9 (−23)	−15 (−26)	−22 (−30)	−27 (−33)	−34 (−37)	−40 (−40)	10 mph (16 km/h)
−18 (−28)	−25 (−32)	−31 (−35)	−38 (−39)	−45 (−43)	−51 (−46)	15 mph (24 km/h)
−24 (−31)	−31 (−35)	−39 (−39)	−46 (−43)	−53 (−47)	−60 (−51)	20 mph (32 km/h)
−29 (−34)	−36 (−38)	−44 (−42)	−51 (−46)	−59 (−51)	−66 (−54)	25 mph (40 km/h)
−33 (−36)	−41 (−41)	−49 (−45)	−56 (−49)	−64 (−53)	−71 (−57)	30 mph (48 km/h)
−35 (−37)	−43 (−42)	−52 (−47)	−58 (−50)	−67 (−55)	−74 (−59)	35 mph (56 km/h)
−37 (−38)	−45 (−43)	−53 (−47)	−60 (−51)	−69 (−56)	−76 (−60)	40 mph (64 km/h)
−38 (−39)	−46 (−43)	−54 (−48)	−62 (−52)	−70 (−57)	−78 (−61)	45 mph (72 km/h)

The SCIENCE of WEATHER

Fire and water
*The sun (left) is the cause of all the earth's weather,
it providing the energy that makes clouds form and
winds blow. Another vital element of weather is
water (above). The water on this leaf will eventually
evaporate and return to the air.*

To UNDERSTAND HOW THE
weather works and why
weather happens, it is
important to find out the
answers to some basic
questions: how does sunlight
pass through the earth's
atmosphere? How do ice and
snow pass from solid to liquid
to gas? Where does air
pressure come from? And
how is all this affected by the
earth's place in space?

LEARNING BASIC PRINCIPLES

WEATHER MAY SEEM SIMPLE, but many questions have to be answered before we can even begin to learn how it works. What is air? Where does the water come from when it rains in places far from the sea? Why does it sometimes feel warmer when it is snowing and colder when it thaws? Questions keep tumbling out, and to understand the weather, all of them must be answered.

Scientists have been seeking these answers for thousands of years, and there are still questions. There is much to be learned, because very often the answer to one question raises another. Long ago, people believed that air can turn into water, water into earth, and earth into stone. Air, earth, water, and fire were the four "elements" from which everything was thought to be made. This is what the Greek philosopher Aristotle believed. He lived from about 384 BC to 322 BC, and the idea was already several centuries old when he wrote about it.

Early discoveries

It was not until about 1600 that air was found to contain gases. Carbon dioxide was the first to be discovered, by the Belgian scientist Jan Baptista van Helmont (1577–1644). He called it gas sylvestre, and in 1754 the Scottish chemist Joseph Black (1728–99) showed that this gas forms part of ordinary air. It was not until 1894, nearly 300 years after van Helmont's discovery, that argon was identified by Lord Rayleigh (1842–1919) and Sir William Ramsay (1852–1916). A year later, Ramsay discovered helium, another ingredient of air, and in 1898 he discovered neon, krypton, and xenon.

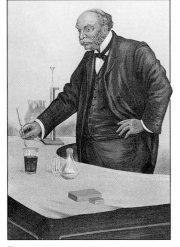

Prize winner
Lord Rayleigh (1842–1919) discovered how air molecules scatter light rays, making the sky blue. He was awarded a Nobel Prize.

Hail storm
Hailstones are formed as water droplets inside a cloud change from a liquid to a solid state. Hailstorms like this one can cause serious damage.

If air is made from substances, it must be a substance itself. In that case it should weigh something. Galileo (1564–1642) was the first person to weigh air. He also showed that air resists bodies moving through it—less strongly than water resists the movement of boats and swimmers, but in the same way.

Air and water

Air is a substance, a mixture of gases, and you can weigh it. Once scientists realized this they were able to think of the air in a new way. Suppose the atmosphere is like a very deep ocean and we live on the ocean floor. The weight of all the air must press down on the surface, and on us, but if you climb upwards the pressure should grow less because there is less air above you. A French scientist, Blaise Pascal (1623–62) had this idea, and in 1648 a friend tested it for him by climbing a mountain and measuring the air pressure at the top (pp.24–25). Most of the mysteries of the air had been solved, but still it was not possible to explain why we have weather. To do that, scientists needed to learn more about water, another of the ancient "elements." Everyone knew, of course, that water freezes when it is cold and boils when it is hot, but Joseph Black, after his work with carbon dioxide, discovered something more interesting. In about 1760 he found that when ice is warmed to melting its temperature remains the same. This is because ice absorbs a quantity of heat to provide the energy for melting; it releases the same amount of energy when it freezes. This much was known about the properties of water, but it was not until 1800 that an English chemist, William Nicholson (1753–1815) passed an electric current through water, collected the gases produced by this procedure, and

What makes air?
Sir William Ramsay (1852–1916) was the Scottish chemist who discovered four of the rare gases present in air.

showed that water is simply made
of hydrogen and oxygen.

Heat and the sun

The discovery of latent heat—the
potential heat that a substance
can absorb—helped reveal the
difference between temperature
and the amount of heat. The
difference is important, because
the amount of heat required
to produce a given rise in
temperature varies from
substance to substance.
In particular, it takes
more heat to raise
the temperature of
water than to raise
that of soil and
rocks, which means
that air over the
ocean is often
at a different
temperature from
air over land.

A final set
of questions
remained to be
answered before
scientists could begin to describe
the way the weather works: They
needed to know more about the
warmth we receive from the sun.
A first step came with the

Water

The moon | *The sun*

The earth

The earth in space
*This machine, called an orrery,
demonstrates how the moon
orbits the earth and the earth
orbits the sun.*

realization that the earth circles
the sun, rather than being circled
by it. It was not a new idea, but it
was revived and stated clearly by
the Polish astronomer Nicolaus
Copernicus (1473–1543)
in a book published
shortly before his
death. In two
books published
in 1609 and 1619,
the German
astronomer
Johann Kepler
(1571–1630)
moved on to
describe the path
planets follow
as they move
around the sun.
The earth's own
axis is slightly
offset in relation to the sun and
the axis itself turns slowly
about its own center. This
movement was discovered long
ago by the Greek astronomer

Liquid   *Gas*

Hipparchus (c. 190–120 BC),
but it remained a mystery to
scientists until Sir Isaac Newton
(1642–1727) explained why
it happened.

Basic science

Little by little scientists were
beginning to draw a clear picture
of the earth in space, of the
energy it receives from the sun,
and of the way the earth's orbit
and rotation cause the amount
of energy reaching the surface
to vary from place to place and
from season to season.

The unfolding story
provided the basis for
much of our weather
science. It tells of what
happens when gases are
heated or cooled, of the
properties of water,
of the earth as one of
the planets moving
around the sun, and
of the sun itself.

Today we know a myriad
of scientific facts about the
weather. The sun warms the
surface of the earth. Air touches
the surface of land and water
and is warmed by contact with
them. Warm air rises (cooling
as it ascends), and draws in cool
air to replace it near the surface.
This flowing of air is what we
feel as wind.

Water evaporates in the
warmer air and condenses in the
cooler air, forming clouds, which
are made from tiny droplets of
water. When the droplets are
large enough they fall as rain,
hail, or snow. The warmth of the
sun provides the energy that sets
this entire process in motion.

The states of water
*Water can exist as a
gas, liquid, and solid at
ordinary temperatures.
Gas molecules move
freely, liquid molecules
slide past one another,
and ice molecules lock
into open crystals.*

Simple thermometer
*A thermometer is a
narrow, calibrated tube
containing a liquid that
expands and contracts
as its temperature
increases and
decreases.*

Weather in our atmosphere
*All of the weather on earth takes place in the atmosphere—a thin veil covering the
earth and protecting it from the harsh conditions of space. The clouds in this satellite
photograph are over the Amazon region, where warm, moist air produces a wet
climate. Note how thin the atmosphere looks at the edge of the picture.*

The earth in space

THE EARTH SPINS on its own axis, completing one revolution every 24 hours. Day and night move around the earth as it turns. Our planet also circles the sun, taking a year to complete one orbit. The reason we have seasons is that the earth's axis is tilted. This means that as the planet orbits the sun, first one hemisphere receives more light and then the other, and the sun appears to move north and south during the year. In the hemisphere receiving more light and heat from the sun it is summer, and it is winter in the hemisphere receiving less. On certain days the sun is directly overhead at a given place. When this occurs at the equator it is called an equinox (the equinoxes are on approximately March 21 and September 21). When this happens at the Tropic of Cancer on June 21 and at the Tropic of Capricorn on December 21, it is called a solstice.

■ DISCOVERY ■
Johannes Kepler

The German astronomer Johannes Kepler (1571–1630) worked as an assistant to the Danish astronomer Tycho Brahe. Brahe asked him to calculate the orbit of Mars. Kepler found it impossible to believe that the orbit of Mars was circular, which he and Brahe had assumed. He concluded that all the planets follow elliptical, or oval-shaped, orbits around the sun. This is one of the laws of planetary motion.

EXPERIMENT
Spreading the Sun's light

The earth receives the same amount of heat and light from the sun on every day of the year, but that heat and light are not distributed evenly. When the sun is high in the sky where you live, it shines more intensely on the surface below, making the weather warmer. When the sun is low in the sky where you live, the same amount of solar radiation, called insolation, is spread over a larger area, so it feels cooler. You can study how this works by intensifying a beam of light from a flashlight (representing the sun) on a curved paper surface (representing the earth).

YOU WILL NEED
● *flashlight* ● *black and yellow poster board* ● *blue paper* ● *white pencil* ● *tape* ● *scissors* ● *ruler*

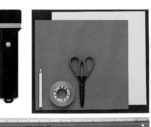

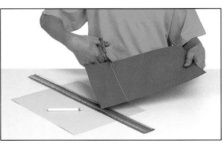

1 CUT an 8 x 8 in (20 x 20 cm) piece of yellow poster board, and then cut an 8 x 8 in (20 x 20 cm) piece of blue paper.

2 DRAW THREE LINES 2 in (5 cm) apart on the paper. Label them 45°, equator, and 45°. Label the edges 90°.

3 TAPE OPPOSITE EDGES of the paper to the poster board, 1 in (2 cm) from the edges, so the paper forms an arch.

4 CUT THE BLACK POSTER BOARD to 9½ x 9½ in (24 x 24 cm). Draw a 2-in (5-cm) square in its center, and cut it out.

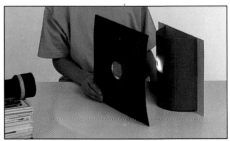

5 HOLD THE "EARTH" and black board parallel. Shine the "sun" on each line by sliding the "earth." Which is brightest?

EXPERIMENT
Day and night

The number of daylight hours is the same all year at the equator. In other places the length of the day changes because of the tilt in the earth's axis. The difference increases with distance from the equator. Day and night are of equal length during equinoxes. Daylight hours reach a maximum at the summer solstice and a minimum at the winter solstice. On certain days of the year in the Arctic and Antarctic, the sun does not sink below the horizon or rise above it. You can show why this happens.

You Will Need
● ping-pong ball ● modeling clay ● felt-tip pen ● wooden stick ● desk lamp

The earth's tilted axis and elliptical orbit

Because the earth's axis is tilted, first one hemisphere then the other points toward the sun, producing our seasons. At the poles, midsummer daylight lasts 24 hours, but at midwinter the sun does not rise at all. The earth's orbit is an oval shape called an ellipse. The sun is 91.4 million miles (146.2 million km) away on 1 January and 94.4 million miles (151 million km) away on 1 July.

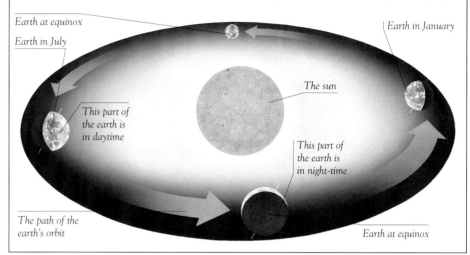

Earth at equinox

Earth in July

Earth in January

The sun

This part of the earth is in daytime

This part of the earth is in night-time

The path of the earth's orbit

Earth at equinox

1 Ask an adult to push the stick through the ball. Mark a line of dots down the ball to show different places.

2 Now place the stick and ball (the "earth") upright in modeling clay. Tilt the stick so it stands at an angle.

3 Turn on the lamp (the "sun"),and darken the room. Point the angled stick toward the "sun." Rotate the axis evenly to bring the dots in and out of shadow.

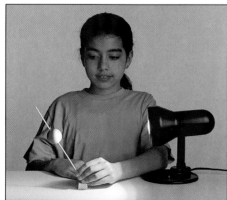

4 Now turn the "earth" so that the axis points away from the "sun." Watch the poles. What is the difference?

5 Finally, turn the "earth" so that the axis points are at right angles to the "sun." This is what happens at the equinoxes.

The atmosphere

WEATHER OCCURS IN the lowest part of the atmosphere, called the troposphere. In this region the air contains water vapor and clouds, and the temperature decreases with height. At about 4 miles (6 km) over the poles and 11 miles (17 km) over the Equator, the tropopause is the boundary between the troposphere and the stratosphere, which extends to the stratopause at about 31 miles (50 km). Stratospheric air is very dry. Air temperature gradually decreases with height but stops falling in the lower stratosphere.

■ Structure of the atmosphere

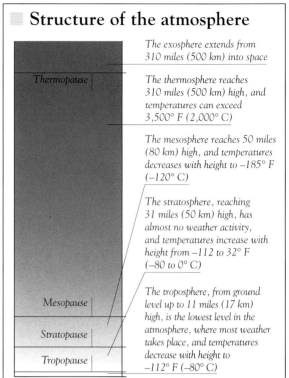

The exosphere extends from 310 miles (500 km) into space

Thermopause

The thermosphere reaches 310 miles (500 km) high, and temperatures can exceed 3,500° F (2,000° C)

The mesosphere reaches 50 miles (80 km) high, and temperatures decreases with height to –185° F (–120° C)

The stratosphere, reaching 31 miles (50 km) high, has almost no weather activity, and temperatures increase with height from –112 to 32° F (–80 to 0° C)

Mesopause

Stratopause

Tropopause

The troposphere, from ground level up to 11 miles (17 km) high, is the lowest level in the atmosphere, where most weather takes place, and temperatures decrease with height to –112° F (–80° C)

Stratospheric conditions influence the weather only by affecting the troposphere. The proportions of gases in the troposphere and lower stratosphere are similar. These change in the upper layers.

EXPERIMENT
Atmospheric ingredients

Below 15 miles (25 km) dry air consists of 78.08 percent nitrogen and 20.94 percent oxygen, with traces of other gases. You cannot see or smell either, and nitrogen does not react readily with other substances, but oxygen is very reactive and you can prove its presence by making it react chemically. When anything containing carbon burns, the carbon reacts with oxygen to form carbon dioxide, which will replace some of the oxygen. In a sealed container, burning will cease when the air contains insufficient oxygen to sustain it. Carbon dioxide is soluble in water, and if there is water in the container its volume will increase as carbon dioxide dissolves.

YOU WILL NEED
● glass dish ● tall glass
● modeling clay
● matches ● small
candle ● water

Adult supervision
is advised for this
experiment

1 PLACE A BLOB of modeling clay in the dish, and stand the candle upright in the modeling clay.

2 HALF-FILL the dish with water. The water will react with the carbon dioxide. Keep the candle's wick dry.

3 NOW ASK AN ADULT to light the candle for you. The flame will provide the carbon. Let the candle burn for a few seconds so that it will not go out too easily.

4 ASK THE ADULT TO PLACE the tall glass over the candle, letting it rest on the bottom of the dish. The candle will quickly be extinguished. What happens to the water level?

EXPERIMENT
Air cooling and warming

Air can be compressed, or squashed, and compression makes its temperature rise. If the pressure on it is released, the air expands and cools as it does so. This is called adiabatic warming and cooling, and it strongly affects the weather. These adiabatic processes occur in the atmosphere whenever air is forced to travel upward or downward—for example, crossing a mountain range.

YOU WILL NEED
● *thermometer*
● *bicycle pump*
● *bicycle wheel and tire*

1 MEASURE THE TEMPERATURE of the air surrounding the wheel. Keep this figure in your mind during Step 2.

2 HOLD THE THERMOMETER near the valve, and open the valve. Compare the temperature to the last reading.

3 INFLATE THE TIRE with the pump. Pump until the tire is as firm as it was before the valve was opened.

4 NOW FEEL THE VALVE. It should feel warm. This is because the compressed air has passed through it.

EXPERIMENT
Air expansion

As a bubble of air rises, the distance from the bubble to the top of the atmosphere becomes shorter, so the weight of air pressing on it is less and the air expands. You can see rising air expand if the bubble is surrounded by a liquid through which it rises fairly slowly. As the bubble rises, the pressure decreases and the bubble expands. Air rising in the atmosphere expands in this way.

YOU WILL NEED
● *tape* ● *3-ft (1-m) plastic tube* ● *tall jar*
● *cooking oil*

2 BLOW GENTLY INTO the other end of the tube. What happens to the size of the air bubbles inside the jar?

1 FILL THE JAR almost to the top with oil. Feed the tube into the jar to about ¼ in (5 mm) from the bottom. Fix the tube to the rim of the jar with tape.

Light and weather

LIGHT AND RADIANT HEAT are both forms of electromagnetic radiation. They travel as waves and differ only in wavelength, which is the distance between one wave crest and the next. At its surface, the temperature of the sun is about 10,300° F (5,700° C), and it radiates energy at many wavelengths and in all directions. About 9 percent of the energy we receive from the sun is invisible ultraviolet light, 45 percent is visible light, and 46 percent is long-wave infrared radiation, which we feel as heat. At the top of the atmosphere, the earth receives about 1,627 watts per square yard (1,360 W/m²) of solar energy. This is called the solar constant.

Scattering of light

Light always travels in straight lines, but light cannot be seen until it strikes something that reflects it. Air molecules and bigger particles scatter light, which "bounces" off them. Sometimes dust particles reflect the light, so you see parallel lines of "sunbeams". Outdoors, dusty air scatters light of all wavelengths, making the sky white.

EXPERIMENT
Blue skies and sunsets

Sunlight is made from light in rainbow colors, which combine to look white. Gas molecules in air scatter the blue light, but not the others, making the sky blue. As the sun sets, light passes through a thicker layer of atmosphere with more dust. Now orangey colours are scattered, but not blue. You can see how this works.

YOU WILL NEED
- lamp with 60-W bulb
- whole milk • glass
- pitcher of water • mixer

1 POUR A LITTLE milk into the pitcher of water. Stir the liquid until it is thoroughly mixed. This makes your "atmosphere," with the particles of milk representing dust and gas molecules.

2 DARKEN THE ROOM and shine the lamp at the pitcher. The lamp represents the sun. Look at the atmosphere from the side, as if you were looking at the sky early in the morning or just before sunset. What color is it?

3 LEAVING THE LAMP in position, look at the atmosphere from the opposite side of the pitcher to the light source, as if you were looking up into a clear sky on a sunny day. Can you detect any difference in the color of the atmosphere?

4 NOW FILL the glass with milky water from the pitcher. Repeat Steps 1 and 2 using the liquid in the glass as the "atmosphere." Is the color different this time? Does the difference in the size of the "atmosphere" have any effect?

EXPERIMENT
Reflecting light

When light strikes water from above, the water appears to be very dark because it absorbs 98 percent of the light and heat (and it reflects only 2 percent). At angles of less than 90°, the amount reflected is 6 percent, and when light and heat shine almost horizontally to the water's surface, most of the light is reflected. This alters the way the oceans warm and cool at different latitudes. Demonstrate this with a flashlight and some water.

YOU WILL NEED
- *wide, shallow container*
- *flashlight ● water*

1 PLACE THE CONTAINER on a table, and fill it with water until it is almost full to the brim.

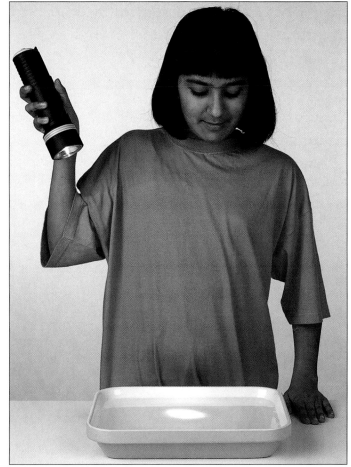

2 TURN OUT THE LIGHTS to darken the room. Turn on the flashlight and shine it at a low angle across the water. How much of the room is lit by reflected light?

3 NOW HOLD THE FLASHLIGHT up high above the water so that its light shines down almost vertically. How much of the room does the flashlight illuminate this time?

EXPERIMENT
Bending light

When light waves pass at a shallow angle from one medium to another with a different density, their speed changes and they bend. This is refraction. Because of it, we see the sunset for about three minutes after the sun has gone below the horizon. Here the different densities of air and water allow you to see what happens when light is refracted.

YOU WILL NEED
- *water ● container*
- *counter or coin*

1 PLACE THE COUNTER or coin on the bottom of the container at the back. Lower your head until you can no longer see the counter. Stay in that position.

2 NOW ASK A FRIEND to fill the container with water. The counter will come back into view because the light from it is bent by the water. In the same way you can see the sun for a while even after it has set.

Water and the weather

WITHOUT WATER there would be almost no weather—no rain, snow, or hail; no clouds or fog; no frost or dew; and no thunderstorms. All that would remain would be warmth, coldness, and wind. Water is a complicated substance because at ordinary temperatures it can exist as a solid, a liquid, and a gas. The solid is called ice, the liquid is called water, and the gas is called water vapor. To change from a solid to a liquid (to melt) or from a liquid to a gas (to evaporate) requires energy. This energy may come in the form of warmth from the sun or from rising temperatures caused by winds blowing from a warmer region. If the wind comes from a colder region, the temperature drops and the water vapor condenses into water droplets. If the temperature falls below 32° F (0° C), the water droplets freeze. Condensation is the opposite of evaporation, and freezing is the opposite of melting. The energy that is exchanged during these changes is called "latent heat." Latent heat is absorbed during the processes of melting and evaporation, and it is released during condensation and freezing.

■ Solid, liquid, and gas

Sometimes you can find all three states of water in the same place. This river is bursting its banks because so much snow and ice have melted into it. The ice is melting to form water, and the water is evaporating; it condenses in the chilled air to form tiny droplets of water, or mist.

EXPERIMENT
Measuring melting ice

When water freezes, its molecules release latent heat, which passes into the air and can be measured with a thermometer. The reverse occurs when ice melts. Exactly the same amount of latent heat that was released when the water was frozen is used to provide energy for the melting, but this time it is more difficult to measure. All of the latent heat is absorbed by the ice until all of the ice has melted. Only when there is no ice left does the temperature rise. You can test this for yourself.

YOU WILL NEED
● *glass*
● *thermometer*
● *cloth* ● *ice cubes*

1 WIPE THE GLASS with a cloth to be sure the glass is completely dry. Now place enough ice cubes inside the glass to make it about ¼ full.

2 WATCH THE GLASS—condensation will appear on the sides. This shows that the frozen water is changing state and absorbing latent heat to do so.

3 NOW PLACE a thermometer in the ice. Check the temperature every 5 minutes. Does it change? Try this again after all the ice has melted.

EXPERIMENT
Freezing warm

The latent heat that is released when water is frozen passes into the air. You can demonstrate this easily by freezing a container of water and comparing the temperature near it to a "control"— where no latent heat is being released.

YOU WILL NEED
● scissors ● tape ● 2 thermometers ● water
● poster board ● plastic container

The three states of water molecules
A water molecule consists of three small parts, called atoms: two atoms of hydrogen and one of oxygen, arranged like a "V." In ice the molecules are locked together in a ball shape with an empty space at the center. Because of this extra space, water expands as it freezes, and ice weighs less than liquid water. As ice melts, the molecules slide past one another and the space disappears. In a liquid the molecules touch but can move freely.

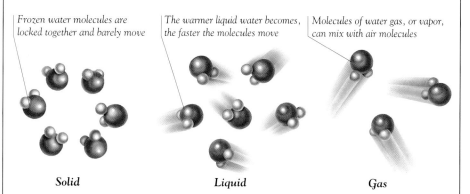

Frozen water molecules are locked together and barely move

The warmer liquid water becomes, the faster the molecules move

Molecules of water gas, or vapor, can mix with air molecules

Solid   **Liquid**   **Gas**

1 CUT TWO POSTER-BOARD strips 1½ in (3 cm) wide, and make them 2 in (5 cm) longer than the thermometers. Tape one thermometer to each strip.

2 FASTEN ONE strip to the inside of the container with a piece of tape. This thermometer will record the latent heat, and the other will be the "control."

3 FILL THE CONTAINER with water to just below the thermometer. Place the container and control far apart in the freezer. Compare readings every 5 minutes.

EXPERIMENT
How much latent heat?

Evaporation and condensation require a large amount of latent heat. If water evaporates directly from the bulb of a thermometer, the latent heat will be taken from the bulb, so you can measure the exact amount.

YOU WILL NEED
● glass of water
● cloth
● rubber band
● thermometer

1 LET THE THERMOMETER stand for a minute or so, and make a note of its temperature. Wrap the cloth around the bulb, using the rubber band to hold it.

2 SOAK THE CLOTH in a glass of cold water. Hold the thermometer by its top, and wave it in the air. Read the temperature—is it higher or lower?

Pressure and the weather

LIKE EVERY SUBSTANCE, air has its own weight. The atmosphere (pp.18–19) is over 370 miles (600 km) thick, and the weight of all that air presses on the earth's surface. The downward force exerted by the weight of the air is called its pressure. Air molecules are squeezed together by the weight of the air above, making the air denser near the bottom of the atmosphere than it is at higher altitudes. Air density and pressure are greatest at sea level. Heat also makes air less dense—and thus less heavy—by moving its molecules. The warmer the air, the lower the air pressure, and the reverse is also true.

EXPERIMENT
Is air heavy?

Adult supervision is advised for this experiment

You can quite easily prove for yourself that air does have weight. Simply take two containers of air, both weighing the same, then remove the air from one of them and see which container is heavier—the one with air or the one without it. Ordinary balloons are the best containers to use.

YOU WILL NEED
- thin pole
- 2 balloons
- scissors
- string
- tape
- pin

Not enough air

The higher up in the atmosphere you go, the less dense the air becomes, and the less oxygen there is to breathe. At high mountain elevations, mountaineers like this one must use special breathing equipment that adds extra oxygen to their air supply.

1 TIE A PIECE OF STRING to the center of the pole. Hold the pole by the string, and adjust the two until the pole is balanced on the string.

2 BLOW UP the balloons and tape one to each end of the pole. Adjust the string as needed to maintain the balance. Put a piece of tape on one balloon.

3 ASK AN ADULT to use a pin to prick a hole through the tape into the balloon. The tape will stop the balloon from popping. As the air slowly escapes, watch the pole and the balloons. Does the pole stay balanced? Which side is heavier?

EXPERIMENT
Measuring air pressure

Air pressure is measured with a barometer. The most common type is called an aneroid barometer. This instrument measures the expansion and contraction of an airless metal box as air pressure changes. You can make a simple aneroid barometer to use at home.

YOU WILL NEED
- ruler ● large balloon ● large jar
- 2 drinking straws ● scissors ● pen
- tape ● poster board ● notepad

■ DISCOVERY ■
Evangelista Torricelli

The Italian Evangelista Torricelli (1608–47) invented the mercury barometer in 1644. He sealed one end of a tube, filled it with mercury, and put the open end in a dish of mercury. Air pressure prevented the mercury flowing out of the tube.

1 CHOOSE A JAR with a very wide opening, and find a very large balloon. Use a pair of scissors to cut off the balloon's neck so that you can stretch the rest over the mouth of the jar. Fasten the balloon to the jar with tape, and make sure there are no leaks.

2 TAPE TWO STRAWS together. Cut a small poster-board triangle, and tape it to one end of the straws. Tape the other end of the straws to the center of the balloon. The barometer is complete.

3 TO MEASURE THE CHANGES in air pressure, hold a ruler upright next to the pointer. Check the position of the pointer every few hours, and write down each measurement. How does the reading vary over a week? Is there any difference between sunny and rainy days?

If the pointer moves up, then pressure is rising, and if the pointer moves down, then pressure is falling

Heat and temperature

YOU CAN FEEL the sun's warmth on your skin. Sunshine also warms rocks and walls that are directly exposed to it, and they feel warm when touched. In hot climates the packed earth, sand, or concrete at midday may be too hot to walk on in bare feet. On the hottest day, though, you can walk barefoot on grass. Heat is what we feel when the energy radiated by the sun strikes an object. This energy is like light, but it cannot be seen. When heat strikes an object, some of that energy is transferred to molecules in the object. When touched, these energized molecules transfer some of their energy to molecules in your skin, so the temperature of your skin rises—this is why the object feels warmer. Warmed objects lose energy. They may radiate it, like a fire; pass it to another object by conduction; or warm a gas or liquid, which carries heat away by convection. All these different sorts of heat help to produce our weather.

■ Heat conduction

The molecules that make up a solid object are touching. If one molecule vibrates faster because it has absorbed energy, its vibration makes its neighboring molecules vibrate —so the energy spreads. This is conduction. Different materials have different structures, and this affects how their molecules pass energy. Materials also vary in the amount of heat they can absorb before their temperature rises. This is called their specific heat capacity. Grass feels cooler than stone because grass contains water, which has a high specific heat capacity.

Specific heat capacities
Put a metal tray, a wooden board, and a piece of plastic on a table. Leave them there for an hour so that they equalize in temperature. Now feel them. Which object feels warmest?

EXPERIMENT
Convection: warming fluids

When a fluid—a gas or a liquid—is warmed, its molecules move apart. The fluid takes up more space, but the number of molecules remains the same, so it becomes less dense than its cooler surroundings. This means it weighs less, so it rises through the fluid surrounding it until it reaches a level where the substance above—such as the air above a liquid—is less dense than it is. The fluid then cools and sinks. You can demonstrate convection with hot and cold water.

YOU WILL NEED
● *large jar* ● *water*
● *small cup* ● *food coloring* ● *rubber band*
● *plastic wrap*
● *stick*

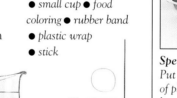

1 FILL A CUP with colored hot water. Cover it with plastic wrap, secured with a rubber band. Put the cup in the jar.

2 NOW FILL THE JAR with cold water so that the water goes over the level of the cup and nearly to the top of the jar.

3 POKE A HOLE in the plastic wrap with the stick, and watch the warm colored water rise. What happens next?

EXPERIMENT
Making air expand

When air is warmed, its molecules move faster and press harder against whatever surrounds them. If the increased pressure is enough to push the surrounding material aside, the air expands to occupy a greater volume. This can be seen using warm water and a cold glass covered in plastic wrap.

YOU WILL NEED
- water ● plastic glass
- bowl ● plastic wrap

1 PUT A PLASTIC GLASS in the refrigerator for an hour. Take it out, stretch some plastic wrap over it, and then stand it in a bowl.

2 POUR SOME HOT TAP WATER into the base of the bowl. What happens to the plastic wrap? What happens if you put the glass back in the refrigerator?

EXPERIMENT
Radiation

The sun warms the earth's surface, and the warmed surface heats the air in contact with the earth. Heat from the sun reaches us by radiation across space. Radiant heat travels in waves just like those of visible light. Nearly half the radiation we receive from the sun is in these "infrared" wavelengths—so called because they are next in length to those of visible red light. An ordinary lamp also radiates heat, and here you can see how a "planet's" surface can be warmed.

YOU WILL NEED
- lamp ● black poster board ● 2 wooden sticks
- scissors ● tape
- modeling clay

1 CUT TWO 3-in (8-cm) squares of black poster board. Tape each square to the end of a small wooden stick.

2 STAND THE STICKS in modeling clay 1 and 4 in (3 and 10 cm) away from the lamp. Which square feels warmer?

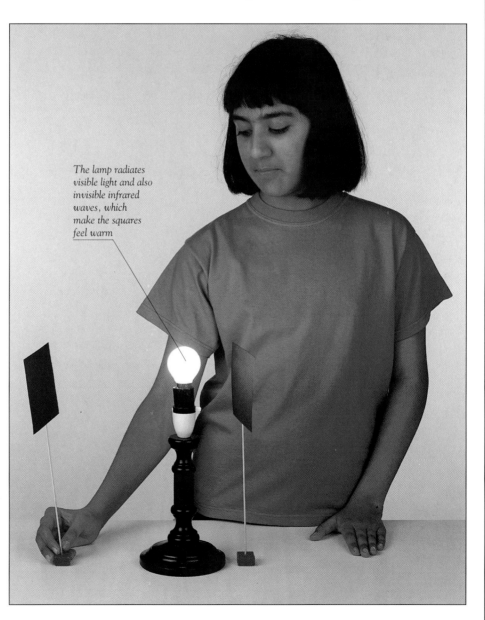

The lamp radiates visible light and also invisible infrared waves, which make the squares feel warm

The albedo effect

WHEN FRESH SNOW covers the ground and the sun is shining brightly, you may be dazzled by the brilliance of the light and glad to rest your eyes on a road from which the snow has been cleared. Fresh snow shines brightly because it reflects about 75 percent of the light falling on it. A road reflects only about 10 percent of the light that falls upon it, so it appears to be darker—it absorbs 90 percent of the light and of the heat. The percentage of the sun's energy that a particular surface reflects is called its albedo. Most clouds have an albedo of about 80 percent, while a field of grass has an albedo of only about 15 percent.

EXPERIMENT
Insulation

In cold weather you put on extra layers of thick clothes for warmth. The clothes trap a layer of air close to your body. Your body warms the air, which makes it less dense. This air cannot escape from among the fibers into the cooler surrounding air, and cold air cannot penetrate to replace it. This effect is called insulation. Dark clothes with a low albedo absorb all the available heat radiation. It is not only our bodies that can be kept warm by a layer of insulating material. We also save energy by insulating our homes and wrapping insulation around hot-water tanks, and we insulate water pipes to prevent them from freezing. You can discover for yourself just how effective insulation can be at preventing heat loss.

YOU WILL NEED
● *water* ● *2 jars with lids* ● *towel*

Comparing temperature
Fill each jar with hot tap water (at the same temperature). Wrap one of the jars in a towel. Place both the jars in the refrigerator for half an hour. Remove the containers and unwrap the towel. Which jar feels warmest?

Celsius and Fahrenheit

The centigrade (°C) temperature scale was devised in about 1742 and is usually credited to the Swedish astronomer Anders Celsius (1701–44). In this system, pure water freezes at 0° and boils 100°.

Gabriel Fahrenheit (1686–1736) was born in what is now Poland. In 1714 he made the first successful mercury thermometer. In his scale, salt water freezes at 0°; pure water freezes at 32° and boils at 212°.

The thermometer

A thermometer is a fine tube from which air has been removed, with alcohol or mercury in a reservoir at the bottom. As the air temperature changes, the liquid expands or contracts in the tube, and you can read the temperature from a scale. Try measuring the temperature in different places inside and outside your home.

Why igloos do not melt

The igloo was invented by the Inuit people and was used as a winter dwelling where no other building materials were obtainable. It is still sometimes used in Canada, Alaska, and Greenland as an overnight shelter. Using snow cut with a long-bladed knife, someone can build an igloo in an hour by fitting snow blocks together to form a dome. A slab of freshwater ice makes a skylight. Inside, lamps burning animal fat provide warmth and light. Because the house is made from snow, with a high albedo, it reflects heat and light. This, along with the very cold temperatures, prevents it from melting.

EXPERIMENT
Comparing albedo

If a surface reflects heat, nothing underneath the surface can be warmed. However, if the surface absorbs heat, anything touching the underside of the surface will become warmer. This is why people wear pale colors in summer and dark colors in winter. You can measure the albedo effect of two surfaces yourself.

You Will Need
- notepad ● white
pencil ● thermometer
- pen ● thick black
and white paper
- scissors ● tape
- sand ● 2 jars

1 STAND the jars top-down, one on the white paper and one on the black paper. Trace the outlines of the jars onto the papers.

2 USE THE SCISSORS to cut out the paper tops so that each fits snugly atop its jar, closing it completely. Set the paper tops to one side.

3 FILL BOTH JARS to the brim with dry sand. Cover one jar with the white paper top and the other with the black top, and seal both jars with tape.

4 STAND BOTH JARS side by side in warm sunshine, and leave them for half an hour. Then measure the air temperature just above each paper top.

5 NOW MEASURE the temperature just below the surface of the sand. Where was the air temperature highest? Which jar has warmer sand?

WEATHER BASICS

Precipitation
An individual snowflake (above) is made of ice crystals. Ice crystals are tiny, but they can join together in elaborate and beautiful patterns. Snow and rain (left) are two of the forms that water in the atmosphere can take.

THE FOUNDATIONS OF OUR weather are light, air, and water. Different quantities of these ingredients give us the basic weather phenomena—sunshine, clouds, rain, wind, fog, snow, and frost. Measuring rainfall, snowfall, air moisture, and wind speed will help you understand why these forms of weather occur. It will also give you an idea of what to expect from the weather in the future.

EVERYDAY WEATHER

LOOK OUT OF THE WINDOW. Is it sunny or cloudy, dry or raining, warm or cold, calm or windy? In other words, what is the weather like today? The "weather" is what is happening in the atmosphere above you right now, but why is it happening? How do clouds form, and why does rain, hail, or snow fall from some clouds but not others? Why is it sometimes windy and sometimes calm?

These questions have always been very important ones. A hail storm or too much heavy rain can ruin farm crops, and when that happens people may go hungry. A sudden storm at sea can sink fishing boats, with loss of life as well as food. Yet too little rain is as bad as too much, for drought also destroys crops and may leave people short of water to drink—thirsty as well as hungry.

The scientific study of the weather is called meteorology, from a Greek word meaning "description of what happens in the air." The first person to write about it was Aristotle, more than two thousand years ago. He believed the best way to find out why things happen is to observe them closely. If one event is always followed by another, then perhaps one causes the other. This was not the only way of thinking about weather, however, nor even the most popular one. In ancient Greece and Rome, for instance, most people believed the weather was caused by the gods, who could be persuaded to change it.

Folk beliefs

All over the world, people used to believe the weather could be controlled, often by convincing the forces producing it to behave themselves better. In North America the Omaha people tried to bring rain to their withering corn by a ritual performed by members of the sacred Buffalo Society, who began by dancing four times around a large pot filled with water. Then one of them took a mouthful of water, squirted it into the air as a spray and upset the pot, spilling the water on the ground. The others drank the water and also squirted some of it into the air to imitate falling rain.

We know now that we cannot control the weather by magic or by appealing to the gods, or even by punishing them. Sometimes, however, rain can be made to fall from a cloud by cooling it with solid carbon dioxide, called dry ice. Clouds can be made to form by "seeding" them with small particles of dry ice, salt, or silver iodide on which water vapor will condense until the clouds form.

Many people who performed weather ceremonies observed the sky carefully and learned to recognize signs of changing weather, so their rituals often appeared to be successful. It was quite likely that rain would fall or cease, because they were about to do so anyway. These people knew a great deal about the weather, but their

Desert drought
The eland lives in semi-arid climates. These died from lack of water in the Kalahari Desert, where annual rainfall can be as little as 5 in (127 mm).

ideas about the way the weather worked gave way to other ideas which explained things in a more clear and logical way.

Scientific methods

At first scientists were concerned mainly with the way gases such as air behave, a topic they could study in their laboratories. In 1660 the British chemist Robert Boyle (1627–91) published his discovery that when the force pressing on air was doubled, the volume of the air was halved. This means that provided the temperature remains constant, air pressure and volume are inversely proportional to one another. This became

Watering the atmosphere
Much water enters the atmosphere via transpiration—whereby plants release water through their leaves.

Thunderclap
Thunder is the sound of air exploding. A paper banger creates a loud bang in the same way.

known in Britain and the United States as Boyle's law (in France it is called Marriotte's law). Then in 1787 the French physicist Jacques Alexandre César Charles (1746–1823) discovered that if pressure remains constant, the volume of a given amount of gas increases as its temperature rises. Boyle's law and Charles's law provided a basis for understanding what happens when air is heated and cooled and when air pressure increases or decreases. This was a very important step in the study of the forces that control the weather.

Scientists do more than watch. They measure things, and to do this they need instruments. The first hygrometer, to measure humidity (the amount of water vapor in the air), is believed to have been made around 1500 by Leonardo da Vinci (1452–1519). The first barometer, to measure air pressure, was made in 1644 by Evangelista Torricelli (1608–47), an assistant to Galileo. Not until 1714 did scientists have a reliable thermometer to measure the temperature of the air. It was invented by the German instrument maker Gabriel Daniel Fahrenheit (1686–1736), who also devised a scale of degrees for recording temperature.

Forecasting

Still it was not possible to forecast weather, because there was no way to gather reports of local conditions from widely scattered places. Weather systems occupy very large areas and it was impossible to build up overall pictures of them until the last century, when telegraph networks were installed to provide almost instant communication across and eventually between continents.

Little by little we have learned that weather can be forecast. The new ideas came from scientists who worked out explanations for what they saw happening in the world around them and then used experiments to test their explanations.

Over many years, as each discovery raised yet more questions, and these were answered in turn, the description of how weather happens grew more complete.

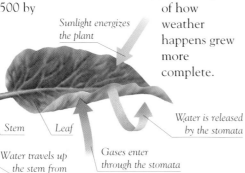

Sunlight energizes the plant

Stem   Leaf

Water travels up the stem from the roots

Gases enter through the stomata

Water is released by the stomata

How transpiration works
Water and gases pass in and out of a leaf through small pores—called stomata—on the underside.

Even so, much of our present more detailed understanding of the weather is surprisingly recent. A team of Norwegian meteorologists, led by Vilhelm Bjerknes (1862–1951), discovered in the years around 1920 how fronts form between masses of air at different temperatures, and how raindrops grow inside clouds. More recently still, satellites orbiting the earth have provided measurements and photographs of weather systems over half the world at a time. Using these observations, modern meteorologists track the development and movement of the clouds and weather systems on a global scale.

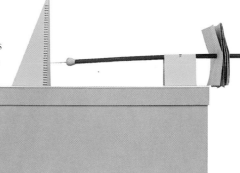

How humid?
When substances absorb water, the water makes them heavier. Humidity testers work on this principle, taking their water from the atmosphere. On dry days the reading is low, and on wet days the pointer gives a high humidity reading.

Daily changes

In this section you will find out how water moves from the sea into the air and back again to the sea, and the important part that plants play in moving it. You will discover how clouds and fog form when moist air is cooled, and what happens inside clouds to make water droplets turn into rain or snow. On clear evenings, water from the air may coat plants and the ground as dew or, if the temperature is low enough, as frost. It is not difficult to work out whether dew or frost is likely to form. Frost is more common in some places than others and you will find out what makes a frost hollow. Frost hollows are one example of the way weather in one place can be quite different from the weather just a short distance away, and there are many more. As you will learn, everyday weather can be more varied and fascinating than you might expect. Changes can happen very quickly, and areas very close to one another can experience very different weather conditions.

A windy day
The Beaufort scale (pp.58–59) measures wind strength. This picture appears to show Force 7 winds.

Sunshine

WEATHER STATIONS use a sunshine recorder to measure the hours of sunshine each day. The most common type of recorder consists of a glass sphere, mounted in the center of a metal bowl to which a strip of cardboard with a scale is attached. When the recorder is set facing the sun, the sphere focuses the sun's rays on the cardboard, making a scorch mark. At the end of the day, scorches on the strip reveal the hours of strong sunshine. A sunny day is frequently a warm one. Direct sunshine warms every surface on which it shines. If you place a thermometer in the shade, it will measure the temperature of the air, but if you place it in direct light, the sun will warm the materials of the thermometer itself—and that is the temperature it will show. This is why you should always measure temperature in the shade.

■ Aztec Sun god

Many people have worshipped the Sun as the sustainer of life. This 16th-century turquoise mosaic mask was made by the Aztecs to represent Quetzalcoatl, the Aztec god of the dawn.

EXPERIMENT
Focusing heat

👥 *Adult supervision is advised for this experiment*

Mirrors and lenses reflect and focus heat just as they do light, so you can use a magnifying lens as a "burning glass" to demonstrate the strength of the heat we receive from the sun. It is best to do this experiment near a window, or outdoors on a sunny day. As you perform this experiment, be careful never to look at the sun, or you may damage your eyes.

YOU WILL NEED
- glass jar ● scissors
- cotton thread ● modeling clay ● magnifying glass
- wooden stick

NEVER look at the Sun because it can damage your eyes

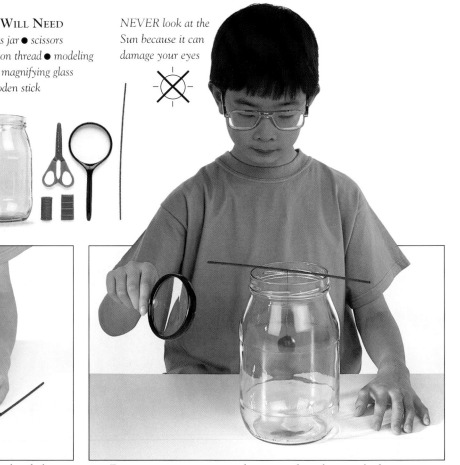

1 CUT A LENGTH of cotton thread, and tie one end tightly around the center of the stick. Attach a blob of modeling clay to the other end of the thread to form a weight.

2 PLACE THE STICK across the jar so that the weight hangs inside. Use the magnifying glass to focus the sun's heat and light on to the thread. What does this energy do to the thread?

EXPERIMENT
Aiding evaporation

Crops grow well in sunny climates, but farmers must water the crops frequently because water evaporates quickly in the sunshine. Even in cool climates the temperature is much higher in direct sunshine than when clouds shade the ground. This means water evaporates faster and the ground is drier. In warm climates water may evaporate before it reaches plant roots, so underground pipes may be used instead. You can measure the difference between the rate of evaporation in direct sunshine and shade.

YOU WILL NEED
- water ● 3 saucers of the same size
- food coloring
- grease pencil

The Odeillo-Font-Romeau solar power station

This solar furnace in the French Pyrenees concentrates the rays of the sun. Its 63 large mirrors turn to follow the sun, reflecting its light and heat on 9,500 smaller mirrors. These in turn focus the rays on the central tower, which houses a furnace, where temperatures can reach up to 6,872° F (3,800° C). This heat is used to vaporize water, producing steam to drive turbines that generate electricity.

1 ADD A FEW drops of food coloring to a pitcher of water and pour equal amounts of water into three saucers.

2 MARK THE WATER level in each saucer. Put one saucer outside in sunlight, one in shade, and one inside.

3 CHECK THE SAUCERS twice a day. As the water evaporates, mark the new levels. See which evaporates most quickly, and make a note of how long it takes to empty each saucer.

EXPERIMENT
Making metal grow

The heat of the sun can make certain materials—such as roads and bridges—expand. You can see this expansion for yourself by leaving a piece of copper outside for a few hours on a sunny day.

YOU WILL NEED
- scissors ● tape
- pen ● ruler
- poster board
- copper pipe

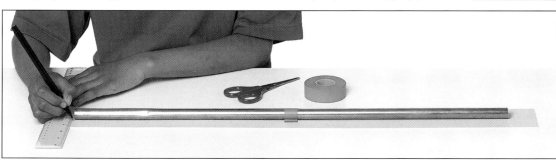

Measuring metal
Place a length of copper pipe on poster board. Tape them together in the middle, and mark the pipe ends on the board. Put them in the sun for a few hours, then check to see if the pipe has grown. Measure the difference.

Optical effects

LIGHT AND HEAT from the sun pass through the atmosphere to the surface of the earth. Although the air is transparent, it does affect the solar rays. As light passes through the air, it encounters air molecules, water droplets, ice crystals, dust, and many other particles. The smallest of these scatter rays, sending them in various directions according to their wavelength. Larger particles may reflect rays or refract them (pp.20–21), and some diffract them—spreading and bending the rays so they interfere with one another. By the time sunlight reaches us, it has usually changed from the pure white light radiated by the sun. We may see a rainbow. Objects may shimmer. If light passes through two layers of still air at different densities, we may see a mirage.

EXPERIMENT
Refracting and reflecting light

As light enters a water droplet it is refracted, or bent. On the far side of the droplet some of the light may be reflected, and as it leaves the droplet it is refracted again. Different wavelengths of light are refracted by different amounts, separating white light into its rainbow colors (pp. 20–21). If the light is reflected once inside the droplet, there may be a rainbow. If light is reflected twice, a secondary rainbow could appear (see opposite). Here you can play with light inside a giant "raindrop" to see how rainbows work.

YOU WILL NEED
- spice powder
- scissors ● mixer
- water ● flashlight
- bowl ● cardboard

1 CUT A THIN SLIT in a piece of cardboard. The slit should be no more than ⅛ in (3 mm) wide, and it should be as tall as the lens of the flashlight.

2 FILL THE BOWL with water, and add a pinch of spice powder. Stir the water so the powder is mixed in thoroughly. The water should look cloudy.

3 DARKEN THE ROOM. Shine the flashlight through the slit, and look into the water from above. Move the light to change the number of reflections.

EXPERIMENT
Using a prism

In 1665 Sir Isaac Newton (1642–1727) passed a narrow beam of light through a prism. The prism separated the light into its rainbow colors, forming a spectrum. You can copy this famous experiment. If you have two prisms, you can also pass the light through both, first separating and then recombining the colors.

YOU WILL NEED
- flashlight ● scissors ● paper ● prism

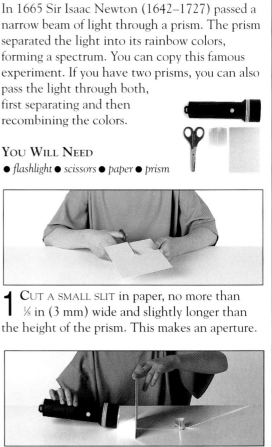

1 CUT A SMALL SLIT in paper, no more than ⅛ in (3 mm) wide and slightly longer than the height of the prism. This makes an aperture.

2 ARRANGE THE FLASHLIGHT, aperture, and prism in a line. Darken the room and shine the flashlight through the slit to form a spectrum.

EXPERIMENT
Shimmering heat

Heat shimmer occurs when a layer of rising hot air refracts the light passing through it. This creates a shimmering effect. You can test this at home. Ask an adult to light a candle and to hold a checked cloth about 6 ft (2 m) from the candle. Look at the cloth from the other side of the candle to see the effects on the pattern of the cloth.

YOU WILL NEED
- saucer ● checked cloth
- candle ● matches
- modeling clay

Adult supervision is advised for this experiment

The heat shimmer will be more pronounced if the flame is moving—blow slightly to make it flicker

Experiment with checks of different sizes, other patterns, or even a newspaper headline

Stay about 6 ft (2 m) from the candle for the best effect

Look at the cloth just above the flame

▦ How rainbows work

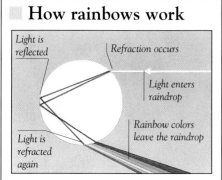

Light is reflected

Refraction occurs

Light enters raindrop

Light is refracted again

Rainbow colors leave the raindrop

Primary rainbow
Ordinary, or primary, rainbows are caused by reflection and refraction. As light enters a raindrop, it is refracted, or bent. It is reflected inside the drop and refracted again as it leaves. Different wavelengths bend by different amounts, breaking the light into colors.

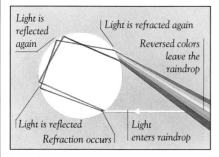

Light is reflected again

Light is refracted again

Reversed colors leave the raindrop

Light is reflected

Refraction occurs

Light enters raindrop

Secondary rainbow
A reversed, or secondary, rainbow is formed in much the same way as a primary rainbow, but the order of the colors is reversed. The light inside the drop is reflected twice, instead of once; the second reflection reverses the colors.

EXPERIMENT
Making a rainbow

A prism breaks light into its rainbow colors because glass refracts light to almost exactly the same degree as water—including rain—does. Because a prism is like an imitation water droplet, you can use water as a prism; by adding a mirror to reflect light inside the water you can make a rainbow in much the same way as a real one is made. However, your rainbow will appear on the wall or on the ceiling, while real rainbows appear only in the sky.

YOU WILL NEED
- water ● flashlight ● bowl ● mirror

1 PLACE THE MIRROR in the bottom of the bowl so that it rests at about a 45° angle. Fill the bowl with water.

2 SHINE A FLASHLIGHT directly down at the mirror from overhead, and look for the rainbow on the wall opposite.

The water cycle

WATER EVAPORATES from the land and ocean, then condenses and falls as precipitation; the water that falls over land either returns to the air by evaporation or plant transpiration, or it flows back to the sea. This ceaseless movement is called the water cycle. Today we know approximately the amounts of water at each stage in the cycle and that, on average, a water molecule spends nine or ten days in the air between its evaporation and its return to the surface. Of all the water on earth, only about 0.35 per cent is in the air at any time, yet this small proportion brings us all our clouds, fog, rain, snow, and hail. If precipitation were distributed evenly, every place on earth would receive 33.8 in (857 mm) a year. In fact, about 77 percent of all precipitation falls over the sea. Edmund Halley (1656–1742), the English astronomer, calculated that evaporation from the Mediterranean Sea removes as much water as flows into it from rivers.

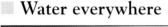

Water everywhere

The vast waters
Seas and oceans cover 70.8 percent of the earth's surface and contain 330 million cubic miles (1,370 million cubic km) of wate—97 percent of all the water on earth.

Frozen assets
Of all the earth's fresh water, 98 percent is to be found in glaciers and the polar icecaps. Were these to melt, the seas would rise about 260 ft (80 m), flooding enormous areas of populated land, such as Bangladesh, Holland, and Florida.

Much of the total precipitation falls into the sea without ever reaching the land

The water cycle

A tiny amount of water reaches the upper atmosphere and is lost into space. It is replaced by water vapor released from volcanoes. Overall, the water cycle balances: the amount that goes back to the sea as precipitation or from rivers is exactly equal to the amount that evaporates. This is about 545 cubic miles (2271.6 cubic km) every day. About 62½ cubic miles (260.5 cubic km) falls as precipitation over land, and 38½ cubic miles (160.5 cubic km) evaporates from the ground or is transpired by plants.

As air is forced to rise by hills and mountains, some of the water vapor in the air condenses into clouds

Precipitation caused by physical features like hills making the clouds rise is called orographic. High mountain ranges, such as the Sierra Nevada in California, can keep rainfall from reaching inland areas, giving them an arid climate

Precipitation does not just mean rain. Snow, sleet, hail, and dew are all included. Precipitation has fallen as snow on this high mountain top

Water is essential for all living things. Much of the water in the cycle is held inside plants, as they draw ground water through their roots and up through their bodies. Eventually the water is evaporated away from their leaves. This process is called transpiration

The water in the oceans stores a lot of heat. Water heated at the equator moves in currents, carrying that heat to colder regions a long way from the equator. Areas near warm ocean currents can receive more precipitation than areas near cold currents, which bring water away from the polar regions

Water that does not sink into the ground water becomes run-off. Surface water and ground water eventually return to the sea through small streams that can grow into rivers as large as the Amazon in South America, which at its mouth is over 100 miles (160 km) wide

Plants and the weather

OVER FORESTS, GRASSLANDS, and fields with growing crops, some of the water that is released into the air comes from plants. In some places this makes the weather cloudier and wetter than it would be if there were no plants. Plants also shade the ground, making it cooler, and they slow down the wind. Plants take in water, containing nutrients, from the ground through their roots. This water rises through the stem, enters the leaves, and evaporates from tiny openings in the leaves called stomata. As water is lost through this process, called transpiration, more water is drawn into the roots. Plants move so much water from the ground to the air in this way that they significantly affect the weather.

■ DISCOVERY ■
Stephen Hales

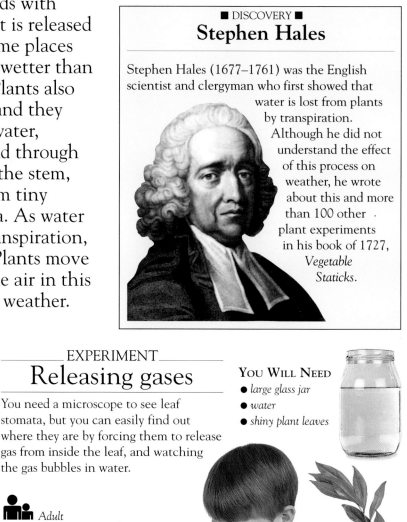

Stephen Hales (1677–1761) was the English scientist and clergyman who first showed that water is lost from plants by transpiration. Although he did not understand the effect of this process on weather, he wrote about this and more than 100 other plant experiments in his book of 1727, *Vegetable Staticks*.

▦ Cloud forest

Forests are sometimes called the "lungs" of our planet because their many plants release gases, including water vapor and oxygen, into the atmosphere above. Climbing up a forested mountain, you will pass through lowland forest. Higher up, at the same altitude as the clouds, you will see the vegetation begin to change to plants that thrive in more humid conditions. The trees in a "cloud forest" like the one above are small with thick, dense crowns and covered with ferns, mosses, and other plants that grow on them.

EXPERIMENT
Releasing gases

You need a microscope to see leaf stomata, but you can easily find out where they are by forcing them to release gas from inside the leaf, and watching the gas bubbles in water.

YOU WILL NEED
- *large glass jar*
- *water*
- *shiny plant leaves*

Adult supervision is advised for this experiment

Coaxing the gases out of the stomata
Ask an adult to boil some water and then to pour the water into a jar. Leave it for a few minutes until any bubbles have disappeared. Now drop a few leaves into the hot water. Heating the leaves makes the gases inside them expand and squeeze out. Watch the undersides of the leaves to see if any small bubbles appear—behind each bubble is a stoma.

Taking water in

Plants draw water up through their roots and stems. This is the very first step in the process of transpiration. You can demonstrate this very simply using a pale-colored flower and some colored water.

The flower will change color over a few days

Water is drawn up through the flower's stem

Colored flower
Pour some water into a glass and add a drop or two of food coloring. Place a cut flower in the glass. Check the flower twice a day. Has it changed in color? Where has the color come from?

Transpiration

Sunlight gives the plant energy

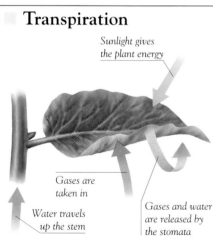

Gases are taken in

Water travels up the stem

Gases and water are released by the stomata

Water passes from the roots, through the stem, and out through the leaves. On the underside of each leaf are the stomata, which allow gases to enter the plant and water vapor to evaporate. Each stoma has "guard cells" that open and close the pore. Desert plants have few stomata, which helps them save water. Other plants have many stomata to release water; the average birch tree transpires about 80 gal (302 l) of water each day.

EXPERIMENT
Catching water

All plants transpire. You can prove this by watering a plant and catching the water as it is released. This experiment requires a control—a duplicate in which no transpiration occurs—to distinguish the moisture from the plant from any that is already in the air.

YOU WILL NEED
- water ● houseplant
- 2 plastic bags
- string ● scissors
- dish

1 START WITH the control. Fill one bag with air by holding it open (do not blow in it). Seal the bag tightly with string, then set it to one side.

2 TIE THE OTHER PLASTIC BAG around the base of the plant—over the stems, not over the pot. Set the plant in a dish, and water it until the soil is moist.

3 PLACE THE PLANT and the control bag next to each other in a warm place, and leave them for a few days. Now check for signs of water—how do the two bags compare? How much of the water in the plant bag do you think is from transpiration?

Water in the air

YOU CANNOT SEE, smell, or feel water vapor, but it has very important effects on the weather. The center of Antarctica is the driest place on earth, but even there the air contains water molecules. Warm air can hold much more water vapor than cold air. When air can hold no more water vapor, it is said to be saturated, and if you cool down warm, unsaturated air, it will eventually become cold, saturated air. When the air becomes saturated, the water vapor will usually condense into water droplets, which take the form of clouds, mist, or fog. To find out how close the air is to saturation, you need to measure its relative humidity (humidity is the amount of moisture in the air). Saturated air has 100 percent relative humidity, and air with no water vapor at all has 0 percent relative humidity. Relative humidity tends to decrease during the day and increase at night, when the air is cooler.

■ Dew beetle

Desert animals have found clever ways to obtain water, even in the driest places. Dew beetles live in the Namib desert in southern Africa, where on some nights fog drifts inland from the sea. When this happens, the beetles climb to the top of a sand dune and stand in a line facing the sea, with their heads down and their abdomens lifted. Water droplets from the air then trickle into their mouths, where they can sip them.

EXPERIMENT
Humidity tester

Some materials, including paper, absorb water from moist, humid air and lose water when the air is dry. The varying amounts of water held affect the weight of the material, and you can tell from this whether the material—and the air around it—is wetter or drier. A humidity tester is easy to make and will show changes in humidity. Use a soft, porous paper, such as newsprint.

YOU WILL NEED
- ● *paper* ● *poster board* ● *toothpick*
- ● *modelling clay* ● *paper punch*
- ● *scissors* ● *pins* ● *pen*
- ● *drinking straw*
- ● *ruler* ● *box*

1 CUT SOME PAPER squares measuring 2 x 2 in (5 x 5 cm), and punch a hole in the center of each. Thread all of the squares onto the drinking straw.

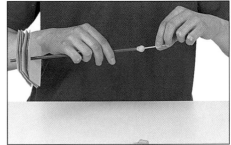

2 TAKE A PIECE of modeling clay and use it to fasten the toothpick to one end of the straw. This makes the pointer for the humidity tester.

4 CUT TWO NOTCHES in the top of the pivot, as shown. Fold the triangle in half lengthwise, and mark an even scale with a pen on one side of the fold.

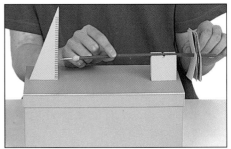

5 GLUE THE PIVOT and the scale to opposite ends of the box top. Stick a pin through the straw, and balance the pin in the notches of the pivot.

EXPERIMENT
Making a hygrometer

A hygrometer is an instrument that measures humidity. The most accurate type of hygrometer consists of two thermometers: one dry and one with its bulb kept wet. This wet bulb is chilled because the water evaporating from it absorbs latent heat—the energy the water needs to change from a liquid to a vapor (pp.22–23). The drier the air, the faster water will evaporate, and the more the bulb will be chilled. Readings from both thermometers can be used to look up the percentage relative humidity in a table (p.185). Once you have made your hygrometer, be sure to keep the wet bulb moist by refilling the container every few days. Your readings will be most accurate if you keep the hygrometer in the shade.

YOU WILL NEED
- *2 pieces of poster board*
- *small piece of muslin*
- *2 thermometers* • *glue*
- *small container*
- *distilled water*

1 GLUE THE THERMOMETERS to pieces of poster board about half the length of the thermometers. Glue these to a 6 x 12 in (15 x 30 cm) poster-board rectangle. Glue the container so that it sits beneath one of the thermometers.

2 NOW THAT THE STRUCTURE of the hygrometer is complete, make two "feet" to stabilize it. Cut two small triangles of poster board, and glue these to the base.

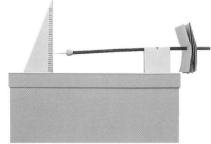

3 CUT A poster board triangle 6 in (15 cm) tall, 4 in (10 cm) at the base. Fold a 6 x 2 in (15 x 5 cm) poster board into a pivot for the pointer.

6 NOTE THE POSITION of the pointer. In moist air it will be low, and in dry air it will be high. Mark the scale "wet" at the bottom and "dry" at the top.

3 HALF-FILL THE CONTAINER with water, and put the piece of muslin inside. Wrap one end of the dampened muslin around the bulb of the thermometer.

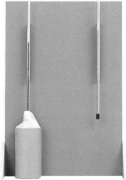

4 AFTER 10 minutes, take readings from both thermometers.

Clouds and fog

WHEN RELATIVE HUMIDITY (pp.42–43) reaches 100 percent, the air becomes saturated and water vapor begins to condense into droplets. At ground level, mist or fog forms. Above the ground clouds start to appear. Water vapor will normally condense only onto a surface—in this case, tiny particles of dust, salt, soot, or sulfate. These particles are called cloud condensation nuclei, or CCN. Over land there are usually 5 or 6 million CCN in every liter of air, and over the oceans there are about 1 million. The bigger the particle, the bigger the droplet.

■ Fog and mist

The droplets in this fog are large and close together. Visibility is less than 1,100 yd (1 km). Mist is thinner, with smaller droplets, and does not feel as wet.

■ Quick cloud

Expanding air cools. If it cools to below its dew-point temperature (pp.52–53), water vapor will condense. To see this happen, you need to make moist air expand rapidly. Fizzy soft drinks are held in cans under slight pressure. When you open the can, this pressure is released and a little moist air escapes, expanding as it does so. Watch very carefully as you open a soda can, and you will see the resulting cloud.

A small cloud will swirl for a few seconds as the pressures between the can and the outside air equalize

EXPERIMENT
Making clouds

Anything that cools air sufficiently will cause water vapor to condense. If warm, moist air comes into contact with a cold surface, the air will be chilled. You can make water vapor condense to form a cloud by chilling air.

YOU WILL NEED
● *warm water*
● *jar* ● *ice*
● *metal dish*

1 PLACE ICE in the metal dish, Let it stand until the dish is really cold. Place 1 in (2.5 cm) of warm water in the jar.

2 PLACE THE METAL DISH over the top of the jar, and watch what happens inside the jar. A cloud will form near the top as the warm water evaporates, rises, and then condenses.

EXPERIMENT
Clouds and nuclei

Adult supervision is advised for this experiment

Except in supersaturated air, water vapor will condense only if condensation nuclei are present. You can make water droplets form faster by adding big particles to the air.

YOU WILL NEED
● *matches* ● *warm water* ● *plastic bottle with cap*

1 FILL THE BOTTLE with 2 in (5 cm) of warm water. Screw on the cap, squeeze the bottle hard, and release to make the air contract and expand. You may see a mist.

2 ASK AN ADULT to light a match, blow it out, and quickly drop it in the bottle. Seal the bottle. The smoke will provide condensation nuclei.

3 SQUEEZE THE BOTTLE hard and slosh away any condensation; the air inside will be clear. Release the bottle, and a cloud will be visible. Repeat to form more clouds.

▓ The birth of a cloud

Clouds form when air is cooled below its dew-point temperature and CCN are present. This sequence shows the formation of a small cloud on a fine day. It begins when rising air cools and water vapor starts to condense.

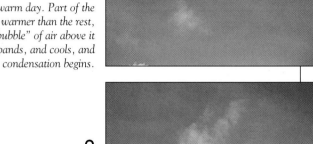

1

It is a warm day. Part of the ground is warmer than the rest, and a "bubble" of air above it rises, expands, and cools, and condensation begins.

2

Just below the cloud, the air is still too warm for water vapor to condense. Above it the water droplets evaporate in the sunshine.

3

A pattern is developing. Warm air rises, cools, and descends again. The descending air warms. Its water evaporates, making a gap in the middle of the cloud.

4

The cloud is growing. Condensation releases latent heat, which warms the air, making it expand and rise higher to where more droplets condense.

5

Wind blows fragments of cloud into drier air, where they dissipate. The part of the cloud that is growing is in air where the temperature is below its dew point.

Rain

WATER FALLING FROM THE SKY in any form, whether as fog, sleet, snow, hail, or rain, is called precipitation. Rain is the name given to water droplets more than 1⁄50 in (0.5 mm) across. Widely separated droplets smaller than this may still be called rain, but tiny droplets that fall close together are called drizzle. It is easy to tell the difference between the two: raindrops make a splash when they fall into puddles, but drizzle droplets do not. Droplets usually form when water vapor condenses around tiny particles of matter called condensation nuclei. Dust, smoke, sulfate, and salt can all become condensation nuclei. Over land there are usually up to 16,400 condensation nuclei per cubic inch of air (up to 1,000 condensation nuclei in every cubic centimeter). Very clean air may contain too few condensation nuclei to form droplets, so the air usually becomes very humid.

A rainy day

This man has been caught in the heavy rain that often falls from a warm cloud, in which the temperature is above freezing. The cloud is thick, so droplets at the top have a long way to fall. As they fall they collide, merge temporarily, then break apart again into smaller drops, which collide with still more small droplets. This produces a cascade of falling drops, all growing bigger as they fall, until they leave the bottom of the cloud.

Making raindrops

Once tiny water droplets have formed inside a cloud, they are carried around by air movements, but they are too small and too light to fall out of the cloud. As they move they collide with one another, which makes them merge to form larger droplets. When these droplets get to a certain size, they are too heavy to be supported by air currents and they fall from the cloud. That is rain. You can make your own raindrops more simply by breathing on a cold mirror.

Heavy breathing
Place a mirror in the freezer for an hour, then take it out and breathe on it until it fogs over. Continue breathing on it to see if you can make the "raindrops" merge and run down the mirror, collecting more as they go.

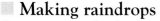

Water vapor collects around tiny condensation nuclei

Some water droplets join together

As the water droplets become bigger, they increase in weight

The heaviest droplets fall fastest within the cloud, and they become raindrops as they fall out of the cloud

How raindrops form

A cloud consists of tiny water droplets. They fall very slowly and are often lifted again by air inside the cloud. Some falling droplets collide and merge. This makes them bigger and heavier, so they fall faster, until they drop from the cloud as rain.

EXPERIMENT
How much rain?

Adult supervision is advised for this experiment

To measure rainfall, meteorologists use a rain gauge set into the ground. Rain falls into a funnel and flows through it to a container from which the water cannot evaporate. A scale on the side of the container shows the level of the water that has fallen over the area of the funnel. It is easy to make a simple rain gauge by using a straight-sided container.

YOU WILL NEED
- ruler ● plastic bottle ● scissors
- marbles ● colored tape ● water

A desert transformed by rainfall

Many desert plants survive dry periods as seeds. The desert landscape looks lifeless, but rain transforms it. Seeds germinate and grow, the plants flower, and finally they reproduce—all in the week or so that the ground is moist.

1 ASK AN ADULT to cut a plastic bottle at a point where its width is the same as its base and then to cover the cut edges of both pieces with tape. These pieces will form the main body and the funnel of the rain gauge.

2 MAKE A SCALE by attaching seven strips of colored tape to the side of the bottle, using a different color for the bottom strip. Check the strips against a ruler to be sure they are equally spaced.

3 TO ADD STABILITY, place a large handful of marbles in the bottom of the rain gauge to act as weights. Now insert the funnel upside down into the mouth of the rain gauge.

4 POUR WATER into the rain gauge up to the bottom mark, which is your starting point for measurements. Place the gauge outdoors in the open, and measure the daily rainfall on the scale.

Snow and sleet

WHEN WATER FREEZES, its molecules join together to form crystals. The word "crystal" comes from the Greek *kryllos*, meaning frost. If these crystals fall from a cloud, they may attach themselves to other crystals, forming snowflakes. A single snowflake may be made of more than 50 individual ice crystals, each so tiny that you would need a microscope to see it. If the air is extremely cold and dry, ice crystals fall as fine, powdery snow. At temperatures around –40 °F (–40 °C) crystals can form in clear air, and snow can fall from a clear sky. In some parts of the world, such as North America, ice pellets smaller than ⅕ in (5 mm) in diameter are called sleet. In other places, such as Britain, sleet is a mixture of rain and melting snow.

■ Mountain of snow

Mount Rainier in Washington state, USA, is snow-capped all year round. In the winter of 1971–72 the weather there broke all records with a total snowfall of 102 ft (31.1 m). This is the largest amount of snow ever to have fallen in one year—a record that has yet to be beaten.

EXPERIMENT
Snow crystals

Each tiny snowflake is made up of many ice crystals joined together. Snowflakes are difficult to study because they are so small and melt very quickly. To get around this problem, you can make an enormous "snowflake" in your freezer. Study your artificial snowflake carefully before it melts, and you will see how it is constructed.

YOU WILL NEED
- *glycerine* ● *jar of water*
- *dish detergent* ● *baking dish*
- *tablespoon* ● *teaspoon* ● *wire*

1 BEND SOME WIRE to make a 4-in (10-cm) loop with a handle. Combine 5 teaspoons glycerine, 1 tablespoon dish detergent, and 3 tablespoons water in the baking dish. Stir.

2 DRAW THE LOOP through the liquid so it holds a film. Place the loop in the freezer, and in a few hours you will have a giant snowflake. To see the very fine detail, use a magnifying glass.

■ DISCOVERY ■
Wilson W. Bentley

People have always been fascinated by snowflakes. The first person to describe their hexagonal structure was Swedish archbishop Olaus Magnus, in 1555. The American farmer and meteorologist Wilson W. Bentley (1865–1931) took more than 5,000 photomicrographs of snowflakes. In 1931 over 2,000 of these were published in his book, *Snow Crystals*.

EXPERIMENT
Measuring snowfall

Some kinds of snow pack down more densely than others, though all snowflakes contain air pockets. As a general rule, divide the depth of snow by 10 to find the equivalent amount of rain. You can measure this more accurately by making a snow gauge.

YOU WILL NEED
- ruler - straight-sided cylindrical container
- stiff cardboard

1 FIND A SNOWY SPOT out in the open that is sheltered from strong winds, and where the snow has not drifted. Measure the depth of snow with the ruler.

2 PRESS THE OPEN END of the cylindrical container through the snow until it reaches the ground. This will give you a sample of snow to measure.

3 SLIDE THE CARDBOARD under the cylinder. Bring the snow inside. When it has melted, compare the water level with the snow to find the equivalent amount of rain.

EXPERIMENT
Sleet versus snow

Large snowflakes fall slowly and gently. Sleet falls much faster. This difference is due to the greater air resistance on the larger surface area of snowflakes. Sleet is much more compact than snow, so it creates less air resistance. It is simple to demonstrate how the different shapes of snowflakes and sleet affect the speed with which they fall.

YOU WILL NEED
- sheet of paper - scissors

3 GATHER ALL the "sleet" and "snow" into your hands. Stand on a chair or stool, and let go of them together. Which reaches the floor first—the snow or the sleet?

1 TAKE A SHEET of paper, and cut it into 32 identical squares. Divide the squares into two piles: one for sleet, the other for snow.

2 NOW CRUMPLE EACH of the squares in the sleet pile into a little ball. Leave the snow pile alone to represent big snowflakes.

Hail, thunder, and lightning

ON HOT DAYS air near the ground is heated rapidly and becomes buoyant, pressing on the air above. "Bubbles" of hot air begin to float up, creating convection currents, with warm air rising at the center and cool air sinking at the sides. If the upper air is relatively cold, convection currents can climb up to 5 miles (8 km) above the ground. If the air is sufficiently moist, this can create towering storm clouds, often resulting in thunder, lightning, torrential rain, and sometimes hail.

■ How hail forms

If rising air currents are strong enough, water droplets are carried up. Before gravity forces them to drop down, they freeze. As they fall they partly melt, then rise again, and then refreeze in layers.

EXPERIMENT
Making lightning

A thundercloud has a strongly positive electrical charge at the top and a negative charge at the bottom. The air in between is a good insulator, so no current flows between the top and bottom of the cloud; the charges are known as static electricity. Static electrical charges are very common. You can produce one for yourself.

YOU WILL NEED
● *rubber glove*
● *dishcloth*
● *screwdriver*
● *metal baking pan*

👥 *Adult supervision is advised for this experiment*

1 USE a gloved hand to rub the pan lightly on the cloth for several minutes. This will build up an electrical charge.

2 DIM THE LIGHTING. Slowly bring the metal tip of a screwdriver close to the bottom of the pan. You will see a spark jump and may hear the crackling sound of "thunder."

■ Static uplift

Static electricity can be created easily with a balloon. Blow up a balloon, then rub it vigorously on your hair or clothing. Now place the balloon against your hair, your clothing, or even something in your home (such as a wall, a lamp, or a piece of furniture). What happens to the balloon?

EXPERIMENT
Exploding air

The difference in electrical charge between the bottom of a thundercloud and the ground may be more than 305 volts per foot (1,000 V/m), so a lightning spark releasing that potential has a huge amount of energy. Some of this heats the air through which the lightning flashes and makes the air explode. The sudden expansion of air, followed by its rush back into the partial vacuum it has created, sends shock waves in all directions. It is those shock waves—the sound of the explosion— that we hear as thunder. You can make a similar explosion by popping a balloon or by flicking a paper banger.

YOU WILL NEED
● *12 x 16 in (30 x 40 cm) sheet of paper*

1 FOLD the two longest edges of the paper together. Then open the paper out so that it is flat on the table again.

2 INDIVIDUALLY FOLD down each of the four corners to the first center fold. Make sure that they meet the centerline exactly.

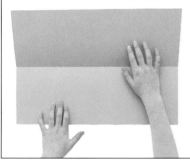

3 FOLD THE PAPER toward you along the center fold so that you enclose the flaps of the previous step. Do not damage the flaps.

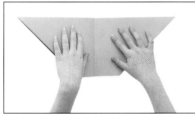

4 FOLD THE PAPER in half as shown so that the tips of the opposing sides meet. Open out the paper again so the fold line shows.

5 BRING THE TWO top corners down toward you so that they meet and are parallel with the previous fold from Step 4.

6 FOLD THE PAPER back on itself so that the two points face you. This will make a triangle shape. The banger is now ready to go.

Conducting lightning

The American inventor, Benjamin Franklin (1706–90) proved that lightning is caused. He flew a kite in a thunderstorm, with metal at each end of the string. When the string got wet, a spark jumped from the key at the bottom.

7 HOLD THE TWO top corners together. Swish the banger down with a quick flick of the wrist. A loud bang will occur as the air is compressed.

Dew and water vapor

HOW DEW FORMS was a puzzle for a long time. It was solved when scientists discovered that air is never completely dry. Even in deserts, air contains water vapor. During the day, the ground is warmed and warms the air near it. At night, the ground cools by radiating its heat into the sky. If the sky is cloudy, most of the radiant heat is reflected back, slowing the rate at which the ground cools—but if the sky is clear the heat is lost and the ground cools quickly, chilling the air next to it. If the air is cooled to its dew point (pp.42–43), water vapor will condense on surfaces and dew will form. When you see dew in the morning you know the night has probably been cloudless. Measuring how much water condenses as dew is difficult because the quantity is so small. But in dry climates it probably accounts for a significant proportion of all precipitation. One device scientists use to measure dew consists of a slab of gypsum. This is weighed dry, then weighed after dew has formed.

Making the most of the dew

Most bromeliads, from the pineapple family of plants, have stiff, overlapping leaves that form a tank in which dew collects. From there, the dew is absorbed through hairs on the leaves or roots that grow upwards. This is an *Ananas bracteatus*, a house plant closely related to the pineapple. Another type of dew-collecting bromeliad is the air plant. It grows only on the surfaces of other plants and has scaly, leafy hairs, no roots, and absorbs water vapor directly from the air. This allows air plants to thrive in very dry deserts, where other plants would die.

EXPERIMENT
Dew evaporating from grass

Dew forms only on clear nights and evaporates quickly in the morning sunshine. If you know the time of sunrise and note the time when the grass feels dry, you can calculate how long this takes. You can also spray "dew" onto grass cuttings, then measure how quickly it dries in light and shade in the controlled enviroment of your home.

YOU WILL NEED
● *tray*
● *modeling clay*
● *cut grass* ● *poster board* ● *desk lamp*
● *plant mister*

1 SPREAD THE grass cuttings over the tray. Fill the plant mister with water, and spray the grass as evenly as possible to make "dew" fall on the grass cuttings.

2 DIVIDE THE TRAY in half by propping the poster board upright with modeling clay. Set the lamp at one end of the tray as the "sun," so it shines on one half of the grass, leaving the other half in shade. Switch on the lamp and see which side of the tray dries out first, and how quickly.

Predicting the dew point

Dew starts to form soon after sunset, most commonly in spring and autumn. You can predict when it will form on a particular night. On a clear, still evening about an hour before sunset, as the air cools, use the wet- and dry-bulb hygrometer (pp.42–43) to take the air temperature and the relative humidity; and use the dew point table in the glossary (p.187) to work out the dew point temperature. Take the measurements again in the morning to find when the dew will evaporate, using the table on p.187.

Wet web
Water vapor needs a surface on which to condense, and a spider's web offers many surfaces, making the water easy to see. The dew soon evaporates, so it does not damage the web. Dew-covered spiders' webs are most frequently seen in early autumn.

How to work out the dew point
Subtract the wet-bulb from the dry-bulb temperature to find the "wet-bulb depression." Then locate this number in the top row of horizontal numbers in the dew point table and the dry-bulb temperature in the left-hand vertical column. The figure where the column and row intersect is the dew point. An hour later measure the dry-bulb temperature again. Subtract this from your earlier reading to calculate how fast the air is cooling, then calculate when it will reach the dew point. Assume the temperature will continue to fall at the same rate (in degrees per hour), and you can work out how many hours will pass before it falls below the dew point.

Feel your way

Dew forms on plants in the evenings because the plants radiate their heat energy rapidly, until they are cooler than the surrounding air. Water from the atmosphere then condenses on to them. In a similar way, you can make your own dew using a tray as a "plant."

Capturing dew
Place a room-temperature metal tray outside on a clear evening. Return to it a couple of hours later and run your finger across the tray—it should be wet with fresh dew. The metal tray, like plants, cools more quickly than air, so dew can form.

The effect of shade

You can demonstrate the effect of shade on dew formation by using two sheets of black paper and an umbrella. Late in the day, when dew is likely, place both of the sheets of paper on the ground in the open, and set up the umbrella so that it shades one of the sheets. At sunset, start checking both sheets every half hour. Dew will form on one but not on the other—but which one? Repeat this experiment on several evenings; there may not be dew every evening.

For the best results, first let the exposed paper warm in the sun during the day

Frost and ice

WHEN WATER FROM THE ATMOSPHERE freezes, frost and ice are formed. A dew-point temperature (pp.52–53) below freezing is called the frost point. At this temperature soft, white "hoar" frost forms as the water vapor changes directly into ice without first condensing into liquid form. The reverse can also occur: ice can change into water vapor without going through the liquid stage. This is called sublimation. The ice crystals that make hoar frost grow loosely and reflect light in all directions. This is why the frost looks white. Sometimes water droplets are "supercooled," remaining liquid even below the freezing point. On contact with a cold surface they form frost. Tiny particles of fog will turn into a hard, white frost called rime, while larger raindrops will turn into a hard, clear ice that is sometimes called glaze. Another type of ice, called white ice, is made from snow that has become pressed down and condensed.

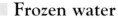

■ Frozen water

When frost is formed, water molecules join to make six-sided crystals. Light is reflected by the crystals, making the frost look white. The top left of this picture shows partly frozen water, and the bottom right shows the crystals.

These icicles have formed in a cave in the Antarctic. During the summer, melting snow has trickled over the lip of the cave, freezing into icicles.

EXPERIMENT

Make your own frost

YOU WILL NEED
● salt ● glass
● stirrer ● ice

In winter, salt (sodium chloride) is often spread on roads to melt ice. Chlorine atoms in the salt attach themselves to hydrogen atoms in the ice. Each atom of hydrogen can also form a weaker bond to a second atom of chlorine, separating it from its sodium atom, which then attaches itself to an oxygen atom. This breaks the ice crystals apart so the ice melts. The latent heat needed to give the molecules enough energy to separate is taken from the air. If you mix salt with crushed ice, the ice will melt, chilling the air around it as it does so, and more ice may form in the cold air from water vapor containing no salt. In this way you can make your own frost.

2 NOW WATCH to see the action. After a few minutes you will see frost form on the outside of the glass. Scratch the frost off, and see if it reappears.

1 FILL A GLASS with ice. Put your hands over the glass. The air will feel cool because latent heat is being taken from the air to melt the ice. Add a dash of salt to the ice, and stir the mixture.

EXPERIMENT
Why ice is slippery

When water freezes, its molecules join together to make hexagonal (six-sided) shapes with a space at the center of each. Strong pressure on the ice can squeeze out these spaces, crushing the crystals. When that happens the ice turns into liquid water but freezes again as soon as the pressure is released. This means that—under abnormally high pressure —water freezes at a lower temperature than usual. When you walk on ice or hard-packed snow, your own weight is enough to melt the ice beneath your feet, which is why the ice is so slippery. You can see for yourself how ice will melt under pressure and then freeze again. Hang a weighted wire across an ice cube, and watch it travel through the ice— without cutting the ice cube in half.

YOU WILL NEED
● *thin wire* ● *ice cube* ● *2 mugs of equal size and weight* ● *bottle*

Skating away

Skaters use the slippery quality of ice to help them go farther and faster. An ice skate has a thin, sharp metal blade. The whole weight of the skater presses on the ice through that small surface, exerting great pressure, which melts the surface of the ice. This allows the skater to glide through a thin layer of water, which freezes again after he or she has passed.

1 MAKE a weight with the two mugs. Take a 12-in (30-cm) length of the wire, and tie one end of the wire to each mug. Fasten the wire to the handles of the mugs, and make sure it is securely tied.

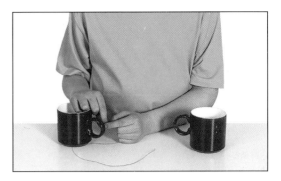

2 PLACE an ice cube on the mouth of a tall bottle. Position the weight so that the middle of the wire sits across the center of the ice cube. Let go of the mugs so that the wire exerts pressure on the ice cube.

3 NOW SIT BACK and watch the action. The wire will slowly move through the ice cube as the pressure of the weight melts the ice, without changing its temperature. When the wire has gone halfway through, try picking up the weight by lifting the mugs—what happens to the ice cube?

Make sure the ice cube cannot fall off or inside the bottle

The wire is thin, so the weight of the mugs is concentrated in a small area on the ice cube

Make sure that the mugs do not touch the table

Wind: air that moves

AIR MOVES FROM AREAS of high atmospheric pressure to areas of lower pressure. In an area of high pressure, the air molecules are closer together than they are in an area of lower pressure. Air molecules tend to move from high to low pressure, and it is this movement of air that we feel as wind. The greater the difference between the two pressures, the stronger the wind will be. The earth's rotation adds a curve to this flow from high to low pressure, creating a gentle spiral that twists inward.

EXPERIMENT
Slowing the wind

Wind near the ground is slowed by friction—it sticks to the ground. The farther away from the ground the wind is, the less pronounced the effect of friction. You can demonstrate this effect using a liquid. Liquids behave like gases (because they are both fluids) but at a slower rate.

YOU WILL NEED
● scissors ● tape
● milk ● eye
dropper ● food
coloring ● baking
dish ● plastic bottle

1 ASK AN ADULT to cut off the top and sides of a plastic bottle and cover the sides with tape, to make a long scoop. Pour some milk into the scoop.

2 USE THE EYE DROPPER to make a line of food-coloring drops on the milk. Put the drops across the bottle, close to the end you are holding.

3 TILT the bottle slightly so that the milk flows slowly into the dish. The food coloring will form a "V" pointing toward the dish as friction causes the milk near the sides to move more slowly than the milk in the middle.

■ DISCOVERY ■
Christoph Buys Ballot

Christoph Buys Ballot (1817–90) was a Dutch meteorologist who founded the Netherlands Meterological Institute in 1854. In 1857 he showed that—except near the equator—winds flow counterclockwise around low-pressure areas and clockwise around high-pressure areas in the Northern Hemisphere (in the Southern Hemisphere, clockwise around areas of low pressure and counter-clockwise around high-pressure areas). According to "Buys Ballot's Law," if you stand with your back to the wind in the Northern Hemisphere, pressure is on your left. In the Southern Hemisphere, the reverse is true.

The food-coloring "V" shows that fluids are slowed by contact with a solid surface. This is why winds are much stronger in air well above the ground

EXPERIMENT
Flowing wind

Air flows from a high-pressure area to a low-pressure area, much as water flows from a higher to a lower level. You can demonstrate this at home.

Adult supervision is advised for this experiment

YOU WILL NEED
- scissors ● food coloring
- modeling clay ● tape
- 2 plastic bottles
- plastic tube
- hand drill and bit
- water

1 ASK AN ADULT to drill a small hole near the bottom of each bottle (in the same position each time) and then to cut off the top of each bottle.

2 ASK THE ADULT to seal the bottle edges with tape. Stick strips of tape at equal intervals on both bottles to make a rough scale.

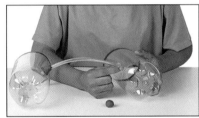

3 CONNECT the two bottles by placing the ends of the plastic tube in the holes. Use some modeling clay to seal the joints.

4 FILL ONE BOTTLE with colored water to the level of the tube, and fill the other completely. What happens to the water levels?

The water will level out as the pressure difference between bottles evens out

EXPERIMENT
A breath of wind

When you inhale, your chest expands and the movement of your ribs and diaphragm allows your lungs to expand. The air pressure inside your lungs is then lower than the air pressure outside your body, so air flows—like a wind—from the region of high pressure to the region of low pressure in your lungs.

YOU WILL NEED
- balloon ● plastic bottle

1 PUSH MOST of the balloon into the bottle. Squeeze the bottle and gently stretch the neck of the balloon over the mouth of the bottle.

The balloon behaves just like a lung

2 RELEASE THE SIDES of the bottle, and the balloon will inflate as air rushes in Squeeze the bottle's sides, and the balloon will deflate.

Measuring the wind

MANY PEOPLE need to find out what the wind conditions are each day. Aircraft crews need to know the strength and direction of the wind on takeoff and landing. Winds make waves at sea, so sailors need to know what conditions to expect. The direction from which the wind blows is measured with a wind vane. Speed is measured with an instrument called an anemometer. In weather forecasts, wind speed is usually reported in miles or kilometers per hour, or—for ships and aircraft—in knots. One knot is equal to 1.15 mph (1.85 km/h). The Beaufort Wind Scale gives wind speed as a "force."

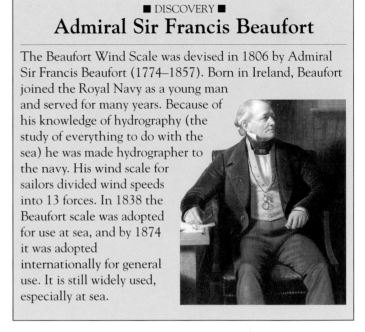

■ DISCOVERY ■
Admiral Sir Francis Beaufort

The Beaufort Wind Scale was devised in 1806 by Admiral Sir Francis Beaufort (1774–1857). Born in Ireland, Beaufort joined the Royal Navy as a young man and served for many years. Because of his knowledge of hydrography (the study of everything to do with the sea) he was made hydrographer to the navy. His wind scale for sailors divided wind speeds into 13 forces. In 1838 the Beaufort scale was adopted for use at sea, and by 1874 it was adopted internationally for general use. It is still widely used, especially at sea.

■ The Beaufort Wind Scale

Originally, the Beaufort Wind Scale described the type and amount of sail a ship should carry in particular winds. Today the scale describes the effects seen on land and relates these to wind speeds. Look for the signs it describes, and you can estimate the wind speed. Use the Beaufort scale to record your own weather observations. In 1955 meteorologists from the US Weather Bureau added forces 13 to 17 to describe hurricane winds ranging from 73 to 136 mph (117–220 km/h).

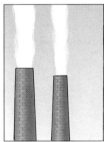
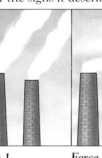

Force 0
Calm: less than 1 mph (1 km/h). Smoke rises vertically, and the air feels still.

Force 1
Light air: 1–3 mph (1–5 km/h). Rising smoke drifts, but wind vanes and flags do not move.

Force 2
Light breeze: 4–7 mph (6–11 km/h). Smoke shows the wind direction.

Force 3
Gentle breeze: 8–12 mph (12–19 km/h). Flags, leaves, and twigs move gently.

Force 4
Moderate breeze: 13–18 mph (20–29 km/h). Loose pieces of paper blow about.

Force 5
Fresh breeze: 19–24 mph (30–39 km/h). Small leafy trees sway in the wind.

Force 6
Strong breeze: 25–31 mph (40–50 km/h). Umbrellas are difficult to use.

Force 7
Moderate gale: 32–38 mph (51–61 km/h). Pressure is felt when walking into wind.

Force 8
Fresh gale: 39–46 mph (62–74 km/h). Twigs are torn from trees.

Force 9
Strong gale: 47–54 mph (75–87 km/h). Slates and chimneys are blown away.

Force 10
Whole gale: 55–63 mph (88–102 km/h). Trees are broken or uprooted.

Force 11
Storm: 64–75 mph (103–120 km/h). Cars overturned. Trees blown a distance.

Force 12
Hurricane: in excess of 75 mph (120 km/h). Widespread devastation. Many trees uprooted. Buildings destroyed. Hurricanes are common at sea but rare over land, except in coastal regions.

EXPERIMENT
Measuring wind direction and wind speed

A wind vane is an instrument that indicates the direction from which the wind is blowing. A simple vane is like an arrow with a very large, flat tail. The head of the arrow points into the wind. Wind speed is measured by an anemometer. The simplest type, invented by Leonardo da Vinci (1452–1519), measures the movement of a flat plate mounted so it faces the wind. This simple combined wind vane and anemometer will show you wind direction and relative speed.

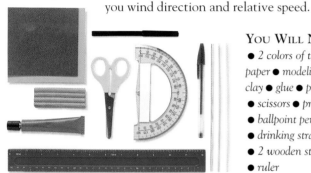

YOU WILL NEED
- *2 colors of thick paper* ● *modeling clay* ● *glue* ● *pen*
- *scissors* ● *protractor*
- *ballpoint pen*
- *drinking straw*
- *2 wooden sticks*
- *ruler*

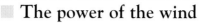
The power of the wind

Wind energy can drive large ships, and it can also be used to generate electricity. Wind turbines like these have large blades mounted on top of tall towers. They are erected in exposed, windy places, often in a group called a wind farm. Many wind turbines are needed for a wind farm to produce as much electricity as an ordinary power station.

1 CUT THICK paper cards: 7 x ½ in (17 x 1 cm) and 4 x 9 in (10 x 24 cm). Draw a center line across each, then add a line on the large card to the right of the first.

2 GLUE A STICK along the second line on the large card, leaving ½ in (1 cm) over one edge. Fold the card along the first line, and glue the sides together.

3 GLUE A ½-IN (1-cm) straw to the line on the small card. Fold the card over the straw and glue it. Thread a 3½-in (8-cm) stick through the straw.

4 WITH A PEN POINT, make a hole in the top corner of the large card, next to the stick. Draw a 90° arc from the bottom corner, marking it at 15° intervals.

5 TAKE THE CARTRIDGE from the pen. Stand the pen barrel upright in clay to hold the stick of the large card. Put the other stick through the corner hole.

6 USE modeling clay to seal the sticks. When a wind blows, the large card will show direction, and the small card, speed.

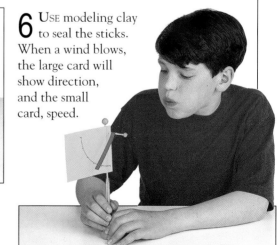

Low-level weather

IN WINTER CONDITIONS may be harsh, but many small animals find ways to survive at low levels. Some live beneath the snow, out of the wind, moving through the grass and herbs. Other animals live below ground, sheltered in the soil. In summer, soil animals can burrow deeper, to where the air is cool and moist. Near ground level and in the soil below, plants and animals experience weather that is very different from the weather above. This is a microclimate. There are other microclimates in places sheltered from the large-scale weather or more exposed to it.

■ Frost hollow

In this valley air has chilled below its dew point (pp.52–53) by radiating heat to a clear sky at night. The still, cold fog is typical of the microclimate of the valley bottom.

EXPERIMENT
Low-level temperature

The microclimates beneath the soil, at ground level, and several feet above the ground differ in many ways. One easy-to-measure indication of this is temperature, which can vary by large amounts and can affect humidity at low levels. Here you can demonstrate this for yourself. Try taking readings in four places: sunshine, shade, under a tree and in long grass.

YOU WILL NEED
● *trowel* ● *thermometer*
● *pen* ● *notepad*

1 MAKE THREE columns in a notepad: soil, ground, air. Dig a narrow hole and leave a thermometer in it for 5 minutes. Write the temperature in the "soil" column.

For each position you check, take three readings so that you can make comparisons

2 NOW FILL IN THE hole and leave the thermometer at ground level for 5 minutes. Write the temperature in the "ground" column.

3 WRITE down the air temperature at chest height. If the three temperatures are different, then so is the humidity.

EXPERIMENT
Soil humidity

Soil contains water that can evaporate only from the surface. Rainwater (or melted snow) moves down through the soil, but water is also drawn up, from deeper levels where the ground is saturated. The relative humidity of air below ground level is usually different from that of air above ground. Measure the difference yourself.

YOU WILL NEED
- *wet- and dry-bulb hygrometer* ● *soil* ● *trowel* ● *notepad*
- *pen* ● *tape* ● *scissors* ● *2 dishpans*

1 CALCULATE AND NOTE the relative humidity (pp.42–43) of the air above the location of your soil sample.

2 PARTLY FILL A DISHPAN with soil and place the hygrometer in it. Do not let soil touch the thermometer bulbs.

3 INVERT THE OTHER pan and tape it on top to prevent evaporation. Leave the pans in a warm place overnight.

4 NEXT MORNING calculate the relative humidity in the container. Is this the same as the humidity measured earlier?

EXPERIMENT
Make a solar trap

A place sheltered from the wind and facing the sun can become very warm. This is a "solar trap," with a microclimate that is brighter, drier, and warmer than its surroundings. You can often tell what a microclimate is like by the different wild plants that grow there. Here you can make a small solar trap.

YOU WILL NEED
- *scissors* ● *thermometer*
- *shoe box*

1 FIND A SUNNY SPOT in an open space, well away from the shelter of trees and shrubs. Hold a thermometer well above the ground, and read the air temperature.

2 REMOVE THE LID of a shoe box and cut away one side to make a three-sided screen. Set the screen above the ground. Leave it for half an hour with the open side facing the sun.

3 WITHOUT MOVING the screen or touching its sides with the thermometer, measure the temperature of the air inside. How does it compare with your previous reading?

Urban weather

CITY AND COUNTRY weather conditions are often very different. You cannot be in two places at once to compare them, but in the city it is often warmer, less windy, and also drier than in the countryside. Cities are built with materials that do not absorb water. When it rains, most of the water is drained away before it can evaporate and condense again as clouds, and there are fewer plants to return water to the air. Less of the sun's energy is used to evaporate water, so the ground in the city is heated more strongly. Buildings slow the wind, and heat from the buildings and vehicles warms the air.

■ Hot city nights

During the day, roads and buildings are warmed by the sun. At night they cool, releasing heat and warming the city air. Plants receive the same amount of warmth, but they are cooled by the evaporation of water from their leaves. Compare heat radiation from a brick and a plant to feel the difference between city and country.

Try holding a thermometer over each—what is the difference in temperature?

Radiating heat
Put a brick and a small houseplant outdoors in the sunshine all day. In the evening, bring them indoors. Hold your hands above them. Which feels warmer?

EXPERIMENT
Humidity in the city

At night, the relative humidity in a city can be as much as 30 percent lower than in the countryside nearby. This dryness affects the temperature. A lot of the sun's energy reaching earth goes into evaporating water. Much air warming is due not to direct solar heat, but to the latent heat of condensation (pp.22–23). Because there is less water more of the sun's heat is available to warm the ground, which in turn warms the air in contact with it. You can find out how quickly a hard surface such as a pavement dries compared to a porous one such as soil.

Adult supervision is advised for this experiment

YOU WILL NEED
- 2 saucers ● desk fan
- blotting paper ● glass ● water

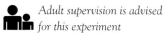

1 PLACE THE TWO SAUCERS next to each other on a table. Place the blotting paper in one saucer to represent the countryside; the other is the city. Pour an equal amount of water into each saucer.

2 STAND THE FAN in front of the saucers, so that it is the same distance from each one. Ask an adult to turn on the fan, set on a low setting, so the air blows across both saucers. Which of the two saucers is the quickest to dry?

▦ Slowed by snow

As seen in this picture of New York City, bad weather upsets the smooth running of a modern city. Snowfall disrupts traffic and pedestrians alike.

EXPERIMENT
City winds

👪 *Adult supervision is advised for this experiment*

When the wind blows at right angles to a building, the air will form eddies around the building—with surprising results. This experiment will show you what happens on the sheltered side of the building.

EXPERIMENT
Wind patterns

Buildings deflect winds, making complicated patterns as the air eddies around them. As wind twists and turns, it also slows, mainly because of friction between the air and the surfaces it passes. Demonstrate this by using milk to represent air.

YOU WILL NEED
- *milk* ● *baking dish* ● *spice powder* ● *modeling clay*

1 STICK SIX BLOBS of modeling clay along one side of the dish to represent city buildings. The clear side represents the countryside. Pour enough milk into the dish to cover the bottom.

2 SPRINKLE SPICE POWDER at one end of the dish away from the "buildings." Tilt the tray and watch the powder to see how the "wind" moves through the "countryside" and "city."

YOU WILL NEED
- *8 x 2 in (20 x 5 cm) cardboard* ● *modeling clay* ● *matches* ● *small candle* ● *saucer*

1 PLACE THE CANDLE on a saucer, using a blob of modeling clay to support it. Ask an adult to light the candle for you.

2 HOLD THE cardboard "building" upright about 4 in (10 cm) from the candle. Blow hard directly at the building. Behind the shelter do you think the wind will blow toward the building or away from it? Watch what happens to the flame.

Local winds

IN MANY REGIONS the shape of the land causes distinctive local winds, while in coastal areas local winds can be produced by the warming and cooling of land and water. Rising and sinking air from mountain or hill ranges are "anabatic" and "katabatic" winds. If air warms by compression as it sinks, it becomes a chinook wind (better known in Europe as a föhn wind). Another well-known local wind is the mistral, a cold katabatic wind funnelled along the Rhône valley in France.

■ Rising and sinking air

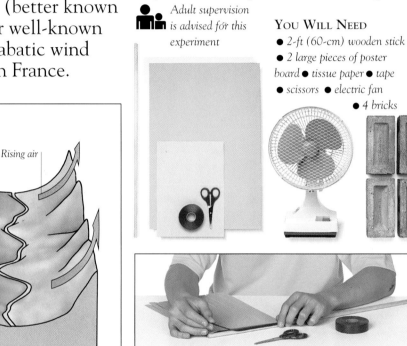

Katabatic wind
As the ground cools at night, air cooled by contact with the ground sinks down the hills and into the valley.

Anabatic wind
As the ground warms during the day, air warmed by contact with the ground rises from the valley up the hillsides.

Wind funnel

A valley or canyon acts as a funnel to wind blowing along it. Wind speed increases and air pressure may fall. In cities, streets lined with tall buildings produce a similar effect and are known as "urban canyons." You can experiment with funneling.

Adult supervision is advised for this experiment

YOU WILL NEED
- *2-ft (60-cm) wooden stick*
- *2 large pieces of poster board* ● *tissue paper* ● *tape*
- *scissors* ● *electric fan*
- *4 bricks*

1 CUT THE TISSUE PAPER into lots of strips ½ in (1 cm) wide and 1 ft (30 cm) long. Tape the strips by their ends to one end of the wooden stick.

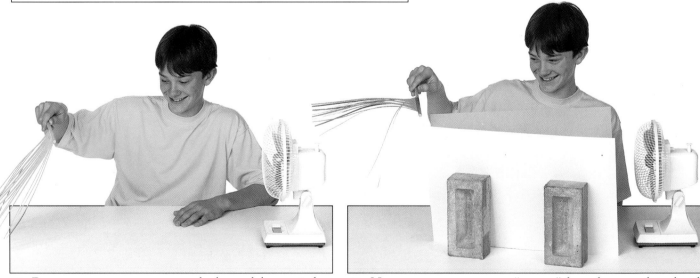

2 PLACE THE FAN ON A TABLE, and ask an adult to switch the fan on to its low setting to make a light breeze. Hold the stick, with the strips at the top, a short way from the fan. How high does the breeze blow the strips?

3 NOW MAKE A NARROWING "VALLEY" from the posterboard and bricks, with the fan at the wide end and the stick near the narrow end. Ask an adult to turn on the fan to the same setting as before. Has the breeze increased in force?

EXPERIMENT
Making a breeze

Water has a much higher heat capacity (pp.22–23) than sand and soil, so much more heat is needed to raise its temperature. Once water has warmed, it also cools more slowly. On a hot day with little wind, these differences produce a breeze from the sea during the day and one from the land at night. Use sand and ice to make your own land and sea breezes.

YOU WILL NEED
- ice ● 2 baking dishes ● cardboard ● tape
- matches ● hotpads ● incense stick ● sand

Adult supervision is advised for this experiment

1 FILL ONE DISH with sand. Ask an adult to warm it in the oven on low heat. Fill the other dish with ice.

Land and sea breezes

Land breeze
During the evening the land cools much faster than the sea. Cool air sinks over the land and flows seaward at a low level. Warmer air rises over the sea and moves landward at a high level to replace it. This is called a land breeze.

As the land heats, warm air rises and begins to cool

Warm air moves over the sea, where it continues to cool

Cool air sinks over the sea

Cool air moves over the land to replace the warm air

Warm sea air moves over land at a high level

Warmer air over the sea rises

Cool air sinks as the land cools

Cooler air from the land moves over the sea

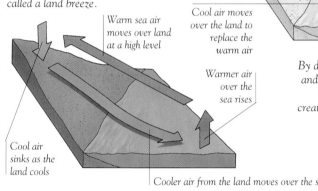

Sea breeze
By day, air cooled by the sea sinks and flows landward at a low level to fill the area of low pressure created by the warm land, causing an onshore breeze.

2 TAPE CARDBOARD PIECES to make a screen. Place the dishes side by side, surrounded by the screen.

The haboob

Some local winds produce visible effects. The haboob wind in northern Sudan causes sandstorms like the one on the right. The name comes from the Arabic word *habb*, meaning "to blow." It occurs when columns of air rise rapidly as they are heated by the sun. The rising air carries desert sand and dust with it.

3 ASK AN ADULT to light an incense stick. Hold it between the sand and ice. The sand warms the air above it, making it rise. Its place is taken by cool air flowing from above the ice. Which way does the smoke move in this sea breeze? Replace the ice with warm water, cool the sand, and use another incense stick to see a land breeze.

The WEATHER MACHINE

Swirling storms
This tornado's twisting vortex (above) is only 100 ft (30 m) across, with wind speeds over 150 mph (240 km/h). By contrast, the Atlantic depression (left) is thousands of miles across, bringing rain and snow but much less violent winds.

WE ALL EXPERIENCE OUR own particular local weather. One day it may be rainy or cloudy, and the next day it may be sunny again. However, each of these kinds of weather is a part of a much larger whole: the weather machine. There are different patterns of weather distributed over the entire Planet Earth. Some of them are ordinary and everyday, but others can be very exciting and dramatic.

WEATHER IN MOTION

THE WEATHER CHANGES day by day, and season by season. In the past, travelers knew that the weather was warmer in some latitudes and cooler in others, but they did not know why the weather was so different. For most of history people assumed that the changes were purely local and that the weather in one place had no influence on weather elsewhere. They thought each region had its very own weather.

Suppose that yesterday it rained and today it is sunny. Nothing in this ordinary observation of the weather suggests that yesterday's rainy conditions have now moved on and the rain is falling somewhere else, or that the sunshine you enjoy today gave the same pleasure yesterday to somebody else. It is easy enough to see that the wind is made of air that moves from one place to another, but it is difficult to see that the entire mass of air to which the wind belongs—and the weather associated with that mass— is moving, too.

Air movements

The whole of the earth's atmosphere is moving all the time, and many people think of it as a kind of machine, working all over the world to produce the weather.

The sun shines more strongly in some places than in others, and the oceans warm and cool more slowly than the continents. As a result, the the air in one place will be warmer or colder, drier or moister, than the air somewhere else. These sections of air are huge—often they extend over most of a continent or ocean. Vast bodies of air like these, if they are more or less at the same temperature, pressure, and humidity, are called air masses.

Air masses do not usually stay in the place where they were

The storm
Very low pressure at the center of this swirling cloud means bad weather for the surface below. This satellite photograph shows that fierce winds are spiraling in, trying to fill in the area of low pressure.

formed. Most of the time they cannot stay still because dense air tends to flow into a region where the air is less dense, like water flowing down a hillside into a lake. The air cannot move in a straight line, however, because the earth beneath it is spinning on its axis (pp.74–75). This makes the movement of air more complicated.

There is another reason why dense air cannot simply flow into a region of less dense air and fill it. If two air masses that have different temperatures and pressures meet, they mix very slowly. Because they do not blend together right away, there is a clear boundary between the two kinds of air, which is called a front (pp.76–77). This front also moves. In addition, a jet stream (pp.126–127) may suck air out of the middle of the depression, either maintaining the depression or intensifying it.

The existence of air masses and fronts was discovered in Norway during the First World War by meteorologists at the Bergen Geophysical Institute, led by Vilhelm Bjerknes (1862–1951). During the Second World War, pilots of high-altitude

U.S. military aircraft sometimes found that they were not moving forward because they were flying against winds that were blowing as fast as their own airspeed. These pilots had discovered the jet streams.

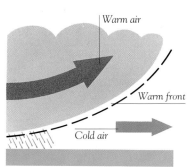

A typical warm front
The shallow slope of an advancing warm front produces sheets of cloud.

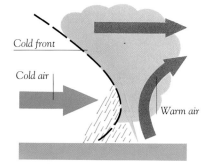

A typical cold front
A cold front slopes more steeply than a warm front, producing heaped clouds and heavy rain on the surface below.

Low pressure   High pressure

Air pressure
Increasing atmospheric pressure crams air molecules more closely together. This means a given volume of air contains more molecules, so the air becomes denser.

Storm clouds

Air can move when very moist air is warmed strongly from below. It can rise to a great height so that its water vapor condenses to form a towering storm cloud.

Inside the cloud air rises rapidly by convection, then cools and sinks again, in convection cells. Water inside the cloud can then become electrically charged. A positive charge collects near the top of the cloud and a negative charge at the bottom. The ground below the cloud becomes positively charged. Eventually huge sparks flash between the charges, neutralizing them. This is lightning, and it releases so much energy that the air through which it passes explodes, making the noise we hear as thunder.

Usually, but not always, the thunder and lightning are accompanied by heavy rain, hail, or snow, plus strong winds. The storm ends, usually after an hour or two, when the cloud has lost most of its water through precipitation.

Thunderstorms are more common in some places than in others, but at any moment of day or night nearly 2,000 are occurring throughout the world.

Violent weather

In some parts of the world the weather can be very violent, causing a great deal of damage and injury to people. Hurricanes are huge tropical weather systems in which winds reach tremendous speeds. They are called typhoons when they occur in Southeast Asia and cyclones when they occur in the Indian and Pacific Oceans in the Southern Hemisphere.

Tornadoes, which are part of very large thunderstorms called supercells, are smaller than hurricanes, but strong ones are even more violent, and many thousands of people have been killed by them.

Tornadoes over water are called waterspouts. The very low pressure inside a waterspout causes water vapor to condense, so it looks as though the spout is drawing water from the surface—but the water in a waterspout comes from the moist air.

Weather maps

Today we have weather maps and use photographs taken from satellites to show how weather systems are moving, but these "satpix" are recent inventions. The first weather map was drawn by Edmund Halley (1656–1742) in 1686. He is best known as an English astronomer, but he was also interested in many other branches of science, including weather. In addition to his map, Halley suggested a way that air pressure was related to height, and he spent several years studying the evaporation of water from lakes.

Not until the Great Exhibition of 1851 in London was it possible to display a map showing the kind of weather recorded at the same time in many different

Typhoon detector
This baryocyclometer, an instrument that shows pressure and wind direction, was once used by sailors to warn them of approaching typhoons so that they could calculate a course to avoid them.

Sun sign
People have used many instruments, including sundials such as this one, to study the sun. The sun's energy powers the weather machine.

places. Before this, people could not have known about other weather, because there was no way to communicate such information. As a result, much of what scientists understand about the weather was learned during the last 150 years. Improved communication has allowed knowledge about the weather to be quickly moved and better used.

In the period from 1850 to 1875, many nations established their own meteorological services. Conferences that were held at Brussels; Belgium, in 1853 and at Vienna, Austria, in 1873 helped build international cooperation. These meetings established methods for exchanging information among national services and standardized the way weather observations were made.

Home wrecker
This house was destroyed by a hurricane. These giant storms can lift roofs, tear trees from the ground, and sometimes drive the sea inland, causing devastating floods. The sudden difference between high pressure and low pressure outside can make buildings explode.

Air masses

A LARGE BODY OF AIR that is more or less constant in temperature and humidity is called an air mass. Air over a continent becomes dry, and hot or cold depending on the latitude and the time of year. The temperature of air over the oceans is less changeable, and the air is moister. This is why the weather near the sea is relatively mild compared to weather in land-locked regions. An air mass is called continental (dry) or maritime (moist) depending on whether it formed over land or sea, and it is either polar (cold) or tropical (warm) depending on the latitude at which it formed. However, the characteristics can change if continental air passes over water, and maritime air passes over land.

■ Where major air masses flow

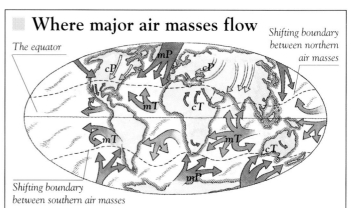

The equator

Shifting boundary between northern air masses

Shifting boundary between southern air masses

The four types of air masses are known as continental polar (cP), continental tropical (cT), maritime polar (mP), and maritime tropical (mT). This map shows the movements of the main air masses. Polar air masses generally move toward the equator, and tropical air masses move away from it.

EXPERIMENT
Heat capacities

Land warms and cools faster than water because water absorbs more heat (it has a higher heat capacity) than land. This affects air masses above land and water by making them drier or moister. Try comparing heat capacities of sand and water.

YOU WILL NEED
● 2 similar baking dishes ● 2 desk lamps with identical bulbs ● sand ● 2 thermometers ● water

👥 Adult supervision is advised for this experiment

1 FILL BOTH BAKING DISHES to about 1 in (2.5 cm) from the top, one with sand and the other with water. Make sure the sand is dry. The sand represents land, and the water is the sea.

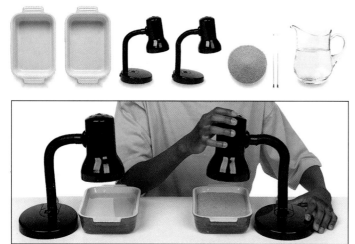

2 PLACE THE DISHES a little way apart. Set one lamp above each to shine down directly on the dishes. Check that the distance is the same between each bulb and the substance below. Note the time, and measure the temperature in the sand and in the water (it does not matter if they are different).

3 SWITCH ON BOTH lamps. Every 15 minutes, measure their temperatures. See how long it takes for the temperatures of the sand and water to rise by 10°. Which one heats most quickly? Now switch off the lamps, and let the sand and water cool. Which reaches its original temperature first?

EXPERIMENT
Do air masses mix?

Warm and cool air masses do not mix readily because their densities are different. A layer of warm air lying above cooler air prevents the cooler air from rising into the warm air mass above. On a large scale, this is known as a temperature inversion. You can use water to demonstrate this effect.

YOU WILL NEED

- *heatproof glass container* • *water*
- *2 bricks* • *mixer* • *spice powder*
- *matches* • *small candle*
- *food coloring*

Adult supervision is advised for this experiment

1 MIX A DASH of spice powder with some cold water. Half-fill a heatproof glass container with this mixture.

2 MIX A LITTLE food coloring with some warm water. Gently pour this over the cold water to form a layer.

3 ASK AN ADULT to light a candle and set it between two bricks. Place the container on the bricks, and watch the spice powder. What happens when it reaches the warm, colored layer above?

EXPERIMENT
Comparing different air masses

Each type of air mass has different characteristics. CP is dry and cool, cT is dry and warm, mP is moist and cool, and mT is moist and warm. You can tell which is which by comparing their relative temperatures and humidities. Here you can make all these air masses on a small scale and measure the differences between them to give each its correct name. Then try to imagine the kind of weather they would bring. Remember that rain is likely only when the relative humidity is approaching 100 percent, but also that as warmed air rises it will cool, and its relative humidity will increase.

YOU WILL NEED
- *water* • *2 wet- and dry-bulb hygrometers*
- *plastic wrap* • *small tray* • *notepad* • *pen*
- *2 dishpans*

1 MAKE THE "OCEANS" by pouring about 1 in (2.5 cm) of water into each pan. Put the hygrometers on trays to keep them dry, place them in the pans, and cover with plastic wrap. Place one in the sun and the other in shade. In half an hour, measure their temperatures and relative humidity.

2 MAKE THE "CONTINENTS" by drying the pans. Put the hygrometers inside and cover with plastic wrap. Place one in the Sun and the other in shade. After half an hour, take their readings. Now compare the readings for all four air masses.

Remove the plastic wrap to see the readings clearly

High- and low-pressure regions

WHEN AIR IS WARMED from below, its density decreases and it rises. If the warming continues, a large mass of air becomes less dense than the air surrounding it. Because the air is less dense, its mass is smaller and it weighs less than the surrounding air. This means it exerts less pressure on the ground, creating a low-pressure region. The cooling of air produces the opposite effect, resulting in a region of high pressure. As cool air sinks, more air is drawn in behind it, which also sinks. As the air sinks, the pressure increases because of the weight of air above, and the lower air warms by compression. The words "warm," "cold," "high," and "low" are relative. Warm air is warm only in relation to cooler air nearby. High pressure usually brings dry weather because when air sinks and warms, its water evaporates. Low pressure, in which air is rising and cooling and water vapor is condensing, often brings rain or snow.

■ Anticyclonic gloom

Fog that forms when pressure is high may be lifted by the wind to produce low clouds. The lifting process is soon counteracted by the general sinking of air in the high-pressure region. The result can be an "anticyclonic gloom"—a misty low-level cloud that blocks out light.

■ Moving molecules

The molecules in warm air move fast and are farther apart

Cold air molecules move slowly and are closer together

The warmer air is, the more energy its molecules have, so they move faster and are farther apart. This means that a given amount, or volume, of warm air contains fewer molecules than an equal amount of cold air, making the air less dense and making it weigh less. The mass of air will rise until it reaches air with the same density.

■ Weather and pressure

The kind of weather you will experience when pressure is high or low depends partly on where you live, but you can learn what to expect by keeping your own accurate day-by-day records of weather conditions.

Forecasting

Check your local weather forecasts, and wait until you are right inside an area of high or low pressure. Then go outside and measure the air temperature, relative humidity, and amount of rain or snow which falls in a day. Write down your measurements. Repeat this for both low and high pressure, in all seasons, and try to take your measurements at the same time of day. Once you have a set of records, you will know the kind of weather that different pressure systems produce.

EXPERIMENT
Amazing expanding air

If you warm a large number of air molecules, they will move faster. The distance between the molecules will increase, so they will occupy a greater volume. This is another way of saying that air expands when it is heated and contracts when it is cooled. As air expands and contracts, its density changes, and that alters the pressure it exerts. Warm some cold air, and you can demonstrate this quite easily.

YOU WILL NEED
- *dishpan*
- *plastic bottle*
- *balloon* • *water*

The cold air in the bottle is warmed by the water and starts to expand. What happens to the balloon?

1 PUT A PLASTIC BOTTLE in a freezer for an hour. Remove it and stretch the balloon over the neck of the bottle.

2 FILL THE DISHPAN with hot tap water. Put the bottle in the water, and watch the balloon as the air expands.

▨ Isobars and pressure regions

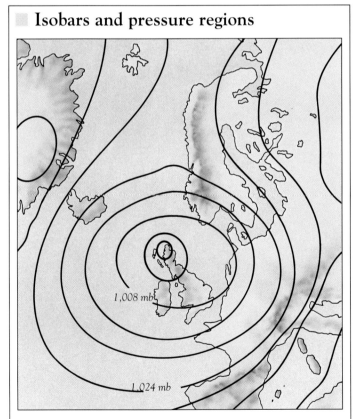

1,008 mb

1,024 mb

Isobars are lines on weather maps joining places of equal atmospheric pressure. They resemble height contours on an ordinary map: high-pressure areas become hills, low-pressure areas hollows. If you draw isobars like this you will see how pressure ridges and troughs earned their names.

EXPERIMENT
Mountains and valleys of air

Isobars on a weather map enclose areas of high and low pressure. A tongue of air separating two areas of high pressure is called a trough. A tongue of high-pressure air between two low-pressure areas is a ridge. You can draw a section across the isobars.

YOU WILL NEED
- *pen* • *graph paper* • *newspaper weather map* • *ruler*

Showing the ridges and troughs
Draw a straight line across a weather map that has isobars (see left). Try to cross both high- and low-pressure areas. Prepare a graph that shows distance along the horizontal scale and pressure in millibars along the vertical scale. Plot the readings taken from the weather map on your graph. Join the marks with a curved line. Now can you see the ridges and troughs?

The earth's rotation

As air moves towards or away from the equator, it drifts east or west, and before long it is flowing around areas of high and low pressure, rather than straight towards or away from them. This drift is called the Coriolis effect, and it is due to the rotation of the earth. As the earth rotates, places on the equator travel faster than places at higher latitudes because the earth's circumference is greatest at the equator, so they have further to travel in the same time than places nearer the poles. Air that is moving away from the equator is still travelling at equatorial speed, so it overtakes the ground beneath and appears to drift eastwards. When the air moves in a circle it has "angular momentum."

■ Angular velocity

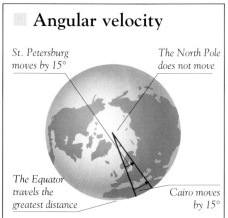

St. Petersburg moves by 15°

The North Pole does not move

The Equator travels the greatest distance

Cairo moves by 15°

The Earth turns on its axis 15° in every hour. This is its "angular velocity". If you mark a 15° angle by drawing two lines from the North Pole to the Equator, you can see that a place on the Equator travels further during one hour than a place much further north. A person standing at the Equator is travelling eastwards at about 1,670 km/h (1,038 mph), and someone at latitude 60° is moving at 722 km/h (449 mph).

EXPERIMENT
Angular momentum

Angular momentum is the total energy of a spinning body. It is a combination of the mass of the body, its rate of spin (this is called its angular velocity), and its radius of spin (the distance from the axis, or center). If one of these elements changes, the others change to compensate so that the total energy remains the same. Thus, angular momentum is "conserved." No matter how fast a body rotates, the energy stays the same. This is easy to demonstrate.

You Will Need
● *stick*
● *scissors*
● *roll of tape*
● *string*

1 Cut 1 yd (1 m) string, and tie one end close to one end of the stick, as tightly as you can. Tape the string to the stick to make sure it is secure.

The faster speed of the roll compensates for the shorter length of the string

2 Tie the roll of tape to the other end of the string. When you spin it, the roll will provide almost all the mass of the spinning body, and the length of the string will determine its radius of spin.

3 Swing the roll until it makes a circle at a fairly constant speed. Using the same force to keep it turning, let the string wind itself around the stick, reducing the radius of spin. At what stage does the roll of tape travel most quickly?

EXPERIMENT
The Coriolis effect

The Coriolis effect was once called a force, but the movements it describes are not caused by pushing or pulling. No force is involved. The effect is simply the result of two bodies, such as the earth and a mass of air or water, moving at different speeds. It can be difficult to understand, but it is very easy to demonstrate.

YOU WILL NEED
- *2 pieces of colored cardboard* ● *pen*
- *scissors* ● *2 push-pins* ● *string* ● *ruler*

Circular motions

In 1835 French physicist Gaspard Coriolis (1792–1843) discovered the "Coriolis effect", which explains the circular motion of ocean currents and air masses. It has caused the swirling clouds on the Equator in this picture.

1 DRAW A LINE along one edge of a piece of cardboard to mark a strip 1 in (2.5 cm) wide. Cut off this strip with scissors.

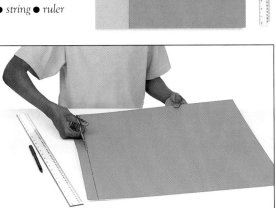

2 WITH THE STRING and a pin, draw the largest circle possible on the card. Cut out the circle with your scissors.

3 PUT THE CIRCLE over the cardboard piece. Pin one end of the strip through the center and the other end outside the circle so the circle turns freely.

4 ASK A FRIEND to turn the circle slowly, in either direction. Use the pen to draw a straight line down one edge of the strip, all the way across the circle. What happens to the line? This is the Coriolis effect.

Fronts

DIFFERENT AIR MASSES do not mix readily, so there is a boundary between them—a front. When both bodies of air are moving in the same direction—usually at different speeds—the front slopes as warm air rides up over colder air ahead of it, or as cold air undercuts and lifts warmer air. If the air behind the front is warmer than that ahead of it, it is a warm front. If the air behind the front is cooler, it is a cold front. Often a wave develops in a front, with a center of low pressure (a "cyclone" or "depression") at the crest, and the system divides into separate warm and cold fronts. If the cold front then overtakes the warm front, lifting the warm air clear of the ground, the front is "occluded."

Warm and cold fronts

At warm fronts air rises up a gentle slope, with the moisture in the air condensing into clouds from which rain or snow might fall. Cold fronts wedge underneath warmer air, lifting it rapidly. Heaped clouds form with clear weather behind.

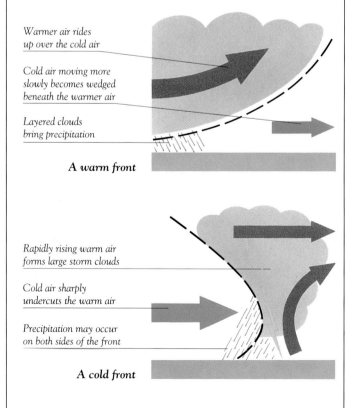

Warmer air rides
up over the cold air

Cold air moving more
slowly becomes wedged
beneath the warmer air

Layered clouds
bring precipitation

A warm front

Rapidly rising warm air
forms large storm clouds

Cold air sharply
undercuts the warm air

Precipitation may occur
on both sides of the front

A cold front

EXPERIMENT
Sinking and rising air

In warm air the molecules move fast and are far apart, so the air is less dense than cold air, in which the molecules move more slowly and are closer together. Air that is less dense than the surrounding air will rise through it. If the air is denser than surrounding air, it will sink. The rising and sinking of air produces clouds of different types. You can see here the strength of this effect.

YOU WILL NEED
● 20 x 20 in (50 x 50 cm) acrylic sheet ● cardboard ● scissors ● tape
● matches
● incense stick ● box
● modeling clay

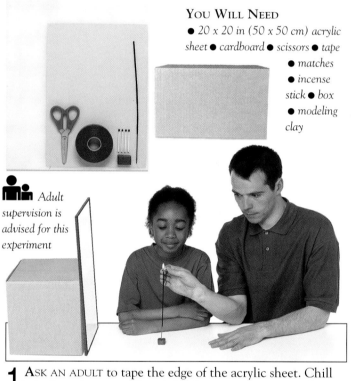

Adult supervision is advised for this experiment

1 ASK AN ADULT to tape the edge of the acrylic sheet. Chill it in the refrigerator. Stand the sheet upright against the box, then stand the incense stick in modeling clay. Ask an adult to light the incense and fan the smoke onto the sheet with the cardboard. What happens?

2 EXTINGUISH THE INCENSE, but do not remove it. Warm the acrylic sheet in hot water. Ask an adult to relight the incense. Stand the sheet against the box as shown, and fan smoke toward it. What happens to the smoke now?

EXPERIMENT
Making a front with water

Bodies of air will not mix if their densities are different. The usual reason for this difference is that one body is warmer than the other. You cannot see the boundary, or front, between them, but it is quite sharply defined. Eventually, the air temperatures and densities will equalize, but it takes quite a long time. This is true for all fluids, liquids as well as gases. Warm water will form a clearly defined layer above cold water. You can demonstrate this quite simply. You will see how clearly the front is marked and how long it takes to disappear.

YOU WILL NEED
- tall, clear jar
- water
- food coloring
- eye dropper
- thermometer

1 HALF-FILL THE JAR with cold water, and put it in the refrigerator. Fill a pitcher with hot tap water, and color it.

How long do the two layers of water stay separate?

3 USE THE THERMOMETER to measure the temperature of the warm water. Move it down to measure the cold water. See if the thermometer can detect the front. Can you can feel it by dipping your finger into the jar?

See if you can take the temperature at the front

2 TRICKLE THE WARM water carefully down the side of the tilted jar. Leave the jar to see if the two waters mix.

Depressions, ridges, and troughs

COLD AND WARM FRONTS (pp.76–77) move at different speeds. Warm air can overtake and rise above cold air, or cold air can undercut and lift adjacent warm air. In these situations, a wave develops in the fronts, with a wedge of warm air intruding into cooler air as it rises. A roughly circular area of low pressure forms at the apex of the wedge. This is called a cyclone, a low, or a depression. As weather systems move, two depressions can follow one another, separated by a tongue of higher pressure air, called a ridge. Similarly, two high-pressure areas may be separated by a tongue of air at a lower pressure, known as a trough.

■ Monitoring ridges and troughs

Time	10 am	12 pm	2 pm	4 pm
Date				
Pressure				
Temperature				
Relative humidity				
Wind direction				
Wind speed				

As it passes, a ridge or trough often brings a brief but marked change in the weather. You can record this by measuring the pressure, temperature, relative humidity, and wind speed and direction, all of which will change sharply. Keep track of your measurements using a chart like the one above. Wait until the TV or newspaper weather map shows a ridge or trough nearby and heading your way. Take measurements every two hours or so, because ridges and troughs can cross quickly. Remember to note the date and the time you take each set of measurements, and your chart should tell you precisely when the ridge or trough arrived and how long it took to move away.

EXPERIMENT
Making a cold front

The air masses that produce our weather are huge, but you can use very small masses of air at different temperatures to make your own cold front which turns into an "occlusion" as the advancing cold air lifts the warm air out of the box.

■ Front symbols

Weather maps use a variety of symbols to indicate different weather conditions and to show their position. Triangles on a weather map indicate the position of a cold front, and semicircles indicate the position of a warm front. Alternating triangles and semicircles indicate an occlusion—an area where one air mass has been lifted up by another moving beneath it. Warm fronts are usually shown in red, cold fronts in blue.

Occlusion

Warm front

Cold front

YOU WILL NEED
● ice ● small box
● large box
● large tray ● pen
● thermometer
● notepad

1 MEASURE THE AIR temperature in the room and write it down. Be sure all the windows and doors are closed, so that the air in the room is quite still.

2 PLACE THE BOXES side by side as shown, so that the large box is closed and the small box is open. Place the thermometer in the open box.

3 FILL A TRAY WITH ICE, and put the tray on top of the closed box (cold front). What happens to the air temperature in the open box?

How occlusions work

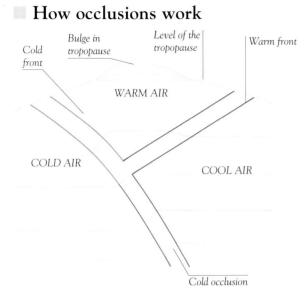

In this cross-section of the atmosphere up to the tropopause (pp.18–19), an advancing cold front has lifted a warm air mass so that both the warm and cold fronts are high above the surface of the earth. The lower part of the front is a cold occlusion between cool air and advancing colder air. The horizontal lines show the heights of air at particular temperatures. In a warm occlusion, the trough of warm air is lifted as the cold front rides up the warm front (with cool air behind it).

Advancing and receding fronts

At a front, warm air rises above cooler air. As the warm air rises, its temperature falls below the dew point and water vapor condenses. The type of clouds produced varies according to the rate at which the warm air rises, and this depends in turn on the gradient up which it is moving. A warm front has a shallow slope. The air is lifted slowly and its water vapor condenses to form sheets of cloud, starting with fair-weather and progressing to rainclouds. A cold front slopes more steeply and produces cumulus clouds (see pp.92–93). Here, rain clouds are in the warm sector, and fair-weather clouds are in the cold sector.

Cross-section through a depression

When a cold front is advancing faster than the warm front, it eventually will overtake it, lifting all the warm air away from the ground and forming an occlusion. In this diagram warm air is rising at both fronts, and cloud is forming. High clouds may appear 12 hours or more ahead of the warm front. Rain falling from high rainclouds evaporates in the cold air, but rain from low rainclouds reaches the ground. The warm sector is cloudy but dry. Rain begins again on the cold front.

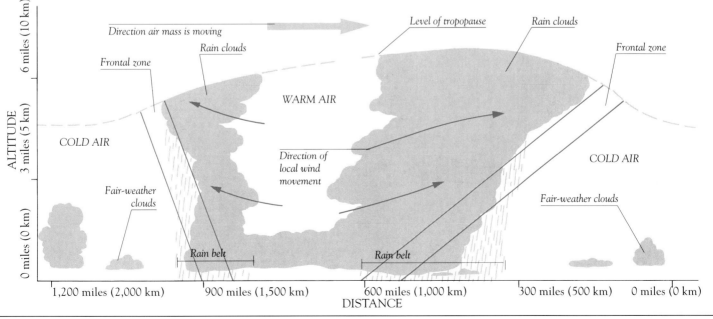

Thunderstorms

As warm, moist air rises, its water vapor condenses. This releases latent heat which helps to maintain the warmth of the air, so the air continues to rise until a towering storm cloud develops. Storm clouds can also be formed by the ground being heated; by winds that flow toward one another so the air converges, triggering the lifting of surface air; and by air climbing over high ground. These kinds of lifting produce isolated storms. More violent storms occur ahead of cold fronts (pp.76–77) when winds converge over a broad area, or zone.

EXPERIMENT
Tracking the storm

Thunder and lightning occur at the same instant, but the light reaches you almost instantly, while sound travels more slowly. You can work out the distance to the storm by measuring the interval between seeing lightning and hearing thunder.

You Will Need
● local map ● pencil
● notebook ● compass

Use a compass to plot the direction of the storm accurately

Plotting the course
Look for lightning, start counting seconds, and stop when you hear the thunder. Sound travels 5 seconds/mile (3 seconds/km), so you can plot where the flash occurred, and trace the storm's movement.

■ How lightning is formed

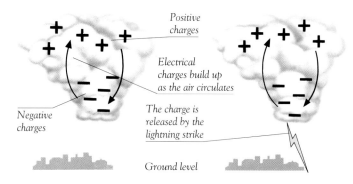

Positive charges

Electrical charges build up as the air circulates

Negative charges

The charge is released by the lightning strike

Ground level

Inside a thunder cloud warm air rises rapidly, cools at the top of the cloud, starts to sink, warms as it sinks, then rises again. This forms convective cells. The turbulent motion causes the top of the cloud to acquire a positive electrical charge and the bottom of the cloud, a negative charge. Scientists are not sure how this happens, but it may be due to collisions between small ice particles as they move up and down inside the cloud building up a static electric charge. Small positively charged ice crystals accumulate at high level, and falling hailstones acquire a negative charge. This static electricity builds to very high levels in the cloud until it eventually sparks—and the spark is lightning.

■ Lightning power

Lightning starts when energy sparks from the bottom of the cloud to the positively charged ground. This energy is met by a returning flash carrying a positive charge upward along the same path of air traveled by the first spark. Flashes continue until the charge between cloud and ground has been equalized by the lightning.

Destruction
Lightning can be very destructive. It blasted this tree and can cause forest fires. Lightning also kills about 100 people a year in the United States alone. The golfer Lee Trevino was once hit by lightning during a game of golf in 1975. Amazingly he was not killed, but the heat of the lightning badly damaged his spine.

EXPERIMENT
The strength of the wind

Inside a storm cloud, raindrops move up and down because of air updrafts and downdrafts. Eventually the drops grow as they merge with other drops and water particles. At the top of the storm cloud the temperature is very low because of the high altitude, making the water droplets freeze and become hailstones. They then get too heavy for the updrafts to support them, so they fall as either rain or hail. You can show this simply for yourself.

YOU WILL NEED
● hair dryer ● tennis ball ● ping-pong ball

Balls in the air
Point the hair dryer vertically upward. Balance the ping-pong ball, representing a small drop of rain, in the updraft. It will be supported. Now see what happens with the heavier tennis ball, representing a larger drop of rain or a hailstone.

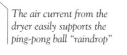

The air current from the dryer easily supports the ping-pong ball "raindrop"

▨ Types of lightning

In fine weather the ground surface is negatively charged, the ionosphere (a very high level of the atmosphere) is positively charged, and a slight current flows between them. A thundercloud intensifies this field locally by at least ten times. Typically, a flash of lightning lasts about 0.2 seconds. It occurs when the difference between the positive and negative charges is large enough to overcome the insulation of the air between them. We think of lightning as flashing between a cloud and the ground, but this is only one direction the spark can take. More often, lightning flashes inside the cloud or between one cloud and another, never reaching the ground.

Sheet lightning
Sheet lightning consists of a white flash that seems to cover a wide area of sky. It is the reflection of a lightning flash that is hidden by the clouds.

Ball lightning
Ball lightning is very rare and appears like a spherical light. It hovers or moves slowly a little way from the ground, then vanishes.

Fork lightning
When lightning flashes, the energy travels along the path which offers least resistance. This is usually irregular, which is why a flash between a cloud and the ground is forked or jagged. The first flash ionizes the air, charging it electrically. This makes a path for the much brighter return flash.

Tornadoes

TORNADOES ARE THE MOST VIOLENT of all wind storms. At their spinning centers wind speeds can reach over 120 mph (180 km/h)—and sometimes much higher—while the body of a storm moves over the ground at 25–40 mph (40–65 km/h). Each tornado is only a few hundred meters in diameter, yet it contains as much energy as one night's street lighting in New York City. Most objects such as cars, houses, and other buildings are completely destroyed if touched by the bottom of a funnel. Worldwide, tornadoes are fairly common, but they are most frequent and most severe in the Great Plains of the United States, along a track through nine states called Tornado Alley. There they kill, on average, more than 200 people a year. Tornadoes over lakes or the sea, called waterspouts, are less violent than tornadoes over land.

■ Flying fish

A tornado can lift almost any object, dropping it later as it weakens. If it passes over a lake it may lift some of the water—and some fish. Fish, frogs, and other small animals that sometimes "rain" from the sky are tornado victims. Such events were often seen as ominous signs for mankind.

EXPERIMENT
Make a tornado

When air or water spins, a vortex, or whirlpool, may form at the center (this happens when bathwater swirls down the drain). The vortex begins at the top and moves down, forming a funnel of strong winds or currents flowing around a calm center. You can see how easily this happens using carbonated water and salt. As the salt dissolves, it displaces the carbon dioxide in the water. The carbon dioxide is released as tiny bubbles of gas. This causes a miniature tornado to form.

YOU WILL NEED
● *carbonated water* ● *revolving cake stand* ● *scissors* ● *tape* ● *salt* ● *tall drinking glass*

1 PLACE THE GLASS at the center of the revolving cake stand. Fasten it securely with tape.

2 NOW POUR CARBONATED water into the glass until it is nearly full. Leave a small space at the top.

3 SPIN THE CAKE STAND, and pour a dash of salt into the glass. Watch the tornado form. You can repeat this as long as the water remains fizzy.

The birth of a tornado

Tornadoes are difficult to observe because of their violence, their relatively small scale, and the speed of their movement over the ground. That is why much remains to be learned about them. These pictures trace the history of one tornado.

1
Air, strongly heated from below, rushes upward to form a convection cell, in which air rises at up to 100 mph (165 km/h) inside a storm cloud. The winds high in the top of the storm cloud start the air rotating at a very high speed.

2
More air flows inward and the rotation extends downward, narrowing as it does so. Its spin accelerates to conserve angular momentum (p.74). Very low pressure in the vortex causes water vapor to condense, making the funnel easily visible.

3
Because it is similar in shape to a large brass instrument, the cloud at the top of a tornado is called a tuba. Dust, water, and small objects are lifted into the cloud and may travel all the way to the top. It is the dust in the cloud that makes it so dark.

4
The tornado can demolish almost anything in its path. It will tear roofs from houses, uproot trees, lift cars, and drop them again farther away. When a storm passes over a building, the difference in air pressure can make the building explode.

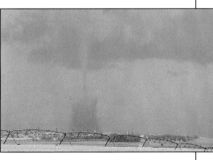

5
The energy spent in destruction weakens the tornado. The surface wind dies down so the base of the tornado is clear of the ground and does no more damage. The supply of moist, rising air dwindles, convection weakens inside the cloud, and the tornado disperses.

Xenia—a town destroyed by a tornado
This is Xenia, Ohio, after a tornado destroyed the town on 3 April 1974. On the same day, 148 tornadoes moved through 13 states killing 315 people and causing $600 million in damage. The storms occurred when a cold front wedged beneath hot, moist air from the Gulf of Mexico.

EXPERIMENT
A vortex in a jar

The vortex that is a tornado begins high in the air and its funnel moves downwards as fast, spiralling winds around a calm centre. Any liquid that turns quickly will form a simple vortex. You can easily make one yourself.

YOU WILL NEED
● *eye dropper* ● *food coloring* ● *spoon*
● *tall jar* ● *water*

1 FILL THE JAR almost to the brim with cold water. Stir the water, keeping the spoon near the top. Make the water spin as fast as possible.

2 NOW watch for the vortex to appear. Add a few drops of food coloring to the water to highlight the shape of the vortex.

How hurricanes work

HURRICANES ARE THE BIGGEST and most powerful of all storms. They are circular and vary in size—many of them are roughly 400 miles (650 km) in diameter, and wind speeds can reach 125 mph (200 km/h) or more. Hurricanes form over warm, tropical seas when the water temperature is above 80° F (27° C). They do not form on the equator, where the Coriolis effect (pp.74–75) is small, or beneath jet streams (pp.126–127). Once formed, they follow a path away from the equator, usually growing in intensity while they remain over warm water. They dissipate over cool water or over land. Such storms are called hurricanes if they form in the Atlantic, cyclones around India and Australia, and typhoons in the western Pacific.

▦ Hurricane danger spots

This map shows the main areas at risk from hurricanes. These storms can travel long distances. The top three regions for hurricane damage are the western Pacific Ocean, the Bay of Bengal, and the Caribbean.

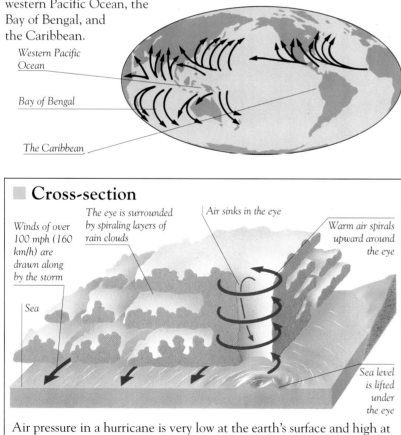

Western Pacific Ocean

Bay of Bengal

The Caribbean

▦ Cross-section

Winds of over 100 mph (160 km/h) are drawn along by the storm

The eye is surrounded by spiraling layers of rain clouds

Air sinks in the eye

Warm air spirals upward around the eye

Sea

Sea level is lifted under the eye

Air pressure in a hurricane is very low at the earth's surface and high at the top of the storm. Warm, moist air, moving to the area of low pressure, rises and forms bands of up to 200 clouds in a vortex of fierce winds around the storm's center (or eye), where calm air descends and warms.

Model hurricane

The clouds around a hurricane form spiral bands. In them, water vapor condenses in the warm, rising air. This releases latent heat (pp.26–27), helping the air to continue rising. At high altitude the air enters the region of high pressure, adding to the pressure difference between the top and bottom of the storm. Some of the energy in the cloud is then transferred to the clear air next to each spiral band and increases the wind speed. You can make a "hurricane" vortex in water showing that spiraling water also forms bands.

YOU WILL NEED
● eye dropper ● food coloring ● mixer ● bowl ● water

1 FILL THE BOWL with lukewarm water. The bigger the bowl, the better. Stir the water gently until it is all moving slowly in a circle around the bowl.

2 RELEASE A FEW DROPS of food coloring into the center of the bowl. Watch the color move out and form bands—just as clouds in a hurricane do.

EXPERIMENT
Storm surge

A hurricane has a great effect on clouds and winds, and it can affect sea water too. Much of the damage caused by a hurricane is due to water. Rainfall is heavy, and winds produce waves up to 50 ft (15 m) high. This effect is widespread and waves are often much larger than normal as much as 900 miles (1,500 km) from the eye of the storm. Fiercely pounding waves ahead of the storm can be 10 ft (3 m) high. When the hurricane approaches a coastline, strong onshore winds cause water to pile up in a "storm surge." If the surge coincides with a high tide, sea water may sweep inland. You can make a storm surge at home.

YOU WILL NEED
- *electric fan* ● *paper*
- *grease pencil* ● *scissors*
- *tape* ● *water*
- *dishpan*

Adult supervision is required for this experiment

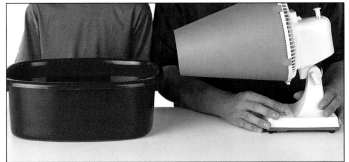

1 MAKE A FUNNEL out of paper, and tape its wide end to fit over the fan. This will concentrate the wind.

2 FILL THE DISHPAN with water to within about 2 in (5 cm) of the brim. Mark the water level at one end of the pan with the grease pencil. Position the fan so that it will blow towards the mark.

3 ASK AN ADULT to switch on the fan so that the wind blows across the surface of the water. How much does the water rise above the mark at the far end? (This is a "storm surge.")

4 NOW REPEAT STEP 3, but tilt the dishpan a little to raise the water level near the mark, creating a high tide. See how much difference the tide makes to the "storm surge."

■ The power of a hurricane

This devastation in Homestead, Florida was caused by Hurricane Andrew—the first hurricane of 1992. Roofs were lifted from homes like this one and smashed to pieces. Buildings can be constructed to withstand the winds of a hurricane, but they can still be damaged by flying debris.

What hurricanes can do

ONE OF THE FIRST SIGNS of a hurricane is thick cirrus cloud (pp.112–113). Light rain soon becomes torrential and driven by a wind that grows rapidly stronger. This is the wind that feeds surface air to the high pressure above the storm. Air sinks inside the eye—the center of the storm. A gallon of water weighs 10 lb (a litre weighs 1 kg), so the force of the wind-driven rain is considerable. Wind speed increases and then, as the eye passes, the sky clears and the wind stops. As the eye moves on, the wind and rain resume. Low pressure raises the sea level, onshore wind drives water into estuaries, and when the storm coincides with a high tide the sea level may rise by 20–30 ft (6–9 m) and flood low areas.

EXPERIMENT
Rising sea levels during a hurricane

Air pressure inside a hurricane can drop by a large amount. The very low pressure at the hurricane's centre allows the sea level beneath it to rise considerably. You can demonstrate this effect in a dishpan.

Daniel Bernoulli

When a fluid flows through a constriction in a pipe, its speed increases and its pressure decreases. This is Bernoulli's Principle, and it explains why the acceleration of air over an aircraft wing generates a lifting force. For the same reason, a strong wind rushing over a house can lift off its roof—something which often happens in hurricanes. The principle was discovered by a Swiss mathematician, Daniel Bernoulli (1700–82). He first qualified as a doctor, but also worked in many other scientific fields, including anatomy, botany and physics.

YOU WILL NEED
● *glass bowl* ● *dishpan* ● *plastic tubing* ● *2 cups* ● *water*

1 HALF-FILL THE dishpan with water. Stand the cups upside down in the pan, and place the glass bowl upside down on them, its rim below the surface.

2 PINCH ONE END of the tube closed, and push it into the air space in the glass bowl. Suck on the tube to reduce the air pressure. The water will rise.

3 REMOVE THE TUBING, and you will be left with a raised wall of water. Lift up the bowl to release the water, and you will create a small storm surge.

EXPERIMENT
Bernoulli's lift

Bernoulli said that when air flows over any obstruction, the difference in pressure above and below the obstruction produces a lifting force. The faster the airflow, the more lift it can generate. By blowing hard you can demonstrate Bernoulli's Principle. Try it with two materials of different shape and weight and see if they move.

YOU WILL NEED
● *8 x 6 in (20 x 15 cm) sheet of paper* ● *small coin*

1 PUT A COIN close to the edge of a table. With your mouth close to the table top, blow hard, and see what the pressure change does to the coin.

2 NOW TRY IT with paper. Hold one end below your lower lip. Blow. What happens to the paper?

EXPERIMENT
Making a vortex

A hurricane is a vortex. This means it is circular in shape, with winds flowing around its center. In the center dry air is sinking from the high-pressure region above the storm, but there is no wind. A vortex in water will also have a calm center, containing no water, surrounded by spiralling currents. If you make one you can find out just how calm it is at the center.

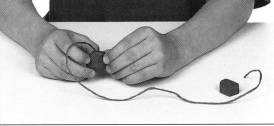

YOU WILL NEED
● *food coloring* ● *scissors* ● *tape*
● *mixer* ● *modeling clay* ● *string*
● *balloon*
● *2 plastic bottles*
● *water*

1 ATTACH THE MODELING clay to one end of a piece of string to make a weight. Tuck any loose ends of string into the clay.

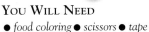

2 ASK AN ADULT to remove a bottle end and tape the edge. Join the bottle necks with a balloon and tape.

3 PLACE THE STRING WITH THE WEIGHT in the top bottle, using the weight to plug the hole between the two bottles. Then fill the top bottle with slightly colored water, to make it easily visible, and give it a circular stir to set it in motion.

4 NOW PULL THE PLUG and then try to suspend the weight in the eye of the vortex. What happens?

CLOUD ATLAS

Cloudy skies
Cloud formations allow meteorologists to track the movement of weather systems. The thunderclouds visible in the satellite photograph above are over the Indian Ocean. Cumulus clouds (left) have formed over the southwestern United States because air heated by contact with the ground has risen and cooled, allowing moisture to condense.

CLOUDS CAN FORM in any climate, at any point on the planet, and can take many different forms. The type of cloud that forms depends on a number of factors and conditions, so recognizing the different kinds of cloud will help you understand what is happening to the air. This in turn will give you an idea of the kind of weather you can expect in the near future.

FORMING CLOUDS

CLOUDS FORM BY THE CONDENSATION or freezing of water vapor, and the way they form depends on their height and on the amount of upward air movement. When pockets of warm air rise rapidly, clouds form in heaped shapes; when air is lifted slowly and evenly over a large area, clouds form as layers. At high altitudes water vapor changes into tiny ice crystals which form thin, wispy clouds high above the ground.

All clouds are made of water droplets or tiny crystals of ice, or both. People have known this since ancient times, and early scientists came close to explaining how clouds form. The explanation stemmed from the belief that all matter is a mixture of four "elements": earth, air, fire, and water.

▮ Early descriptions

In his *Meteorologica*, the first book on weather ever written, the ancient Greek philosopher Aristotle described clouds as mixtures of the element water and varying amounts of the element fire. He believed that when fire and water are mixed, the lightness of fire raises the water from the ground, but if only a small amount of fire is mixed with the water, it is not raised very high. As the fire leaves the water and the two separate, fire rises and the water descends once more, often as dew or—if it is cold enough—as frost. Vapor must be lighter than water, because of the fire mixed with it, so the more fire there is the higher the vapor will rise before it condenses again into clouds.

Aristotle had found an explanation for the way water evaporates and condenses. We know now that fire is not an element that can be mixed with other

Aristotle
Aristotle was a Greek philosopher who lived 2,400 years ago. He was the first person to write about the weather.

Cumulus
Small cumulus clouds (pp. 98–99) like these usually mean fine weather, but if they grow and merge they may bring showers. The larger they grow, the heavier the showers, and the clouds may merge to form thunderclouds.

matter, and what Aristotle called fire is heat—a form of energy. This discovery was made 2,000 years after his death.

Aristotle taught his pupils to study the world by observing what happens in it. Later scholars had different ideas about what went on in the sky; they attributed some events to demons and supernatural forces, and explained others with astrology. Not until the Middle Ages did people begin to describe the weather they saw. Even then scholars were more interested in extreme weather—such as snow, storms, and floods—than they were in the ordinary, day-to-day weather.

An understanding of weather is based on records of numerous meteorological measurements, but early scientists lacked the kinds of instruments they needed to make the measurements. They could

Red sky at night
When the air is dry, dust particles scatter the yellow and red light at sunset, which colors the clouds.

record only what they saw and felt and could only guess at changes in pressure and humidity. There is one class of weather conditions, however, they could have recorded more accurately than they did—clouds. Instruments are needed to measure accurately the height of clouds, but not to describe their appearance. Some clouds look flat and grey, others are very white and fluffy, still others are thin and wispy. To predict whether or not the weather will be good, people also need to know how much cloud there is, whether the amount is increasing or decreasing, how high in the sky the cloud is, and most importantly, what kinds of clouds they are seeing. Are they the kind of clouds, for example, that bring drizzle or steady, persistent rain? Do they bring showers with bright, sunny spells in between? Will they bring thunderstorms? Not all clouds have the same effect. But if you want to tell someone which kind of cloud to expect, you need a name for it, and it helps greatly if everyone agrees to use the same names for the same clouds. You need a system of classification.

▪ Cloud formation

To describe different types of cloud, it helps to know why they are different. Clouds can form in a number of different ways. When air is lifted slowly and evenly over a large area, as it often is in a low-pressure system, its water vapor condenses at about the same height, and layers of cloud form. This is stratiform cloud.

If the ground is heated strongly, a different kind of cloud forms as the warmed air rises by convection in "bubbles" or "pockets," carrying water vapor with it. In this kind of cloud, cumiliform, the water vapor condenses at a certain height, but the droplets continue to be carried upward, and clouds form in heaped shapes.

Buildings, trees, hills, and varying surfaces make the ground

Carolus Linnaeus
The scientific system Linnaeus (1707–78) devised for plant and animal classification has been adapted to classify clouds in genera and species.

uneven. When the wind carries moist air close to ground level the unevenness of the earth's surface mixes the air, causing it to eddy and swirl, and the mixing lifts the air to a higher level where its water vapor may condense to produce fog, stratus, or stratocumulus. Sometimes, water vapor may condense in air that is forced to rise as it is carried over hills. Whether this forms layers or heaps of cloud depends on whether the air is stable or not.

When air is warmed unevenly by contact with the ground, it rises and is carried downwind. The air cools as it rises and also as it mixes with the colder, drier air surrounding it. Its water vapor condenses, slowing the cooling process. This makes the rising air more buoyant relative to the cool, dry air surrounding it, so it continues to rise. This produces high, towering clouds. Warming by contact with the ground starts the process, but once it has begun it continues because of what happens in the cloud: The unstable air inside rises, cools near the top, then descends again.

▪ Luke Howard

The simplest and most useful way to describe clouds was devised in 1803 by the English amateur meteorologist Luke Howard (1772–1864). Howard's method is based on the general shape, appearance, and thickness of clouds, and the heights at which they form. In other words, he described what he saw and where he saw it. Howard devised a system of names for different kinds of clouds, so that when an observer saw a certain kind of cloud and identified it by its scientific name, any meteorologist in the world could understand at once what the observer meant.

The system Howard suggested was so popular among scientists that it was adopted as the basis for an international system in which clouds are grouped as genera and species—the method Linnaeus introduced for classifying plants and animals. Eventually, in 1896, international teams of meteorologists published the first *International Cloud Atlas* using Howard's classification of clouds and the names he had invented. Today, the *International Cloud Atlas* is published by the World Meteorological Organization of the United Nations.

The following pages show pictures of all the common types of cloud, with the ways their appearance can vary, as well as some less common but very beautiful cloud formations. The clouds are named according to the system Luke Howard originated, and they are easily recognizable.

Mares' tails
Cirrus clouds (pp.112–113), or mares' tails, are made from ice crystals swept into strands by the wind.

Streaks of cloud
Fall streaks are ice crystals falling into warmer air, leaving a hole in the cloud and then vaporizing.

Mountain cloud
Fog often forms in valleys at night as air close to the ground is chilled. In the morning the fog may lift to become stratus cloud (pp.94–95), so low that the mountain top is still above it. The thin layer of cloud will slowly evaporate and clear during the day.

CLOUD CLASSIFICATION

THE SEARCH FOR A WAY to classify clouds took centuries. The Greek philosopher Theophrastus (c.372–c.287 BC) tried. He wrote of "clouds like fleeces of wool". The French naturalist Jean Lamarck (1744–1829) divided clouds into categories such as "sweepings," "bars," and "flocks," but it was the Englishman Luke Howard (1772–1864) who suggested a classification that could work.

Luke Howard
Howard introduced the first scientific system for classifying clouds.

Luke Howard worked in London as an apothecary and was keenly interested in meteorology. In 1803 he published an article called "On the Modifications of Clouds." He named four main cloud types, giving them Latin names. Cloud that is wispy and looks like locks of hair he called *cirrus*, the Latin for hair. Heaped, lumpy looking clouds he called

cumulus, which means pile. Featureless sheets of cloud he called *stratus*, from *stratum*, the Latin word for layer. Low, grey rain cloud he called *nimbus*, which just means cloud. In 1874, at the first International Meteorological Congress, scientists agreed on the need for a proper cloud classification. They used Howard's names as a starting point and

published an *International Cloud Atlas* in 1896. As aviation developed during the twentieth century, the need for cloud classification grew more urgent. The modern system is much simpler than it looks. It begins by dividing all clouds into ten genera (see opposite), with each genus (the singular of genera) made of a number of species, plus varieties of the species.

Types of clouds

Clouds that form at very high altitude have names beginning with "cirr-" or "cirro-." Medium-level clouds have names beginning with "alto-," from *altus*, which means high, and they can form as heaps or sheets. The remaining clouds have names beginning with "cumu-" if they are heaped and "strat-" if they form sheets. More generally, cirrus-type clouds can be called cirriform, heaped clouds are cumuliform, and sheet clouds are stratiform.

The names of the ten genera also refer to the height of the cloud base. The cirriform clouds form at high altitude, altocumulus and altostratus at medium altitudes, and the others at low altitude. Nimbostratus is usually a medium-level cloud and sometimes extends through both medium and low altitudes. Every cloud you will ever see

Cirrostratus
Cirrus
Cirrocumulus
Anvil of cumulonimbus
Altostratus
Airplane contrail
Cumulonimbus
Stratocumulus
Cumulus
Nimbostratus
Stratus

Types of cloud
Classification is based on a cloud's height and appearance. Similar clouds at different heights will have different names, even if they look alike.

can be described by one of these names, and for most purposes they are the only names you need to remember. The names of species describe the shape of clouds, and those of varieties describe cloud thickness and arrangement.

Cloud differences

Some names refer only to cumuliform clouds. If the top of a cumulonimbus is anvil-shaped the top is called incus, if it is hairy or streaky it is capillatus, and the dark, threatening, arch-shaped base of cumulonimbus is arcus. Occasionally there may be lumps of cloud attached to the base or the anvil, looking like the udders of a cow. These are called mamma.

Calvus means bald and describes a cloud that has no cauliflower-like lumps on the top. Castellanus describes a cloud that is heaped up into what looks like the turrets of a castle. When a cumulus is growing it may look as though the top is swirling and turbulent; this is called congestus. If the cumulus is small, not growing, and rather flat, it is called humilis. Especially while it is growing, a cumulus may have a flat cloud at its top, rather like a cap. This is called pileus. The cloud that links together the tops of cumulus clouds is called velum.

Fractus looks like fragments torn from other clouds. Sometimes the name is used as a prefix to the name of the original cloud—for example, fractocumulus.

If the fibrous strands of cirrus are tangled together, it is called intortus, and if the cirrus is compact and fairly dense it is called spissatus. The hooked fibers of cirrus that make mare's tails are called uncinus.

Precipitation that evaporates before reaching the ground is called virga or fall streaks.

How the Cloud Atlas works

The cloud classification in this atlas is based on the most widely used international system. Clouds are arranged first according to the height of their bases, and then by their appearance. Generally, the bases of low-level clouds lie below 7,000 ft (2 km), the bases of medium-level clouds lie between 7,000–16,000 ft (2 and 5 km), and the bases of high-level clouds between 16,000–35,000 ft (5 and 12 km). However, medium- and high-level clouds form at a higher altitude in the tropics than in polar regions, and heights anywhere can vary depending on local conditions. The bases can be affected by location, season, or time of day.

Low-level clouds
The low-level clouds are called stratus, which forms sheets; stratocumulus, which forms sheets with rolls and bulges; and cumulus, which forms heaps. Cumulonimbus is categorized as a low cloud, but its top can reach high into the atmosphere.

Medium-level clouds
The medium-level clouds are nimbostratus and altostratus, which form sheets; and altocumulus, which forms lumps. Altocumulus is very variable in appearance and can be difficult to identify. Altostratus produces a watery-looking sky, often bringing precipitation.

High-level clouds
The high-level clouds are called cirrus, cirrostratus, and cirrocumulus. These form at very high levels in the atmosphere where the air contains little water vapor, so they are very thin, wispy, and transparent. They are made from tiny ice crystals.

Stratus

Nimbostratus

Cirrus

Stratocumulus

Altostratus

Cirrocumulus

Cumulus

Altocumulus

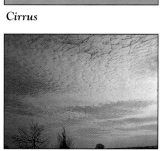

Cirrostratus

Cumulonimbus

Photographing the sky

You can build up your own record of cloud photographs. Try not to take photographs if the sun is shining on the lens. If you can attach filters to your camera, a polarizing filter will improve contrast. Remember, never look at the sun—especially through your camera—because you may damage your eyes.

Low-level clouds

CLOUDS ARE CLASSIFIED by their appearance and base height. Base heights are used because some low-level clouds are very shallow, but others can reach 8 miles (13 km) high. The bases of low-level clouds range in height from ground level to 6,500 ft (2 km). Stratus, stratocumulus, cumulus, and cumulonimbus are low-level clouds. Stratus is smooth and featureless. The others are lumpy, or cumuliform (pp.92–93), and have more shape.

Low-level clouds
*0–6,500 ft (0–2 km)
The heights of cloud
bases can vary
because of the time of
year, the latitude, and
the time of day. All
these factors affect the
air temperature, which
in turn affects the way
that clouds form and
the shape they take.*

Stratus

The base height of stratus is normally in the lowest 2,000 ft (600 m) of the atmosphere. Often stratus shrouds the tops of hills or sea cliffs, and it is then known as stratus nebulosus (from the Latin word for "mist"). It forms in stable air, which has little or no turbulence—so the cloudy air does not mix with the clean air above or below it. As a result an airplane flying through stratus has a relatively smooth ride. If stratus forms in air that is lifting over hills or along a front, it may be followed by rain. People who live in valleys know to expect rain when stratus appears on the hilltops. Stratus can also form at night when moist air moves over land that is cooling. The following morning is cloudy, but if the sun evaporates the water droplets the cloud will soon clear and the day will be fine.

Stratus translucidus ▶
*If stratus is so thin or patchy that
the Sun can be seen faintly through
it, the cloud is called translucidus.*

▲ **False stratus translucidus**
*This false stratus translucidus has
formed on the edge of a thunder
cloud. The sun is actually shining
through a gap in the cloud.*

▲ **Shallow fog developing over a flat valley**
Here, a fine evening ends with fog forming in a valley as the ground
cools faster than the moist air above it. During the night the fog may lift
to form a raised layer of stratus clouds.

▲ **Mountain valley fog**
A temperature inversion—with
a warm layer of air over the
cloud—has caused this stratus to
be trapped as fog in a mountain
valley. If the inversion breaks,
the fog will rise and become a
raised layer of cloud.

Mountain stratus ▷
Moist air has cooled as it has risen
over the hill. Its water vapor has
condensed, forming a layer of
stratus shrouding the peak.

Stratus fractus ▲
When stratus breaks up into
small, tattered fragments, it is
called fractus. Sometimes, as in
this picture, there is more cloud
above the stratus fractus. This
type of cloud is often associated
with bad weather, either recently
past or soon to come.

Stratocumulus

When warm, moist air is mixed with drier, cooler air and the mixture is moving beneath warmer, lighter air above, clouds will often form as rolls or waves. Sometimes, especially in summer, there are gaps through which the Sun can shine. This cloud is called stratocumulus, meaning sheets of lumpy cloud. Stratocumulus is grey, white, or a mixture of both, usually with some darker patches. It is a low-level cloud that can look threatening, but unless it is very thick usually only drizzle or light precipitation fall from it. It can also form in air forced to rise over hills. Its base is typically at 1,000–7,000 ft (300–2,000 m). Although stratocumulus is not usually a bad-weather cloud, its presence may indicate that worse weather is on its way, or is just clearing.

▲ Parallel rolls
The rolls of stratocumulus are caused by the movement of air. Here they appear to be dark and gloomy because the sun is behind them.

Stratocumulus at sunset ▷
This is high-level stratocumulus that is nearly altocumulus (pp.108–109). At sunset the bottoms of the rolls are tinged with color, and the cloud to either side is in shadow. The parallel rolls lie at right angles to the direction of the wind at cloud height. The wind must be light, because strong wind would break up the cloud formation.

▲ **Broken stratocumulus**
Stratocumulus can occur as broken patches of cloud, usually indicating fine weather. This is a merged sheet of stratocumulus that is breaking up, with good weather soon to follow.

▲ **Merged stratocumulus**
When the stratocumulus forms a complete layer —sometimes a thick and dark-colored one covering much of the sky—it is called opacus, which means you cannot see through it.

▲ **Separated stratocumulus**
After a time, a stratocumulus layer begins to separate as its water particles evaporate in warmer air. Breaks appear in the layer, and the stratocumulus forms individual clouds.

◀ **Sheet stratocumulus**
When stratocumulus forms a sheet it is called stratiformis. Here you can see its edge, marking the boundary of a region of warm, descending air in which the cloud has developed.

Stratocumulus from space ▶
We usually see clouds from below, but satellite photographs, covering a very large area, reveal complete cloud patterns. This NASA photograph shows a broad band of stratocumulus marking the boundary of a mass of warm air moving out over the Pacific Ocean from the coast of California. Notice the parallel rolls of cloud, at right angles to the wind direction. Meteorologists can recognize fronts, depressions, and other weather systems from the cloud patterns associated with them, and they can track the movements of these systems by comparing photographs such as these taken at intervals of a few hours.

Cumulus

Puffy white clouds that drift across the sky on a bright summer day, like those on the right, are called cumulus. When they are small and scattered, they are a sign of fine weather. Cumulus means "heaped," and the clouds form in columns of rising air above ground that is being heated strongly by the sun or in air that is made to rise rapidly. As the air rises it cools, and its water vapor condenses onto particles of matter called condensation nuclei. The latent heat of condensation (pp.22–23) warms the air around the droplets, so the air rises further and more water vapor condenses. Air around the clouds descends to replace the rising air. As this air descends, it warms, and water droplets on the fringes of the clouds may evaporate into it. This limits the horizontal growth of the clouds.

◄ **Tibetan cumulus**
Cumulus is not always small. This enormous cloud is over Tibet, where continental polar air has risen as it crossed the mountains, at the same time being warmed by contact with the sunlit ground. The air has become unstable, forming a cloud that has risen to a great height.

▲ **Cauliflower cloud**
Differences in air speeds within the cloud makes the top of a cumulus look like a cauliflower. In bright sunshine the bulges catch the light, emphasizing the effect and making the cloud look very white.

▲ **Cumulus mediocris**
Sometimes a high-level temperature inversion, in which the air temperature increases with height, limits the growth of cumulus because the rising air meets air warmer than itself. This type of cumulus is called mediocris.

Developing cumulus ▶
Cumulus clouds continue to develop as long as there are upcurrents carrying moist air to a height where water vapor condenses and upward growth is not limited by temperature inversion. Clouds that begin to appear early in the morning, as the ground begins to warm, can reach a considerable size by the afternoon.

◄ ▲ *Fractocumulus*
As it begins to form or break up, cumulus can look wispy and ragged. This is called fractocumulus or cumulus fractus, meaning that the cloud is broken into fragments. On the left, small patches of fractocumulus appear between or are attached to larger clouds. In the picture above, different lighting conditions have made the fractocumulus darker.

Cumulus II

▲ Decaying cumulus
As the sun sinks at the end of the day, the ground is warmed less strongly, so the thermal currents are weaker and less air is carried to a height at which its water vapor condenses into droplets. Slowly, the droplets evaporate and the cloud shrinks.

▲ Cumulus congestus
Small cumulus clouds sometimes merge into a larger and darker mass called cumulus congestus. There is intense vertical movement within this towering cloud, and people beneath it may expect a shower, possibly a heavy one. Beneath the cloud are bands of light called crepuscular rays.

Congestus and fractus ▶
Seen from the air, cumulus congestus forms a large but fairly isolated cloud. Near its base it is surrounded by puffy scraps of cumulus fractus.

Development of a large cumulus ▶
Because it forms when air is heated from below, cumulus can grow very quickly. Within a few hours, small "cotton-wool" clouds can develop into a mighty congestus covering much of the sky. This sequence shows a cumulus growing upward, like a tower. When it can grow no taller because of a high-level temperature inversion, the cloud spreads sideways into a mushroom shape, shading a large area.

A massive rain-bearing cumulus ▲
Cumulus tends to grow larger in the
tropics than elsewhere because there is
stronger surface heating to drive it. This
swelling cumulus congestus over Barbados
is 2 miles (3.2 km) deep, and far wider.
Seen from the ground, congestus appears
as a towering wall of cloud. The very
dark base indicates that the precipitation
edge of the cloud is approaching and
producing large amounts of rain.

Cumulonimbus

On a hot summer day with a clear sky and no wind, a large mass of humid air may sit almost motionless over a wide area. People will feel sticky because they cannot cool themselves—their perspiration evaporates slowly into the almost saturated air. Air begins to rise as it is heated by contact with the warm ground. This air forms separate convection cells (pp.50–51), with warm air rising through the centers of the cells and cooler air sinking at their sides. The cloud that forms is called cumulonimbus. It resembles cumulus but towers much higher, with a base at 1,000–5,000 ft (300–1,500 m). Rain starts to fall. Inside this very violent cloud, air rises rapidly in the convection cells and sinks between them. Lightning is produced, causing the rumble of thunder as it strikes.

◀ Anvil detail
The lower part of a cumulonimbus
is made from water droplets, which
may freeze as they rise near the top
of the cloud and melt as they fall
again. The anvil shape is made
entirely from tiny crystals of ice that
fall very slowly. As they fall they are
replaced as more water vapor is
converted into ice.

Anvil detail ▶
Strong winds draw out the top of the anvil, and as its ice crystals mix with drier
air they change, giving the cloud a wispy appearance. Although cumulonimbus
clouds often have anvil tops, you can see them only from a distance.

◀ Mammatus detail
Sometimes you may see large bulges
hanging from the bottom of a cloud.
They are called mamma, which
means "breast."

◀ Classic anvil
Where the cloud top flattens as it
meets the tropopause (pp.18–19), the
cloud spreads. High-level winds may
draw the cloud into the shape
of an anvil.

▲ Mammatus anvil
Mamma are small clouds that form just below the base of the larger cloud and
attach themselves to it. It is usually only when the sun is low enough for its light
to catch the bottom of the cloud or its anvil that you can see the mamma clearly.

Cumulonimbus II

◀ **Precipitating cumulonimbus**
Rain is falling over the sea from this
cumulonimbus. A summer storm like
this one may release as much energy
as an atomic bomb.

Massive cumulonimbus anvil ▲
The air temperature at the top of this cloud
is about –50° F (–45° C). At this
temperature the last of the water vapor
carried up by convection is converted into
the ice crystals that make up this anvil.

Cumulonimbus without anvil ▶
Not every cumulonimbus grows an anvil. If the rising air reaches a layer of warmer air, the growth of the cloud will be stopped. The top will flatten and spread to the sides, and the cloud will be made from water droplets, not ice crystals. The white streaks below this cloud indicate that hail or snow is falling.

▼ **Sunset rainfall**
Heavy rain is falling from the large cumulonimbus on the left, but as the ground cools the cloud may decay, like the cloud to the right of it. Tomorrow the weather may be fine.

Cumulonimbus over Zaire ▶
Notice the size of the shadows cast by these clouds photographed by a satellite over Zaire. Compare the area of the largest anvil with that of the cloud feeding it. One cumulonimbus is fully developed and huge, two more are nearing their full size, and some of the large cumulus may become cumulonimbus. Storm clouds like these are more common and much larger over the tropics than they are elsewhere because the ground is heated more strongly and the tropopause (pp.18–19) is at its highest over the Equator. As a result the cloud tops can reach a much greater height, rising up to 8 miles (13 km) or more.

Medium-level clouds

THE BASE OF MEDIUM-LEVEL CLOUD is usually between 6,500–16,500 ft (2 and 5 km) and is often lower at high latitudes than in the tropics. This group of clouds includes nimbostratus, altocumulus, and altostratus. There is less variety in these clouds than in low-level clouds, because the clouds are farther away from the influences of ground heating and cooling. The variety in medium-level clouds is difficult to see because of their height.

Medium-level clouds
6,500–16,500 ft (2–5 km)
The heights of medium-level cloud bases can vary widely in different regions. Changes in cloud formation are affected by air temperature, latitude, and time of day.

Nimbostratus

On a dull day when it rains or snows gently but ceaselessly, the blanket of grey cloud hiding the sun and any higher clouds is nimbostratus. *Nimbus* means rain, and *stratus* means sheet, so nimbostratus is a sheet cloud from which rain or snow is falling, usually continuously. Although this grey, featureless cloud is classified as a medium-level cloud, its base can be quite low: anywhere from 2,000–7,000 ft (600–2,000 m). The layer is thick enough to block out the sun. Nimbostratus forms when warm, moist air is lifted steadily over a large area. This can happen at a warm front or, less commonly, at a cold front (pp.76–77). Usually the air is stable and there is little turbulence in the cloud, but local conditions can cause cumulonimbus (pp.102–103) to develop inside the nimbostratus.

Nimbostratus ▶
Cloud droplets in nimbostratus freeze if the cloud temperature is low, and precipitation may leave the cloud as snow. If the air temperature below the cloud is above freezing, the snow will melt as it falls and reach the ground as rain.

▲ Nimbostratus patches
Nimbostratus is often patchy, and then it is called fractostratus. Low fractostratus is called scud.

Altostratus

A warm front has a much shallower slope than the cold front overtaking it (pp.76–77), so the warm, stable air behind it is lifted quite slowly over the colder air. At about 6,500–16,500 ft (2–5 km) an altostratus may form from water droplets, which may be below freezing temperature, or supercooled. From the ground this altostratus looks white or slightly blue and watery. It may form a continuous sheet, as in the picture at right, or look as though it is made from soft fibers. Altostratus is light, and the sun is often visible through it, although the cloud may also be thick enough to hide the sun. Rain or snow may fall. Altostratus may not cover the whole sky, but it frequently does. Clouds of other types may be visible at its edges or beneath it.

◀ **Altostratus translucidus**
When people talk of a "watery sky," they are usually describing a wide layer of pale altostratus through which the sun can be seen as a bright blur, as though you were seeing it through frosted glass. Meteorologists call this altostratus translucidus. The sun is partly visible because the cloud layer is not very thick, and above the cloud the sky is clear. The cloud is thicker in some places than others, and from time to time the sun may disappear as a deeper layer crosses in front of it.

Altostratus translucidus above fractocumulus ▶
This thin sheet of altostratus translucidus is moving above wispy bits of fractocumulus. The two clouds may belong to separate air masses and be moving in different directions to one another.

Altocumulus

The small, white, puffy clouds that sometimes slowly drift across the sky can look like dozens of small, loose cottonballs. This is altocumulus, and it forms between 8,000–18,000 ft (2.5–5.5 km). Altocumulus can develop in several ways. Moist air is cooled by turbulence, then lifted up slightly and cooled to form a layer of cloud at that height. Altocumulus usually forms in a layer of moist air, where air currents undulate gently, like waves on the sea. As a wave rises, water vapour condenses, and there is cloud. In the wave troughs, water evaporates. There the cloud is thinner or the sky may be clear, producing the bands of cloud that are sometimes seen. Stratocumulus occasionally appears in the evening or early morning, disappearing during the day.

▲ **Altocumulus texture**
Altocumulus frequently forms patterns, but these may not be very clear when the individual clouds are scattered, as they are here. The sky looks peaceful, but in fact the air close to the clouds is fairly turbulent.

Broken altocumulus ▷
Altocumulus can form from remnants of clouds that have broken up. A sky like this, covered by randomly scattered altocumulus, is of little use in predicting the weather to come. If the cloud has formed on a front it might gradually grow thicker, with the gaps filling in. It is then likely to be followed by rain. A layer of altocumulus that is thinning and breaking up may mark the start of a spell of fine weather.

◄ **Parallel rolls of altocumulus**
When one layer of air lies above another in which the temperature, density, and humidity are different, and if the two layers are flowing in different directions (or in the same direction at different speeds), large waves can be formed. At the colder top of waves water vapor condenses. As air sinks into the warmer troughs, water evaporates. This produces parallel rolls.

Altocumulus castellatus ▲
Altocumulus clouds like these are called castellatus, meaning "like the turrets of a castle." For weather forecasters, these clouds often warn of impending storms.

◄ **Castellatus at sunset**
In altocumulus castellatus, convection is generated inside the clouds by the condensation of water vapor. If sunlight heats the ground strongly, convection from below will add to that at a higher level, possibly bringing thunderstorms.

Altocumulus cumulogenitus ▶
This altocumulus is called cumulogenitus ("born from cumulus") because the large, flat-topped cumulus is its "parent." Some of the warm, moist air that produced the cumulus is moving up and down between layers of air at different temperatures to the sides of the main cloud. This forms altocumulus from the air and moisture from the cumulus.

Altocumulus II

◀ ▲ *Altocumulus lenticularis*

Stable air crossing a mountain range is lifted, then sinks to its former level. This can generate waves like those at sea. Altocumulus lenticularis (meaning "lens-shaped") clouds may form in the wave crests, sometimes in strange shapes.

Mammatus textures ▲ ▼
Mamma attached to the base of a continuous layer of altocumulus can create a variety of textures.

▲ Altocumulus mammatus
Mamma—the breast-shaped protuberances that sometimes attach themselves to the base of a cloud—occasionally form beneath altocumulus. The presence of mamma suggests unstable air, with thicker cumulus shower clouds approaching or moving away.

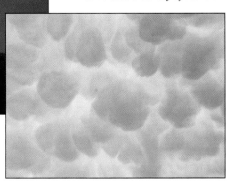

◄ ▲ Lenticular wave
This "pile of plates" (left) has formed downwind of high ground. The other cloud (above) is forming waves and troughs that are moving away from the position of the observer.

Altocumulus floccus ▶
Altocumulus can occur as ragged, tufted fragments called floccus. These may be associated with approaching thundery weather.

High-level clouds

HIGH-LEVEL CLOUDS form at 16,500–45,000 ft (5–14 km), usually at a lower level in high latitudes than in the tropics, because the tropopause (pp.18–19) is higher in the tropics. The high-level clouds all have names beginning "cirr-" because of their resemblance to hair. They are cirrus, cirrocumulus, and cirrostratus. Made by the changing of water vapor into ice crystals, they are as thin and wispy as they look.

High-level clouds
Above 16,500 ft (5 km) Changes in the height of the tropopause, combined with differences in the latitude, air temperature, and the prevailing air mass means that high-level clouds can form at different heights in different regions.

Cirrus

When you see cirrus you can be sure the air is very dry; if the air were moist other types of cloud would form at lower levels. In an otherwise clear sky, cirrus may mean fine weather will continue, but cirrus can also appear at the leading edge of a warm front (pp.76–77). If cirrus increases to cover most of the sky, and especially if it forms a continuous sheet called cirrostratus, wind and rain may soon follow, although you may be out of the direct line of advance of the front (and escape the worst of the weather). Cirrus is made up of falling ice crystals drawn out by the wind into filaments. In this picture (left), crystals falling from a patch of cirrus are being drawn into filaments by the wind. The longer the filaments, the stronger the wind—sailors once used cirrus as a "wind warning."

Cirrus over Norway ▶
These long bands of cirrus appear to converge because of their height, but in fact they form parallel lines.

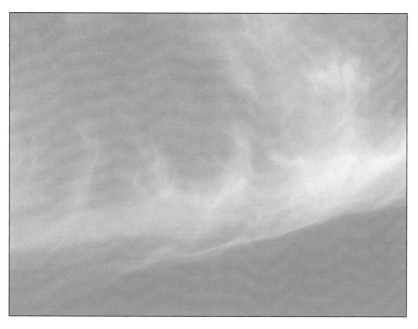

▲ ***Cirrus virga***
Falling ice crystals form streaks called virga. If the wind does not draw them into filaments, they can give cirrus a tattered appearance.

Cirrus shapes ▲ ▶
These cirrus forms have many names, including "mares' tails," "painter's brush," and "hen scratchings." The cirrus tails indicate the direction of the high-level wind.

◀ **Cirrus fibratus**
The variety of cirrus in which the filaments are smooth is called fibratus, meaning "fibrous." Perspective makes distant strands appear to merge into a continuous layer.

Cirrus spissatus ▲
Cirrus spissatus is a dense, compact mass of cloud. In fact it is a cumulonimbus anvil (pp.102–105) that was detached when the main body of the cloud decayed. Now it survives independently. Because of its origin, its full name is cirrus spissatus cumulonimbogenitus, or "false" cirrus. The storm has disappeared, and this cirrus remnant marks the improving weather.

◀ **Cirrus floccus**
Here, scattered patches of cirrus have trailing tails made from falling ice crystals. The sky is visible through gaps in the cloud, so the cloud appears to be ragged. Such clouds look like tufts or flocks of wool, hence the name cirrus floccus. Floccus patches sometimes look like small cumulus clouds.

Cirrocumulus

A patch or layer of cloud consisting of tiny individual cloudlets at high-level is called cirrocumulus. The cloudlets may make a regular dappled or rippled pattern. Sometimes they look like the scales on a fish—a "mackerel" sky that may mean that unsettled weather is on its way. Like all high-level clouds, cirrocumulus is made of ice crystals. It forms when cirrus or cirrostratus is warmed gently from below. This causes air to rise and sink inside the cloud. Some of the ice crystals change into water vapor, and gaps appear. It can be difficult to tell cirrocumulus from altocumulus (p.108). Cirrocumulus has no shading (which altocumulus usually has), and because it is so much higher, the cloudlets of cirrocumulus are much smaller than those of altocumulus.

◀ **Cirrocumulus and cirrostratus**
This small patch of cirrocumulus is below a patch of cirrostratus. The cirrocumulus is very broken and may soon disappear.

Fake cirrocumulus ▲
Aircraft condensation trails form when water vapor from engine exhaust changes into ice, and they can gradually spread to look like this.

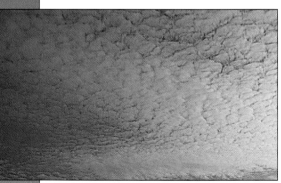

Ripples in the sky ▲
This cirrocumulus is continuous over part of the sky. You can tell the cloud from cirrostratus (p.115) by its rippled texture, and from altocumulus by the size of its ripples.

Cirrostratus

Cirrostratus may cover the sky as a continuous sheet with no features, but it often has a fibrous look. The cloud is so thin it is almost transparent. You can see the sun or moon through it much more clearly than you can through altostratus (p.107), and this is the simplest way to tell one cloud from the other. Also, if the sun or moon is surrounded by a halo, the cloud is almost certainly cirrostratus. It is worth watching cirrostratus, because it often signals changing weather. If it forms from cirrus that grows thicker and more continuous, it may give way to altostratus followed by lower cloud and wet weather. If gaps begin to appear in cirrostratus, so that it slowly changes into cirrocumulus, the weather is probably fair and may remain dry for several days.

◀ **Cirrostratus at dusk**
This is typical cirrostratus. The cloud forms a thin, fibrous veil through which the sun can clearly be seen. Below it is a small patch of stratocumulus. Imagine an enormous board lying on the ground in front of you. Lift the edge nearest you by 1°. This is the angle that a warm front (pp.76–77) approaches. Warm air is rising above a mass of colder air. The stratocumulus is in the cold air below and ahead of the front, and the cirrostratus is in the warm air behind the front. The frontal slope is so gentle that it will be several hours before the cirrostratus gives way to the altostratus, nimbostratus, and low-level stratus following behind.

Halo around the sun ▶
Common with cirrostratus and often heralding rain, a halo like this is caused by the refraction, or bending, of light by ice crystals. As in a rainbow, but less strongly, the refraction breaks light into separate colors.

Atmospheric phenomena

VERY OCCASIONALLY, STRANGE LIGHTS or shapes appear in the sky. "Castles" may float high in the air, a huge, shining cross may hang far above the ground, or there may seem to be two suns at the same height but a bit apart. These phenomena are caused by the reflection or refraction of light (pp.20–21) by water droplets or ice crystals or by light rays passing through layers of air with different densities. The shadow of an airplane cast by the sun onto clouds, or of a person cast onto a bank of fog, may be surrounded by colored rings, like a rainbow. This is a "glory." In fact, these unusual sights can all be explained.

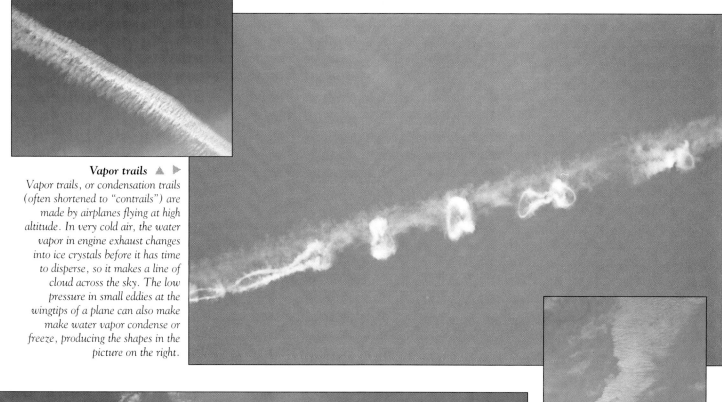

Vapor trails ▲ ▶
Vapor trails, or condensation trails (often shortened to "contrails") are made by airplanes flying at high altitude. In very cold air, the water vapor in engine exhaust changes into ice crystals before it has time to disperse, so it makes a line of cloud across the sky. The low pressure in small eddies at the wingtips of a plane can also make make water vapor condense or freeze, producing the shapes in the picture on the right.

Spreading trails ▲
Vapor trails can often spread widely across the sky.

◀ ***Crepuscular rays***
When the sun is lower in the sky than the clouds, light rays may pass through gaps in the clouds. If smoke or dust particles or water droplets reflect the bands of light, they will appear as huge sunbeams called crepuscular rays.

◄ ▲ Mock sun
Mock suns, or sun dogs, are
common in very high latitudes but
less so elsewhere. They are caused
by refraction of light by ice crystals
and are often seen at the same time
as a halo. Mock moons sometimes
appear for the same reason.

▲ **Icebow off northern Canada**
An icebow is produced in the same way as a
rainbow (pp.36–37), but through ice crystals,
not raindrops. The small particles do not spread
the colors, so the bow is white.

Halo around the sun ▶
Halos around the sun or full moon are produced
by the refraction of light through ice crystals.

▲ **Glory over clouds**
Glories are caused by the diffraction of sunlight
toward the observer by spherical cloud droplets.
They are often seen from airplanes.

Atmospheric phenomena

◄ ▲ Fallstreaks
Precipitation that falls from a cloud but vaporizes before reaching the ground is called virga or fallstreaks. It looks wispy, like strands of hair swept in the wind. Virga produced by altocumulus (above) or cirrus (left) are made from tiny ice crystals. Ice crystals in the cirrus are refracting the sunlight, making the cloud shine brightly. This is a "mock sun," or "parhelion."

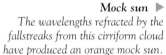

Mock sun ▶
The wavelengths refracted by the fallstreaks from this cirriform cloud have produced an orange mock sun.

◄ Virga from low clouds
At sea you can often see bad weather approaching long before it arrives. Here, a low cumulus casts its shadow over the sea, and a shower is falling from it. The rain is not reaching the surface, however, because beneath the cloud the dew point is low enough for the rain to evaporate. Rising air may carry the water vapor up again, where it will condense to form new clouds.

▲ **Iridescent cloud**
The tiny particles in the upper part of this cumulonimbus capillatus are catching and diffracting the sunlight, making the cloud look slightly colored. This is called iridescence, and it is fairly common with medium-level clouds.

◀ ▲ **Colored clouds**
Iridescence, also sometimes called irisation, can produce beautiful effects. In these altocumulus clouds, it is probably caused by diffraction of sunlight through supercooled water droplets. The colors depend partly on the size of the droplets and partly on the angle between the cloud and the sun. Red and green are the colors most often seen, but sometimes, as here, parts of the cloud are blue or yellow.

Purple haze ▲
Here the sun is just below the clouds, and a purple-colored band of iridescence has occurred.

CLIMATES

Frost ferns and mud mazes
Water can turn to ice at any latitude, even at the equator, where high mountains can be covered in snow. These frost ferns (above), photographed on a window, were caused by moist air coming into contact with cold glass. In the subtropics, dry air sinks to produce deserts. This is Death Valley in California (left), where prolonged drought and high temperatures have dried the soil, making it shrink and crack.

THE KIND OF WEATHER that affects a large area of the earth most of the time is its climate. The world has many different climates, ranging from those of the equatorial regions, where rainfall is heavy and the temperature is constantly high, to the very dry and extremely cold polar regions. Between these contrasting climate types lie those that produce grasslands, temperate forests like those of New England and Europe, and the vast belt of conifer forest called taiga which covers the northern parts Canada, Europe, and Asia. There are also subtropical desert climates and mountain climates.

CLIMATES OF THE WORLD

CLIMATE IS WEATHER averaged over a long period of time. The study of climates is called climatology. Climatology and meteorology overlap because you cannot understand one without knowing quite a lot about the other. By understanding your climate, and the climates of other places, you can learn about the day-to-day weather that affects you. Climates are distinguished from one another by their numerous characteristics, which are extremely varied.

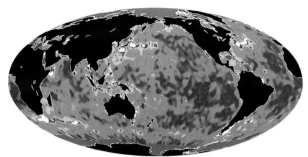

Ocean currents
In this satellite photograph ocean currents (pp.132–133) appear as red, yellow, or white. The Kuroshio current off Japan and the Gulf stream off North America take warm water north.

The whole world can be divided into large regions on the basis of different groups of plants. What grows depends to a great extent on the climate, so the vegetation regions are very similar to climatic regions (although they are not quite the same, because plants are also affected by the kind of rocks from which their soils are made). Knowing what plants grow can help indicate a region's climate.

Rain gauge
This rain gauge is used to measure daily rainfall. Wet climates can receive as much rain in one day as dry climates receive in a year.

Climate areas

Zambia, in tropical Africa south of the equator, is mostly a countryside of grassland called savanna. Savanna is not the same everywhere. In some places the trees grow more closely together, giving the appearance of fairly open forest. Elsewhere only shrubs and stunted trees can survive the long, dry winter. Here and there small acacia trees have retained their leaves.

Acacias grow best in very hot weather. Little water evaporates from their leaves, so they can withstand drought well. In November, as summer begins, the rains come. Empty water holes fill, low ground floods, and seeds lying dormant in the soil germinate. Briefly, the ground is carpeted with flowers. Then the flowers fade, and grasses take their place, soon growing very tall. Great herds of animals arrive on their annual migration to graze on the abundant food, accompanied by the predators that hunt them.

North from the Zambian savanna is the Congo Basin, where it rains throughout the year and the vegetation is tropical rainforest.

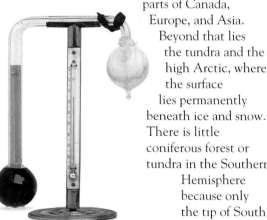

Wet- and dry-bulb hygrometer
This is an antique wet- and dry-bulb hygrometer, used to measure humidity. Humidity is important to climate because it is the level of water vapour in the air that dictates the possibility of clouds and precipitation.

South beyond the savannah is the Kalahari Desert, and still farther south, around the tip of southern Africa, is a climate of wet winters and dry, warm summers, much like that of the countries bordering the Mediterranean.

This pattern of climate and vegetation is repeated north and south of the equator all around the world. In Africa and Asia, the deserts of the Northern Hemisphere are the Sahara, Arabian, and Gobi. North American deserts are in Mexico and the southwestern United States. Beyond the deserts lie forests and more grasslands, called prairies in North America and steppes in central Asia. Still farther north, a broad belt of coniferous forest stretches across parts of Canada, Europe, and Asia. Beyond that lies the tundra and the high Arctic, where the surface lies permanently beneath ice and snow. There is little coniferous forest or tundra in the Southern Hemisphere because only the tip of South America and a few small islands lie in the latitudes where they occur, and Antarctica is covered in thick ice sheets.

Why climates differ

Distance from the Equator is not the only factor that affects the climate, and therefore the vegetation, of any particular region. For instance the city of Birmingham in England is about the same distance from the equator as Goose Bay, Labrador, and Lake Baikal, Siberia, so it is easy to assume that they might have similar climates. But Birmingham has a much warmer climate than the other two. Lake Baikal is at a much higher altitude than Birmingham or Goose Bay, but that is not enough to explain the difference. Labrador is a little closer to the equator than England and both are islands, but Labrador is much colder. This is because a warm ocean current flows past the coast of northwestern Europe, and a cold current flows south past the northeastern coast of North America. Warm currents raise the temperature of the air above them, raising air temperatures over nearby land if the prevailing winds blow over the land. Cold currents cool the land in the same way.

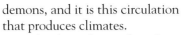

Reading temperatures
Individual climate regions can experience huge fluctuations in temperature.

Global wind systems

Climate is affected by these ocean currents and also by travelling masses of air and the varying amounts of moisture they contain. One of the first writers to suggest how this mechanism worked was the French philosopher William of Conches (c.1100–54). He suggested that the winds are caused by collisions between ocean currents moving in opposite directions, and between the currents and land masses. In fact the winds drive most of the currents, rather than the other way around, but William was correct in supposing that all of the atmosphere and the oceans are circulating, driven by physical forces rather than spirits or demons, and it is this circulation that produces climates.

In the days when sailing ships explored and traded around the world, winds and currents were extremely important. The winds near the equator, blowing from the northeast in the Northern Hemisphere and the southeast in the Southern Hemisphere, are called trade winds (pp.130–131). The English scientist Edmund Halley (1656–1742) explained these winds by suggesting that warm air rises at the equator and is replaced by cooler air drawn in from higher latitudes. He was partly correct, but the circulation he described would produce northerly and southerly winds, and the trade winds blow from the northeast and southeast. The first scientist to suggest why they blow from an easterly direction was George Hadley

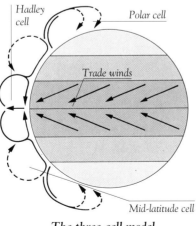

The three-cell model
The Hadley convection cell in the tropics drives the trade winds (pp.130–131). Cold air flows away from the poles and is replaced by warmer air. These air movements affect climates.

(1685–1768), in 1735, who gave his name to the convection cells that drive the trade winds.

Climates change all the time. Subtropical and midlatitude climates are strongly affected by jet streams—strong, high-altitude winds that blow from a westerly direction in both hemispheres. El Niño, a change in the trade winds and Pacific currents, occurs every few years and affects the weather and climates over a large part of the world. Scientists are still searching for a complete explanation for why an El Niño occurs.

Long-term changes

Climates also change over long periods. At present we are living in an interglacial, an interval between the end of one ice age and the start of another. Climates very different from those we know today have existed everywhere in the past. Ice ages are long-term changes, but small climatic changes can be caused by the vast amounts of dust and small particles thrown high into the air by volcanic eruptions and meteorite impacts. The 1991 eruption of the volcano Mount Pinatubo in the Philippines, for example, brought cooler weather to most of the world in 1992.

Pollution already affects some climates, and many scientists suspect that in time it may change climates all over the world. Realizing the difficulties scientists have in understanding pollution will help you see how much we have to learn about the forces that control the weather.

Industrial pollution
Pollution is a serious threat to most climate regions. Factories like this one can have equipment installed to reduce the pollution they would otherwise cause.

Hair hygrometer
The hair hygrometer (shown above), invented in the 17th century, is still used. It is based on the idea that as relative humidity rises, a clean human hair will increase in length. Average humidity can fluctuate rapidly as climates change.

Global convection and convection cells

IN 1735 THE ENGLISH SCIENTIST George Hadley (1685–1768) suggested that air is heated strongly at the equator by contact with the surface of the earth. The warm air rises, moves away from the equator, and cools at a very high altitude. Subtropical air moves towards the equator to take its place, and this movement is what we know as the trade winds. In fact, Hadley's explanation would produce winds from due north and south. Later meteorologists realized the Earth's rotation accounts for the winds' easterly direction. The rising air loses its moisture, cools, and descends over the subtropics, warming by compression as it does so. This is a Hadley cell. Movements of air and ocean currents carry heat away from the equator, and bring cold air and water towards the equator.

Hadley cells

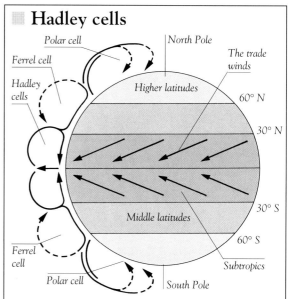

This three-cell model shows the general pattern of atmospheric circulation. In both the Northern and Southern Hemispheres, air rises at the equator and sinks in the subtropics. These convection cells are known as Hadley cells. Part of the subtropical air returns to the equator, but some moves into higher latitudes. In the polar cells, cold air sinks and flows outwards. This air meets subtropical air from the middle latitudes, where the Ferrel cells are driven by warm air.

EXPERIMENT
Make a Hadley cell

👥 *Adult supervision is advised for this experiment*

Although Hadley cells are very large, you can demonstrate how they work on a small scale. Heat a bowl of water around the edges and chill it at its center. Convection cells are formed as warm water rises, moves to the center of the bowl, is chilled, and then returns to the sides to be warmed again.

YOU WILL NEED
● water ● tin can ● glass bowl
● powdered potato ● matches
● modeling clay ● food coloring
● candles ● ice ● brick

1 STAND THE BOWL on the brick, and fill it with colored water to contrast with the white potato powder.

2 FILL THE SMALL tin can with ice, and stand it in the bowl's center. Sprinkle potato powder in the water.

3 SPACE THE CANDLES evenly around the edge of the bowl, and ask an adult to light them. Watch how the powder moves as the water is heated and then cooled. The powder will absorb water and swell, making it more clearly visible.

EXPERIMENT
Circulating air

When warm air rises, cooler air is drawn down to replace it, causing a constant movement of air. This is a convection cell. It is easy to make convection cells, using smoke to indicate movement.

YOU WILL NEED
- cardboard ● incense stick ● tape ● candle ● matches
- scissors ● modeling clay ● clear container

Adult supervision is advised for this experiment

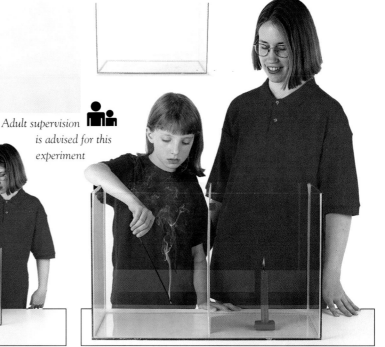

1 CUT SQUARES, about 2 x 2 in (5 x 5 cm), from two corners of the cardboard. Tape it in the center of the container, holes down.

2 THE CONTAINER is now divided into two compartments, with openings at the bottom of the partition. Place the candle in one side and ask an adult to light it for you.

3 ASK AN ADULT to light the incense stick. Hold the stick in the compartment without the candle, and watch what happens to the smoke. It will soon start flowing down into the cool compartment, through the holes at the bottom, and then rise as it is heated.

EXPERIMENT
Changing densities

Oil and water will not mix. Oil is the lighter of the two, so it floats above water. When water is heated, its density decreases; when it becomes lighter than the oil, it will rise through it. When it cools, its density is once more greater than that of the oil, so that it sinks. This demonstrates how air behaves in the atmosphere when heated by convection.

 *Adult supervision is advised for this experiment*

YOU WILL NEED
- candle ● water ● heat-resistant glass jar ● matches
- modeling clay ● food coloring
- 2 bricks

1 FILL THE CONTAINER with water to about 3 in (7 cm) from the top. Color it. Raise the level about 2 in (5 cm) with oil.

2 PLACE THE CANDLE between the two bricks and ask an adult to light it for you. Carefully put the jar with the oil and water on top of the bricks and above the flame without disturbing the oil.

3 LEAVE THE JAR alone for a few minutes, giving the candle enough time to heat the mixture. What happens to the oil and water?

Jet streams and Rossby waves

AIR TEMPERATURE decreases from the equator to the poles, and wind speed in the upper air is proportional to the rate that temperature changes. This is most extreme where polar and tropical air masses meet, at the polar front, and where equatorial and subtropical air masses meet. In these regions narrow belts of winds, called jet streams, often blow with great force. The Polar Front Jet Stream is less constant than the Subtropical Jet Stream, but it is stronger—with winds of 100–150 mph (160–240 km/h), and occasionally over 200 mph (320km/h).

Forming Rossby waves

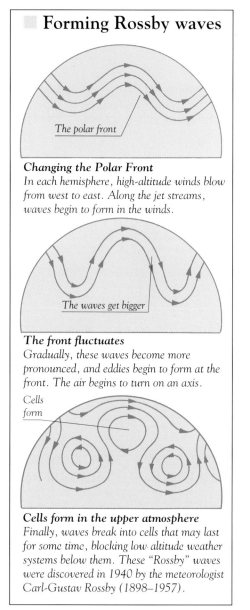

Changing the Polar Front
In each hemisphere, high-altitude winds blow from west to east. Along the jet streams, waves begin to form in the winds.

The front fluctuates
Gradually, these waves become more pronounced, and eddies begin to form at the front. The air begins to turn on an axis.

Cells form in the upper atmosphere
Finally, waves break into cells that may last for some time, blocking low-altitude weather systems below them. These "Rossby" waves were discovered in 1940 by the meteorologist Carl-Gustav Rossby (1898–1957).

EXPERIMENT
Moving jet streams

YOU WILL NEED
- *food coloring* ● *water*
- ● *bowl* ● *plastic tubing*
- ● *2 dishpans*

Except at the equator, air or water moving horizontally tends to form a vortex, or eddy, due partly to the Coriolis effect (pp.74–75) and partly to its own movement in relation to the surface of the earth. Because of this vorticity, a jet stream deflected toward or away from the equator often develops waves which turn into circular patterns, like those of cyclones and anticyclones. Make a stream of water flow through a container of water, and you will see this happen.

1 PUT THE TWO dishpans next to each other. Turn one upside down, and half-fill the other with water. Place a bowl of colored water on the upside-down dishpan.

2 PUT ONE END of the plastic tubing in the bottom of the glass bowl. Then suck the water gently through the other end of the tubing to begin siphoning the water out of the bowl.

3 HOLD THE END of the tube horizontally about ½ in (1 cm) below the water. Swing it gently from side to side of the dish pan to make the patterns appear.

EXPERIMENT
Making waves

Jet streams and Rossby waves seem remote because they occur 6 miles (10 km) or more above the surface in middle latitudes, but they have a strong influence on our weather. Depressions tend to form beneath the peaks of Rossby waves and to be drawn in an easterly direction by them—especially in winter, when the jet streams are strongest. If the cells remain stationary, surface weather beneath will not change until the flow begins again. Jet streams and Rossby waves are produced by atmospheric convection cells. You can demonstrate this movement for yourself in water.

The heart of a jet stream at high altitude

Jet streams are like cylinders of fast-moving air. This diagram shows a front where tropical air lies above polar air. Because it is less dense, the tropical air is deeper. The wind blows parallel to the front, with the cold air on the left.

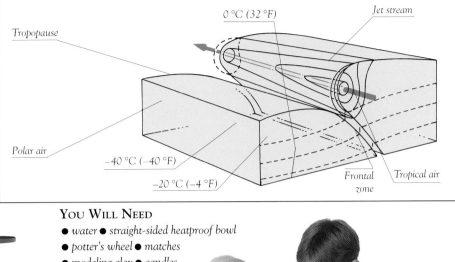

Tropopause
0 °C (32 °F)
Jet stream
Polar air
−40 °C (−40 °F)
−20 °C (−4 °F)
Frontal zone
Tropical air

YOU WILL NEED
● *water* ● *straight-sided heatproof bowl*
● *potter's wheel* ● *matches*
● *modeling clay* ● *candles*
● *potato powder* ● *ice*
● *food coloring* ● *tin can*

Adult supervision is advised for this experiment

1 PLACE THE GLASS bowl on the potter's wheel, and put the candles around the base.

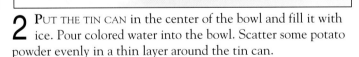

2 PUT THE TIN CAN in the center of the bowl and fill it with ice. Pour colored water into the bowl. Scatter some potato powder evenly in a thin layer around the tin can.

3 ASK AN ADULT to light the candles. The candles provide the heat that causes miniature Hadley cells to form in the water. The currents in the water are shown by the pieces of potato powder following their path.

4 AS SOON AS THE Hadley cells have started to form in the water, slowly start to turn the bowl, like the earth rotating. What happens to the cells?

Salt and sea water

WHEN SALT DISSOLVES in water, the volume of the solution changes only slightly, so the density increases, because there are now more molecules in the same space. Water also becomes denser as it cools, because the molecules crowd together more closely. It reaches its maximum density at 39.2° F (4° C). At temperatures lower than this, the molecules move apart, so density decreases. Think what happens when sea water freezes. Salt molecules are squeezed out, making the water close to the ice saltier, and thus more dense. At the same time, the water near the ice is chilled and becomes denser still. This dense water sinks to the ocean floor and can create currents such as the North Atlantic Deep Water, which flows towards the equator. These currents can influence climate (pp.132–133).

(pp.132–133)

EXPERIMENT
Water purifier

When salt water evaporates, only water molecules escape into the air. The salt is left behind, and—if the vapor condenses—the resulting water is fresh. In some countries this principle is applied to obtain drinking water from sea water. Here you can purify water yourself.

YOU WILL NEED
- water ● marble ● small dish ● salt
- large bowl ● mixer ● plastic wrap

EXPERIMENT
Filling empty spaces

When salt dissolves in water, the sodium and chlorine in the salt molecules separate and attach themselves to the oxygen and hydrogen in the water molecules. The sodium attaches to the oxygen, and the chlorine to the hydrogen, and these new combinations occupy the spaces between the water molecules. This means that a solution of salt in water occupies a smaller volume than the salt and water would separately. You can see this yourself.

YOU WILL NEED
- glass ● salt ● large container ● water
- mixer ● pitcher

1 FILL THE LARGE CONTAINER with tap water, and fill the glass with table salt. The space occupied by the water and salt equals that of the containers.

2 POUR THE SALT into a pitcher, and add all the water. Use the mixer to stir the solution until the salt has dissolved.

3 NOW POUR THE SOLUTION into the container. Is there enough of the solution left to fill up the glass, too?

The chickpeas are bulky, and there are large gaps around them

Tiny grains of rice fit into the spaces between the chickpeas

Chickpeas and rice
Repeat this experiment using uncooked rice to represent the salt and dried chickpeas or beans to represent the water. How do they fit together?

1 POUR SOME WATER into a bowl, and add a dash or two of salt. Place the small dish in the middle of the bowl.

2 COVER THE BOWL with plastic wrap. Place a marble on top of the film, and stand the purifier in the sunshine.

3 AS THE WATER evaporates, it will condense on the plastic wrap and drip into the dish. Taste it—is it salty?

EXPERIMENT
Changing density

The saltiness and density of the sea can create some interesting effects. For instance, it easier to float in the sea than in fresh water. You can show this with an egg and a bowl of water.

YOU WILL NEED
● *water* ● *salt* ● *fresh egg*
● *bowl* ● *mixer*

1 FILL THE BOWL with cold tap water, and gently place a fresh egg in the water. Does the egg float or sink?

2 REMOVE THE EGG from the water. Add salt, stirring to dissolve it, until there is a small amount left undissolved at the bottom.

▨ Leftover salt

Sometimes a shallow sea is isolated from the ocean, and all its water evaporates, leaving only the dissolved salts behind, as "evaporite" deposits. The most famous of these is in Utah's Great Salt Lake Desert. This is the Bonneville Speedway, a vast area of very level salt where attempts are made to break the world land speed record.

3 NOW, PLACE THE EGG into the salty water. What happens to the egg this time—does it sink or does it float?

Wind systems, trade winds, and doldrums

SURFACE OCEAN currents are often driven by the wind. Wind directions change, but for any part of the world they blow more often from one direction than from any other. There is a general wind pattern related to the atmospheric convection cells (pp.124–125) that carry heat away from the equator. In the tropics, winds are generally easterly (blowing from the east). These trade winds are produced by the Hadley cells (pp.124–125). Near the equator, where air converging from north and south meets, there are windless regions called the doldrums. In middle latitudes winds are mainly from the west, and in polar latitudes, from the east. Wind patterns are the same in both hemispheres.

Global wind patterns

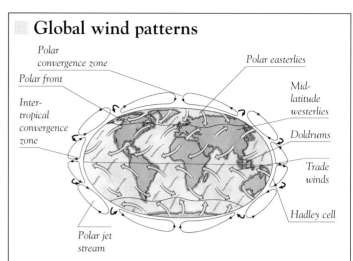

Polar convergence zone
Polar front
Polar easterlies
Inter-tropical convergence zone
Mid-latitude westerlies
Doldrums
Trade winds
Hadley cell
Polar jet stream

This map shows global wind patterns, showing those areas where large-scale convection cells cause winds to flow. The Coriolis effect (pp.74–75) keeps the wind from blowing directly from high to low pressure. The yellow arrows indicate the most common, or prevailing, wind direction.

EXPERIMENT
Make the trade winds

There is more land (with its higher heat capacity) in the Northern Hemisphere than in the Southern Hemisphere, so average temperatures are highest not at the equator, but at about 5° north—the heat equator. The easterly trade winds meet and the doldrums are found here. The zone of high pressure between the trades and the mid-latitude westerly winds is called the horse latitudes. You can make your own heat equator and pattern of trade winds in a glass bowl.

YOU WILL NEED
● water ● matches ● modeling clay ● candles ● 2 different food colorings ● 2 bricks ● heat-proof dish

Adult supervision is advised for this experiment

1 PLACE SOME CANDLES in a row in some modeling clay. Put two bricks on either side of the candles to use as a stand.

2 PLACE A HEAT-PROOF dish across the bricks. Fill the dish about three-quarters full with water. Ask an adult to light the candles.

3 LET THE WATER HEAT for a few minutes. Trickle different food colors into the water at the ends of the dish. The colors will be carried to the center of the dish by "trade winds" on the dish bottom.

EXPERIMENT
A wind rose

The prevailing wind can be shown as the longest line on a wind rose—straight lines radiating from a central point, each showing a particular wind direction. Determine the wind direction with a compass at the same time every day and record it as degrees to the left or right of north, to the nearest 10°. Draw each day's wind as a ½-in (1-cm) line, extending it every time the wind direction repeats. On your protractor, N is 0°, E is 90°, S is 180°, and W is 270°. After a while, one line should be longer than others.

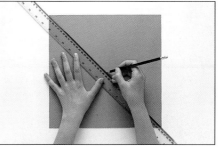

YOU WILL NEED
● compass ● pen ● pencil with eraser ● short ruler ● poster board ● protractor ● long ruler

1 DRAW TWO FAINT pencil lines across the poster board from corner to corner to find the center. Mark this with a dot, and then erase the lines.

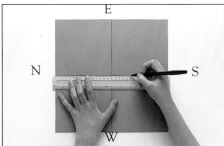

2 LABEL THE EDGES of the card N, E, S, and W as shown. Then find the center of each edge and draw lines to divide the card into 4 separate quadrants.

3 EVERY DAY, find the wind direction with your compass, and draw the direction from which the wind is blowing as a ½-in (1-cm) line from the center dot.

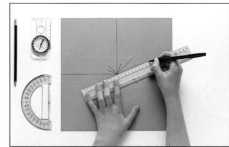

4 WHEN A WIND DIRECTION recurs, make its line ½ in (1 cm) longer. After a few weeks, the longest line will indicate the prevailing wind.

■ The doldrums and the trade winds

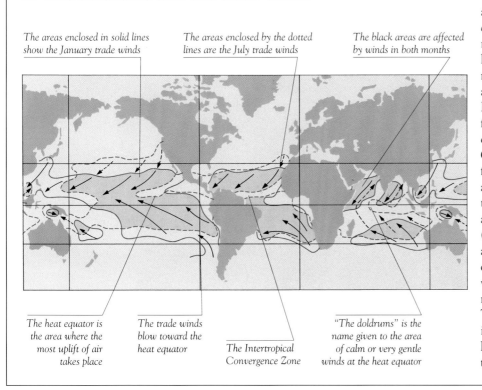

The areas enclosed in solid lines show the January trade winds

The areas enclosed by the dotted lines are the July trade winds

The black areas are affected by winds in both months

The heat equator is the area where the most uplift of air takes place

The trade winds blow toward the heat equator

The Intertropical Convergence Zone

"The doldrums" is the name given to the area of calm or very gentle winds at the heat equator

This map shows those areas of the earth affected by the trade winds and the doldrums. In the area outlined on the map to either side of the heat equator, half of all winds blow from the northeast in the Northern Hemisphere and southeast in the Southern Hemisphere. These are the trade winds, forming the lower part of the Hadley convection cells, influenced by the Coriolis effect. The high-level winds forming the upper part of the cells blow away from the equator and are called the anti-trades. The trade winds meet at the Intertropical Convergence Zone (ITCZ), where air converges and rises, and where gentle easterly winds are common. The rising air can produce windless conditions at the surface, in regions sailors named the doldrums. The rising air at the convergence zone is often associated with thunderstorms. Like the mid-latitude westerlies, the trade winds are strongest in winter.

Ocean currents and climate

WARM AND COLD ocean currents can change the climate of coastal regions, but only when prevailing local winds blow from the sea to the land. Warm currents bring higher temperatures and more precipitation, while cold currents can lower temperatures and shorten growing seasons. Most ocean currents are driven by prevailing winds, but the earth's rotation deflects them into roughly circular paths, clockwise in the Northern Hemisphere and counterclockwise in the Southern Hemisphere. These circular currents, called gyres, are strongest in the largest oceans—the North and South Atlantic and the Pacific. The North Atlantic gyre moves from the warm north coast of South America toward Florida, then east across the ocean, and south off Portugal.

A simple vortex

This vortex has been highlighted with food coloring. It has a calm center that reaches all the way to the bottom of the bowl

Because of the earth's rotation, moving air and water tend to form axes and spin about them. If the movement is large, and directed toward or away from the equator, the Coriolis effect (pp.74–75) will deflect it. Small movements also form vortices, because the earth beneath air and water is also moving. Remove the plug from a basin of water and a vortex will usually form. This is not caused by pulling the plug, but by vorticity. It is too small to be influenced by the Coriolis effect, so it may rotate clockwise or counterclockwise.

Wind-blown currents

The wind we experience from day to day seems to change often, sometimes blowing from one direction, sometimes from another. These prevailing winds are most reliable over the oceans, where there are no land masses to deflect them. In both hemispheres, prevailing tropical winds are from the east, mid-latitude winds are from the west, and polar winds are from the east. These winds drive the surface currents, and consequently the currents move in the same direction as the winds. You can demonstrate this for yourself.

YOU WILL NEED
● *corks* ● *water*
● *dishpan*

1 FILL A DISHPAN with water. Wait until the water is quite still, then float a handful of corks on top of the water, all at one end of the dishpan.

2 BLOW GENTLY ACROSS THE WATER in one direction. The corks will move in the same direction as the water, which follows the path of the current your wind has made. Keep blowing, and see if the current forms a pattern around the pan.

The main ocean currents

This map shows the main ocean currents. Western currents such as the Gulf Stream and the Kuroshio current flow faster than those on the eastern sides of oceans. Off the coast of Florida, for example, the Gulf Stream is 31–47 miles (50–75 km) wide and flows at 2.5–7 mph (4–11 km/h). The Kuroshio current is 50 miles (80 km) wide and flows at a speed of about 7 mph (11 km/h). The Benguela current, flowing northward along the west coast of Africa, flows at about 0.6 mph (0.9 km/h). The most constant current is the Antarctic Circumpolar current, which flows unopposed by land through the southern oceans.

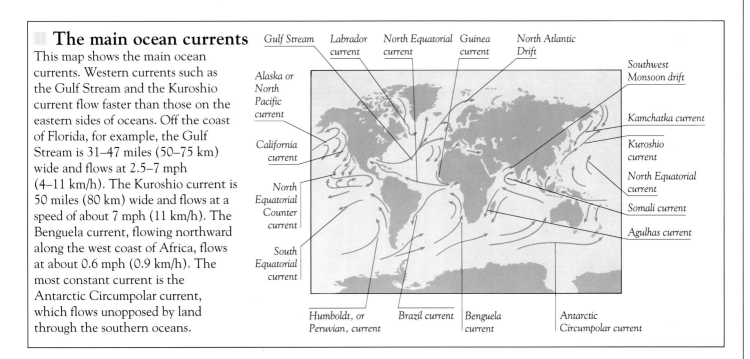

Gulf Stream · Labrador current · North Equatorial current · Guinea current · North Atlantic Drift · Southwest Monsoon drift · Alaska or North Pacific current · Kamchatka current · Kuroshio current · California current · North Equatorial current · North Equatorial Counter current · Somali current · Agulhas current · South Equatorial current · Humboldt, or Peruvian, current · Brazil current · Benguela current · Antarctic Circumpolar current

---

EXPERIMENT

Deep-water currents

The general circulation of water in the Atlantic and Pacific is driven by deep, slow-moving currents of cold water that flow from the poles toward the equator. When sea water freezes, its salt separates from it. Sea ice is fresh, but the water close to it is saltier than other water because it contains the salt that was removed during freezing. This makes the water denser. Water close to the ice is also cold, and this dense water sinks all the way to the ocean floor, flows away from the ice and is replaced by warmer surface water which then cools and sinks. These deep water currents move only 2–3 yards (1–2 m) a day. You can make a deep-water current in a dish.

YOU WILL NEED
- ice ● food coloring ● eye dropper
- water ● glass dish
- aluminum foil

1 FILL THE GLASS DISH with warm water, and leave it until the water has become quite still. This represents a warm ocean such as the mid-Pacific.

2 WRAP SOME ICE CUBES carefully in foil, making sure no melted water will be able to leak out. Put the foil package in one end of the glass dish and leave it until the water is still once again. The ice will start to cool the warm water.

3 PLACE A FEW DROPS of food coloring over the foil so the color trickles into the water. What happens to the color as it sinks to the bottom of the dish? This is how deep-water currents carry water toward the equator from the poles.

El Niño and the Southern Oscillation

THE TRADE WINDS (pp.130–131) drive the South Pacific equatorial current, which carries surface water west and leaves relatively cool water off South America and a much deeper layer off Indonesia. Every few years, however, this normal pattern changes. The trade winds weaken, and temperature and rainfall patterns change over a huge area stretching from the Pacific coast of South America to the Indian Ocean. This is called a Southern Oscillation, and when it happens the equatorial current in the Pacific reverses. Warm water flows east and then south along the coast of Peru. This current is called El Niño. The two changes together are called an El Niño–Southern Oscillation (ENSO) event. This affects weather and climate over other parts of the world as well as the Pacific area.

How an ENSO event works

ENSO events usually happen in December. The strongest one in recent history occurred in 1982–83. It generated a series of changes in the oceans that moved farther and farther from the equator, producing climatic changes that were still being felt in 1994. Another ENSO event lasted two years, in 1991–93. El Niño brings rainstorms to Peru, unusual weather to North America, and may affect crops in Zambia and elsewhere.

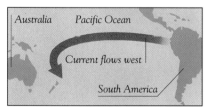

Normal conditions in the South Pacific
In most years the trade winds drive the equatorial current in the South Pacific. The current flows west, carrying the warm water with it across the ocean.

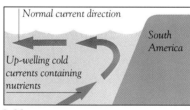

Cold water rising
Normally the trade winds blow westward. This forms a thick layer of warm water in the west and leaves relatively cool water near South America.

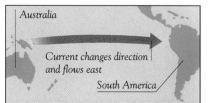

Conditions during an ENSO event
An ENSO event reverses the normal pattern. The trade winds weaken and warm surface water flows east, raising the sea temperature off South America.

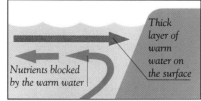

Warm surface water
The thick layer of warm sea water in the west moves to the east. This blocks the cold water that rises from the sea bed, starving the surface sea life of nutrients.

EXPERIMENT
Comparing temperature

An ENSO event raises the sea temperature off South America by 18 °F (10 °C). Cold water, rich in nutrients, cannot penetrate the deeper layer of warm water. This reduces the amount of phytoplankton (tiny plants) in the surface water. The number of animals and fish that feed on the plants also dwindles, affecting the Peruvian fishing industry. You can find out how much warm water it takes to create a mini-ENSO.

YOU WILL NEED
● *2 dishpans* ● *water* ● *tape*
● *scissors* ● *2 thermometers*

1 TAPE ONE THERMOMETER to the inside of each dishpan as shown. Half-fill both of the pans with cold water from the tap.

2 POUR HOT TAP WATER into one of the pans until the thermometer shows a difference of 18 °F (10 °C). This is what happens during an ENSO event. Does it feel very different?

In the Pacific

ENSO events occur in the equatorial South Pacific, although some scientists think similar but much weaker events may sometimes happen in the South Atlantic. These maps show normal conditions versus ENSO conditions. During an ENSO, the Pacific south equatorial current changes direction, leaving a much weaker "gyre" in the South Pacific. A strengthening of the winds and equatorial currents is called La Niña.

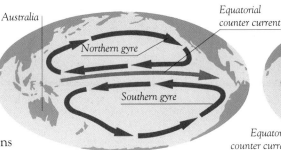

Usual conditions in the Pacific
A high-pressure region over the eastern Pacific and a low over the western Pacific produce the trade winds, which push warm water westward toward Australia.

What happens during an ENSO
The low-pressure region in the western Pacific shifts eastwards, reversing the trade winds and turning the equatorial currents back on themselves. This causes the build up of warm water off the coast of South America.

EXPERIMENT
Making your own El Niño

The trade winds blow warm surface water across the ocean, so it forms a pool on one side and only a thin layer on the other. During an El Niño, the flow reverses. This happens on a huge scale right across the Pacific, but the principle is simple. With the help of a friend you can easily see how it works.

You Will Need
- *food coloring*
- *water* ● *ruler*
- *wide, clear-sided container*

1 FILL THE CONTAINER with cold water to within about 4 in (10 cm) of the brim. When the water is quite still, trickle colored, hot tap water into the container to form a surface layer.

Compare the depth of the colored layer to the level before you started to blow

2 USE THE RULER to measure the thickness of the warm, colored layer of water at either end of the container. This should be the same at both ends.

3 ASK YOUR FRIEND to blow the water to make a "trade wind" that moves the colored water toward one end. To make your El Niño, ask your friend to stop blowing so that warm water flows to the other end.

Climate distribution and vegetation

THE PATTERN of world climates is the result of a combination of factors, including the distribution of land and sea, of mountains and plains, the great wind systems of the atmosphere, and of the ocean currents. Each region of the globe has its own typical climate, and scientists have devised many ways to classify them. The German meteorologist Wladimir P. Köppen (1846–1940) produced his system in 1918. It is based on the distribution of vegetation, which is closely related to rainfall and temperature. The American meteorologist C. Warren Thornthwaite (1899–1963) proposed a different method in 1931, with an important revision in 1948. The Thornthwaite classification is based on the ratio of precipitation to evaporation and plant transpiration (pp. 40–41) taken together. These two systems are the most widely used today.

■ Climate classification

Köppen's climate classification system has five divisions. Thornthwaite's system uses nine divisions, ranging from "arid" to "perhumid." On a global level, climate is closely linked to soil and vegetation. The map on these pages uses a classification system that shows 12 types of climate, based on the vegetation that grows in each area. Use the key below to find the names for each type of climate shown on the map.

Polar climates produce some of the driest regions in the world

Coal deposits off the coast of Greenland show that the past climate (pp. 152–153) was once very different

Temperate grasslands have hot summers and cold winters

Areas close to the poles with frozen soil that melts for at least 2 months each year can support the mosses, lichens, and small shrubs that characterize tundra (pp.144–145)

Volcanic eruptions (pp. 158–159) in places such as Mexico can have short-term climatic effects

Mountainous regions have distinct climates because the temperatures are much lower and winds stronger

Part of South America is covered with tropical rain forests (pp.142–143), but human activity may change that over time (pp.160–161)

Ocean currents (pp.132–133), such as the Brazil current off the coast of South America, can have a decisive effect on climate

Key for climate distribution map

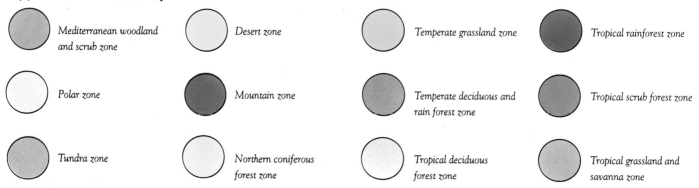

Mediterranean woodland and scrub zone

Desert zone

Temperate grassland zone

Tropical rainforest zone

Polar zone

Mountain zone

Temperate deciduous and rain forest zone

Tropical scrub forest zone

Tundra zone

Northern coniferous forest zone

Tropical deciduous forest zone

Tropical grassland and savanna zone

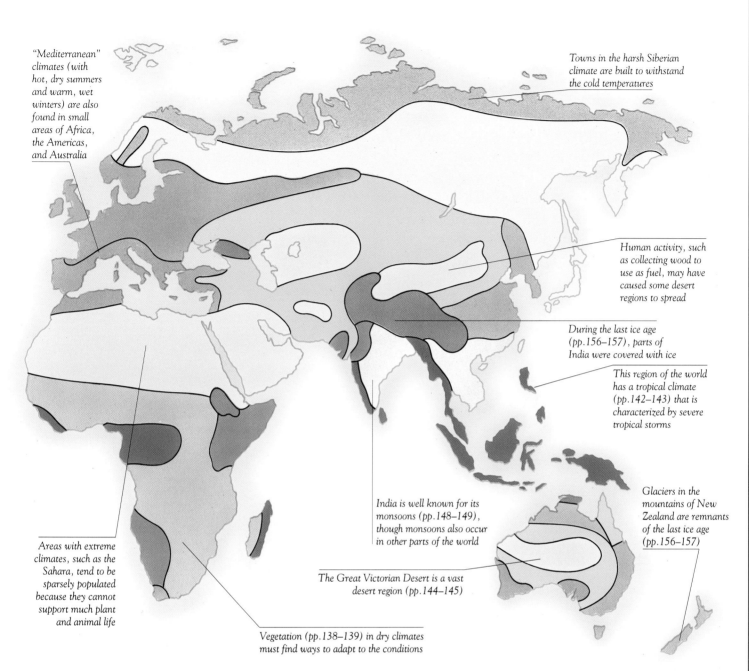

"Mediterranean" climates (with hot, dry summers and warm, wet winters) are also found in small areas of Africa, the Americas, and Australia

Towns in the harsh Siberian climate are built to withstand the cold temperatures

Human activity, such as collecting wood to use as fuel, may have caused some desert regions to spread

During the last ice age (pp.156–157), parts of India were covered with ice

This region of the world has a tropical climate (pp.142–143) that is characterized by severe tropical storms

Glaciers in the mountains of New Zealand are remnants of the last ice age (pp.156–157)

India is well known for its monsoons (pp.148–149), though monsoons also occur in other parts of the world

Areas with extreme climates, such as the Sahara, tend to be sparsely populated because they cannot support much plant and animal life

The Great Victorian Desert is a vast desert region (pp.144–145)

Vegetation (pp.138–139) in dry climates must find ways to adapt to the conditions

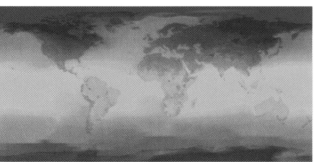

Global temperatures in January
This computerized map shows the world distribution of temperatures in January. It is summer in the Southern Hemisphere, and the warmest regions (orange on the map) are just south of the equator. In July they will be north of the equator. The blue areas are comparatively cooler.

Global rainfall in January
The contrasts in precipitation throughout the world are extreme, as this computerized map shows. The wettest areas are near the equator (dark green) and receive more than 10 m (33 ft) of rain a year, but many years can pass with no precipitation at all in the most arid regions.

How plants adapt to climates

GREEN PLANTS need sunlight for photosynthesis (pp.40–41), the process by which they make food. They need water to make food, to carry minerals, and to provide their cells with the rigidity that gives them their shape. Finally, they need a range of minerals, which they obtain from the soil. The earth provides an abundance of these requirements, but they are not distributed evenly. Some places are too hot, too cold, or too dry for any plants to survive, but away from these extreme climates plants have adapted to most of the conditions the earth offers. In most cases the vegetation typical of a region is also typical of the climate of that region, and a map of vegetation types is very similar to a map of climate types (pp.136–137).

Drying by osmosis

If two solutions of different strengths are separated by a barrier that only water molecules can cross, water will move from the weaker to the stronger solution until the two are equal. This process is osmosis. Because it removes water from one side of the barrier, osmosis has a drying effect. Use this to find out how well different kinds of leaves retain water. Line a tray with newspaper, scatter salt evenly over it, and place some evergreen and deciduous leaves across the tray. The salt will dissolve in moisture it has drawn from leaves by the process of osmosis.

Wet leaves
Press the leaves onto the paper. Leave them for several hours, then remove them. The paper beneath some leaves will be wetter. Which leaf type loses the most water?

EXPERIMENT
Making the most of light

Plants need light to fall on their leaves to provide energy for photosynthesis. Some seek light by growing tall, and all plants arrange their leaves to capture as much light as possible while shading one another as little as they can. You can make an experimental "plant" to try out different leaf positions and see how effective they are.

YOU WILL NEED
- *flashlight* ● *card*
- *wooden stick*
- *scissors*
- *modeling clay*

1 STAND THE STICK upright in modeling clay. Cut eight paper leaves, all the same size.

2 RANDOMLY ATTACH the ends of the leaves to the stem with clay. Shine the flashlight from above.

3 REARRANGE THE leaves until all the light shining on them from above is intercepted, no leaf shades another, and the table is in shadow.

EXPERIMENT
Measuring seed germination

Where the climate is usually very dry or so cold that water freezes, some plants can survive as seeds. When it rains or the ice melts, the seeds germinate at once, and soon the ground is covered with plants that flower and produce more seed before the water disappears. Using cress or other fast-growing seeds, you can see which conditions are best for germination.

YOU WILL NEED
● *blotting paper* ● *box* ● *4 saucers* ● *scissors*
● *cress seeds* ● *straw* ● *cardboard* ● *pin*

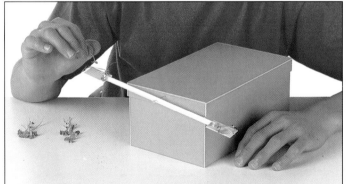

1 PLACE EQUAL-SIZED SQUARES of blotting paper in four saucers, all the same size. Then liberally dampen two of the four pieces of blotting paper with some water.

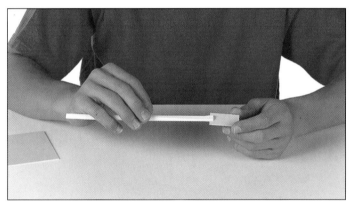

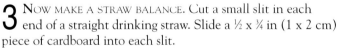

3 NOW MAKE A STRAW BALANCE. Cut a small slit in each end of a straight drinking straw. Slide a ½ x ¾ in (1 x 2 cm) piece of cardboard into each slit.

2 SCATTER THE SEEDS on all four saucers. Put one dry and one damp saucer in a cold spot and the other two in a warm spot. Keep all the saucers away from strong light.

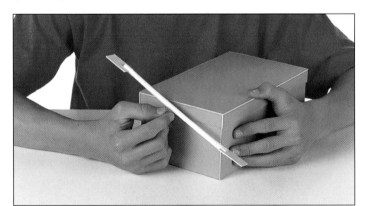

4 STICK A PIN through the middle of the straw. Use the pin to fix the straw to a box, which serves as a stand. Make sure the ends of the straw are evenly balanced. This straw balance shows only that one thing is heavier than another, not the amounts.

5 AT THE END OF 7 TO 10 DAYS, cut the growth from each saucer as close to the level of the blotting paper as possible. Compare the samples. Using the straw balance, work out which saucer provided the best conditions for germination.

Temperate climates

SOME OF THE MOST densely populated parts of the world lie in the temperate (or mild) regions, which extend in the Northern Hemisphere from the northern fringes of North America, Europe, and Asia to the Gulf of Mexico, the southern coast of the Mediterranean, and the deserts of central Asia and China. In the Southern Hemisphere, where there is less land, temperate regions are confined to New Zealand, the south coast of Australia, and parts of South America and South Africa. Climates change throughout this vast area. They differ in the availability of water, and natural vegetation varies, depending on whether rain falls all year or is confined mainly to one season.

EXPERIMENT
Water support

All temperate deciduous plants use water to maintain their structure: when the plant cells are full of water, they are rigid, and when they lack water, they become soft and the plant wilts. Deciduous plants loose water through their stomata (pp.40–41), so they need a constant supply of water to their roots. Watch what happens to a deciduous plant during a drought, and compare it to a cactus, a plant that comes from a dry climate, where water is scarce.

YOU WILL NEED
● water ● sand
● cactus ● 2 plant pots
● deciduous plant

1 PUT A CACTUS AND A DECIDUOUS plant into small plant pots, using dry sand for soil. Do not water the plants.

2 LEAVE THE PLANTS in a sunny place for two days. What happens to the deciduous plant as it loses water? How does it compare to the cactus? Now water both the plants. Is there any change in the deciduous plant?

Temperate trees

When climates change, trees that are not adapted to the new climate die, and other species gradually replace them. As the ice sheets retreated at the end of the last ice age, coniferous forests developed on the newly exposed land. Farther south, broad-leaved species took their place.

Coniferous forest canopy
The dry season is long in high latitudes, because of the long winter, and in some low latitudes, because of low rainfall in the summer. This means the growing season, when liquid water is plentiful, is short. Conifers, such as pines and firs, form vast forests in these regions. They have small leaves, called needles, from which little water evaporates. The shape of the trees helps them shed snow, which might break branches.

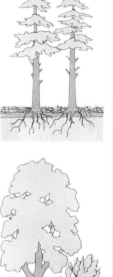

Deciduous forest canopy
Deciduous trees, such as oak, elm, and ash, grow where the dry season is shorter and the growing season is longer. These trees prevent water loss by shedding their leaves ahead of the dry season. They grow new leaves in spring. The leaves have larger surface areas than conifer needles do and can produce food more quickly. Young trees and shrubs can grow beside them, because they are not permanently in shade.

The thick, fleshy leaves of the cactus store the water it needs, and its sharp spines protect the leaves from animals that might raid its supply

EXPERIMENT
The wind and water

Wind can dry out leaves and stunt the growth of temperate plants by drying their growing tips. Plants badly affected by wind may be small, and—if the wind comes mainly from one direction—the drying of their growing tips on the side facing the wind can give them a windswept appearance, as though they were bending before the wind. The drying effect of the wind is very marked near coasts, where the wind carries salt that draws water out of plant cells. In windy areas, temperate plants shelter one another by growing close together. In a forest most trees are the same height for this reason. You can demonstrate the drying effect of wind on leaves.

YOU WILL NEED
● scissors ● string ● 2 leafy twigs from the same tree

How frost can damage temperate plants

Some temperate plants are hardy, but others are comparatively delicate. The ancestors of many temperate garden plants were from warmer climates, and these plants cannot tolerate severe frost. Gardeners protect them against the cold, but they can be damaged or killed by an unexpected late frost in spring or early frost in fall. You can test the vulnerability to cold of two common plants.

In the deep freeze
Place a delicate plant (try a lettuce) and a hardy plant (such as grass) in a freezer for 10 minutes. Now compare their conditions. What has happened to the lettuce?

1 TIE A LENGTH of string firmly around each twig. Go outside on a windy day. Tie one twig in the windiest place you can find, the other somewhere sheltered from wind.

2 INSPECT THE TWIGS twice a day for several days. Continue your inspections until the leaves on one twig are dry and shriveled. Which leaves dried out first?

Frost alert

This map shows the extent of frost—a condition that affects most temperate climates when the temperature drops below 32° F (0° C)—in North America during January (right) and July (far right). Temperatures affect the plants that farmers can grow. Annual plants, such as wheat, must produce seed between spring and the first fall frost, but plants fail to reproduce if frost damages them before the seeds have formed. Seeds are not usually harmed by freezing.

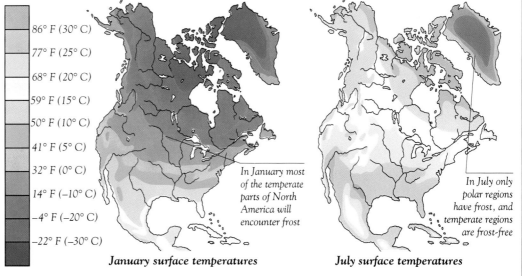

86° F (30° C)
77° F (25° C)
68° F (20° C)
59° F (15° C)
50° F (10° C)
41° F (5° C)
32° F (0° C)
14° F (–10° C)
–4° F (–20° C)
–22° F (–30° C)

In January most of the temperate parts of North America will encounter frost

In July only polar regions have frost, and temperate regions are frost-free

January surface temperatures

July surface temperatures

Tropical climates

THE TROPICS IS THE REGION that lies between the Tropic of Cancer (at latitude 23°30' N) and the Tropic of Capricorn (at 23°30' S). These latitudes mark the boundaries of the area in which the sun is directly overhead on at least one day each year. Near the equator the difference in temperature between day and night is greater than that between one time of year and another, so there is no winter in the usual sense of the word—although some parts of the tropics have wet and dry seasons. In the humid lowlands near the equator, cloud cover reflects up to half the incoming sunlight back into the atmosphere. This is where tropical rain forests grow, with lush evergreen trees and plants that flower and produce fruit all year. In tropical places that have a relatively dry season, and in the mountains, the forest is less luxuriant.

Living on top of each other

In many climates one plant may grow on top of another. In tropical regions this happens frequently because of the high rate of plant growth, decay, and regeneration. This northern tangle orchid is growing high up in a tree.

-------- EXPERIMENT --------
Coping with too much water

If plant leaves are wet all the time, the layer of water may focus the sun's rays, making them too hot. The stomata (pp.40–41) may be blocked by water and debris, making it more difficult for gases to pass through the plant and reducing photosynthesis. The leaves of many tropical plants have "drip tips" that help carry water away, and others have holes through which water can fall. You can make "leaves" of different shapes to see which is best at coping with a very wet climate.

YOU WILL NEED
● *wooden stick* ● *aluminum foil* ● *plant mister* ● *scissors* ● *tape*

1 CUT THREE LEAF shapes from the foil. Make one circular and flat, one with a central rib and a pointed drip tip, and one with several oval holes.

2 TAPE THE "LEAVES" to a stick and hold them as shown. Spray them with the mister. Which leaf is best at shedding water? Can you design a leaf shape that is better at getting rid of excess water?

Drip tip

Root structures

In tropical regions, the soil is usually very deep, but all the nutrients plants need are at the surface or just below it, and the soil itself is often waterlogged. As a result, trees need only shallow roots to obtain nutrients and water. However, the roots must still anchor and support the plant and obtain air for respiration.

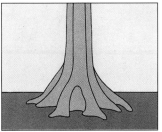

Buttress roots
Buttress roots grow out from the main trunk but are attached to it all the way to the ground. They help to prevent the tree falling.

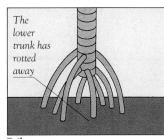

Stilt roots
The lower trunk has rotted away
Stilt or prop roots grow out from the trunk but separate from it; each stilt root has its own smaller roots in the soil.

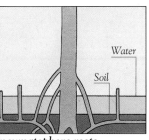

Pneumatophore roots
Water
Soil
In airless, waterlogged soil, peg roots grow upward from the main roots to reach the air. Other roots loop above and below the surface.

EXPERIMENT
Rapid decomposition

High temperatures throughout the year, averaging about 77° F (25° C), and ample water cause dead leaves, plants, and other remains of living organisms to decay very quickly in the humid tropics, releasing nutrients that are taken up at once by growing plants. Plants grow throughout the year, so nutrients do not accumulate in the soil. Most tropical soils supply little nourishment for plants. You can demonstrate the difference temperature makes to the rate at which organic material decomposes into the soil.

YOU WILL NEED
- cotton ● toothpick ● 2 jars
- leaves ● plastic wrap
- fruit peels ● water

1 PLACE A LAYER of cotton on the bottom of each jar. Add enough water to each jar to wet the cotton. Like tropical soil, the cotton will supply moisture, but nothing else.

2 PLACE EQUAL AMOUNTS of leaves and fruit peels into each jar. Bacteria and fungi will begin to decompose the leaves and fruit peels by breaking them down chemically.

3 COVER BOTH JARS with plastic wrap. Use a toothpick to prick a few holes in the plastic. Place one jar in a warm place and the other in the refrigerator. Where is decomposition faster?

Desert and tundra

IF THE AMOUNT of rain falling each season of the year is less than the amount that could evaporate from the ground, the land will be desert. Any place receiving less than 10 in (250 mm) rainfall in a year is almost bound to be a desert, especially if rain falls erratically. In the Sahara the average rainfall is less than 2 in (50 mm) a year; in many places years pass with no rain at all. Deserts are not necessarily hot. The interior of Antarctica receives about 2 in (50 mm) annual precipitation, making that continent the world's largest desert. Tundra is the name for the climate region between the permanent ice of the polar region and the limits of tree growth.

Tundra vegetation

Northern arctic regions support a tundra vegetation, like this in Alaska of shrubs, clumps of grass, sedges, and herbs which flower in the brief summer and survive the harsh winter.

EXPERIMENT
Slowing down the desert

Drought lasting several years in land bordering a desert allows the desert to expand. Then, when the rains return, the desert retreats. If the desert is sandy, the prevailing winds may carry sand that buries the adjacent dry land. Trees that can survive the dry conditions can form a barrier to hold back the sand. This prevents the temporary spread of the desert and hastens the recovery of plants when rain falls again.

You can demonstrate how a barrier like trees can slow down the movement of wind-driven sand. It is best to do this experiment outside.

YOU WILL NEED
● poster board ● scissors
● modeling clay ● tape
● wooden skewers ● pencil
● brush ● sand

Draw a line at the back of the pile of sand so you know where your desert started

1 MAKE A 3-SIDED SCREEN from some poster board. Pour a pile of sand across the open side of the screen and draw a line to mark the edge of the sand closest to the back of the screen.

2 USING POSTER BOARD as a fan, make a wind blow toward the back of the screen. Mark the new edge of the sand with another line. Brush the sand back to its original position.

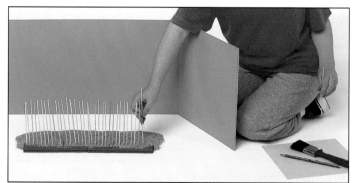

3 MAKE A WIND BARRIER across the edge of the sand with closely spaced skewers held upright in a strip of clay. Fan the sand and see how far it travels now there is a barrier.

EXPERIMENT
Make an oasis

Beneath a sandy desert, water may flow above a layer of rock. Rock hollows can allow water to accumulate close to the surface. Plant roots can reach it, wells can be sunk into it, and there is an oasis. You can make your own oasis.

YOU WILL NEED
- water ● modeling clay
- 2 plastic bottles ● strip of wood
- waterproof tray ● grass seeds
- sharp scissors ● sand
- tape ● block of wood
- nails ● plastic tubing
- scissors ● hammer
- rolling pin

Adult supervision is advised for this experiment

1 TAPE PLASTIC TUBING to the bottom of the tray. Make sure the end of the tube is near one end of the tray.

2 IN THE TRAY make a small ring of modeling clay around the tube end. This is the oasis. Fill the tray with sand.

3 ASK AN ADULT to make a very small hole in the base of one bottle with a nail, and to cut the top from the other.

4 TAPE THE TOP OF THE second bottle to the base of the first bottle. This is so water can drip slowly from the top.

5 ATTACH THE END of the plastic tube to the inverted bottle top using modeling clay to waterproof the joint.

6 MAKE A STAND for the bottle by asking an adult to nail one end of the wood strip to the block of wood.

The stand must be steady enough to support the plastic bottle when it is full of water

7 NOW FIRMLY tape the bottle to the wooden stand. The bottle should be able to stand upright unaided.

Where do you expect grass to grow? Leave the experiment in a sunny place for several days, and then look for plant growth

8 POUR WATER into the bottle so it drips down the tube to the oasis. Scatter seeds over the sand and watch for a few days to see where they sprout.

Continents, islands, and coastal regions

THE FARTHER LAND IS from the ocean, the drier its climate. As a maritime air mass (pp.70–71) crosses a continent, the air loses its moisture. As it crosses mountains, precipitation occurs on the windward side but little or none falls on the other. This dry area is in the rain shadow. By the time the air has reached the center of the continent, it is a dry, continental air mass. A continental climate has hotter summers and colder winters than the maritime climates of islands and coastal regions. Coastal climates are usually moist, with precipitation distributed through the year. Ocean currents bring cool or warm water, also influencing coastal climates.

Now you see it, now you don't

New York City is caught between two air masses. Sometimes it is affected by maritime air from the Atlantic Ocean, sometimes by continental air from the northwest. A change in the air mass means a change in the weather. These two photographs of the skyline show the difference. On the left, continental air formed over northern Canada has brought dry, cold weather and a bright, clear sky. On the right, maritime tropical air has made the sky misty.

EXPERIMENT
Continents and oceans

Water has a higher heat capacity than land, so it takes much longer to warm up and cool down. Summer ends before the sea has warmed to the temperature of the land, and winter ends before it cools to the land temperature. You can measure the different rates of cooling and warming, using sand as a "continent" and water as an "ocean."

YOU WILL NEED
- water
- 4 rubber bands
- sand
- 2 thermometers
- pen ● 2 bowls

When you remove the bowls from the refrigerator, keep a note of which one reaches room temperature first

1 HALF-FILL ONE BOWL with dry sand and the other with water. Stretch two rubber bands across the width of each bowl, and lay one thermometer on top of each. Leave both in the shade until they reach the same temperature.

2 NOTE THE TEMPERATURES and the time. Place the bowls side by side in a refrigerator, and note the temperatures every 15 minutes until both are the same. Which took longest to reach the temperature in the refrigerator?

Moving inland

Northern California receives mainly maritime polar air from the north and maritime tropical air from the south. This produces a moist climate along the coast, but as the air moves inland it crosses two mountainous regions. By the time the air has moved inland as far as Nevada, the air is very dry.

Temperate in the west
Along the narrow coastal strip of California, maritime air masses produce warm summers and mild winters with little snow. Rain falls mainly in the winter months.

Desert in the east
The air loses its moisture over the mountains and is warmed by compression as it descends the eastern side. Here in Death Valley the annual rainfall is about 2 in (5 cm).

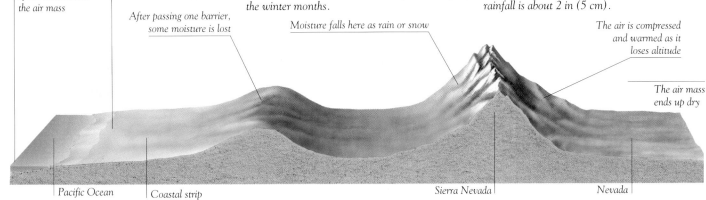

The sea is the source of the moisture in the air mass

Little moisture is lost over the coastal strip

After passing one barrier, some moisture is lost

Moisture falls here as rain or snow

The air is compressed and warmed as it loses altitude

The air mass ends up dry

Pacific Ocean | Coastal strip | Sierra Nevada | Nevada

Advancing air masses

North American climates are produced by six types of air mass. Maritime polar and maritime tropical air masses bring moist Pacific air to the west and Atlantic air to the east. Continental polar air brings drier, cooler conditions to central Canada and the northern United States, and continental tropical air gives the southern central states their hot, dry summers.

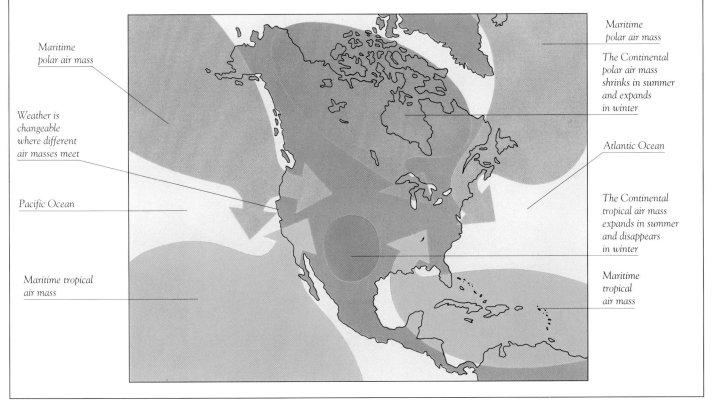

Maritime polar air mass

Weather is changeable where different air masses meet

Pacific Ocean

Maritime tropical air mass

Maritime polar air mass

The Continental polar air mass shrinks in summer and expands in winter

Atlantic Ocean

The Continental tropical air mass expands in summer and disappears in winter

Maritime tropical air mass

Monsoons

MONSOONS are land and sea breezes (pp.64–65) on a very large scale. They are produced by changes in pressure systems. The Asian monsoon is the best known. In winter dry, sinking air forms a large high-pressure area over Asia. The weather is dry, and winter monsoon winds blow away from the coasts. In summer the land heats faster than the sea. The high-pressure system weakens, and the winds reverse direction, bringing moist air from over the sea into the dry continent. The onset of the summer monsoon is usually sudden and dramatic, bringing heavy rains.

■ Where monsoons occur

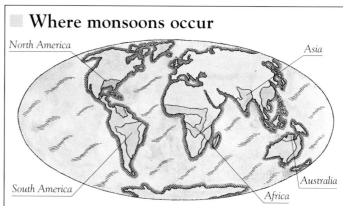

North America   Asia

South America   Africa   Australia

This map highlights the areas that are affected by monsoon winds and rain (shown in pink). The monsoon is more intense in Asia than in other regions, because of the size of the Asian land mass. The monsoon extends over all of southern and southeastern Asia, as well as parts of northern Australia. Large parts of Africa and North and South America experience monsoons of differing intensity.

EXPERIMENT
Rain-bearing winds

Northerly winds blowing from the high-pressure area in central Asia bring dry air to the Indian subcontinent in winter. In January the average rainfall in Cherranpunji is ¾ in (18 mm). In July the continental high pressure disappears, pressure rises over the sea, and at the height of the monsoon moist winds from the sea increase rainfall to 96 in (2,446 mm). You can demonstrate how such a change in wind direction brings dry or moist air.

👥 *Adult supervision is required for this experiment*

YOU WILL NEED
● *2 dishpans*
● *wet- and dry-bulb hygrometer*
● *electric fan*
● *water*

1 FILL ONE DISHPAN with water. Set the other upside down beside the first. Put the hygrometer on the inverted pan, near to the water.

2 ASK AN ADULT TO TURN on the fan so it blows over the hygrometer, and then over the water. This is the "winter wind." Check the humidity reading. The air will be fairly dry.

3 SWITCH THE POSITION of the two pans so the fan blows over the water before reaching the hygrometer. Check the humidity. Your "monsoon" wind should be moist.

EXPERIMENT
Monsoon mud madness

Monsoon rains increase the amounts of water flowing in rivers. In the lowlands, rivers flood surrounding farms. When the floods recede, tiny particles of silt that were in the water remain. Silt makes soil fertile, and farmers rely on the monsoons for this seasonal flooding. You can see how this flooding happens.

YOU WILL NEED
- large board ● bricks
- soil ● water ● spoon

1 RAISE ONE END of the board and support it with bricks. Cover the board with about 2 in (5 cm) of soil, and pack the soil down well.

Take care
This experiment is very messy, so do it outside to keep your home clean.

2 USE THE SPOON to make a hollow "lake" at the top of the board and a "river" channel down the board from the lake. About halfway from the bottom, make the channel meander gently from side to side.

3 POUR water into the lake. When the river is flowing, pour faster until it breaks its banks, then stop. When it dries, where has the silt settled?

Monsoons in Asia

In summer (right) the land warms faster than the sea. Air pressure falls over central Asia and rises over the Indian Ocean. Moist air blows inland, rising as it reaches high ground and bringing heavy rain to India. This is the summer monsoon. In winter (far right) the land cools rapidly, and sinking air forms a large but shallow area of high pressure over the continent. Air pressure is now higher over the land than over the sea, and northerly winds bring dry air to India. This is the winter monsoon.

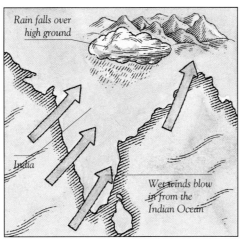

Rain falls over high ground

India

Wet winds blow in from the Indian Ocean

Summer monsoon winds

High pressure in central Asia causes drier winds to blow out over the sea

Indian Ocean

Dry winter winds

Climate and the earth's surface

SOIL IS A MIXTURE of mineral particles and plant and animal remains. The mineral particles may have been deposited by wind, water, or ice sheets in the distant past, but in most soils they come from the underlying rock. It is the weather, however, that changes rock into soil, and the different climates of the world give each region its particular soils. Frost shatters rock into fragments from which rain dissolves chemical compounds that nourish plants. With warm sunshine and moisture, plants grow; their remains decompose to form soil humus. In cold or dry climates these processes operate slowly. When climates change it takes time for soils to respond.

EXPERIMENT
Salination

Adult supervision is advised for this experiment

In some hot climates, salts dissolved from the C soil horizon can be slowly drawn to the surface and left there as the water that carries them evaporates. This process, called salination, can kill plants. You can demonstrate salination for yourself at home.

YOU WILL NEED
- desk lamp ● 2 plastic containers ● water
- soil ● tape ● scissors ● salt ● ice pick

EXPERIMENT
Growing soil

In a mild, moist climate, invertebrate animals living in the soil feed on dead plant material and mix it thoroughly with mineral particles to make rich, fertile soil. Earthworms are the largest soil invertebrates, and there may be hundreds of them beneath every square yard of a temperate grassland or forest soil. Their existence is vital for the formation of air passages in the soil. You can watch them work as they carry material down from the surface and mix it into the soil.

YOU WILL NEED
- soil ● sand ● clear jar
- water mister ● pebbles
- leaves ● earthworms

Beneath the surface

If you cut vertically down to the bedrock from the soil surface you would see a soil profile. In many profiles you can see separate layers, called horizons. Each horizon is given a letter, starting with O and running down through A, B, and C to D. Some soils have more horizons than these basic ones, and others have fewer.

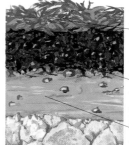

The O and A horizons consist of a thin layer of humus—decaying organic matter

The B horizon consists of humus and mineral particles

The C horizon is mostly weathered bedrock material

The D horizon is the bedrock—the parent material of the soil horizon

1 FILL THE JAR with a 2 in (5 cm) bottom layer of small pebbles, sand to about ¾ of the jar's depth, and finally a 1 in (2 cm) layer of topsoil.

2 SCATTER ENOUGH dead leaves and small twigs to cover the soil surface. Then catch a few earthworms and place them among the leaves on the surface.

3 MIST THE LEAVES. Pump the mister until there is ½ in (1 cm) of water at the jar's bottom. Leave the jar in a warm, dark place and see what happens.

1 ASK AN ADULT to make twenty holes in one container and fill it with soil. Fill the other with water and dissolved salt.

2 PUT THE SOIL container on the water container and tape them together. Flood the soil container.

3 WITH THE LAMP over the containers, wait until the soil dries and the water level drops. What is the white powder?

EXPERIMENT
Drought

Adult supervision is advised for this experiment

When rain falls or snow melts, some water flows into rivers, some evaporates, and some drains through the soil to accumulate above an impermeable layer, such as clay or rock. This is ground water; its surface is called the water table. Water that evaporates from the surface is replaced in the soil by water drawn upward from the ground water through tiny spaces between soil particles. You can demonstrate the effect on soils where you live.

YOU WILL NEED
- *pitcher of water*
- *desk lamp* ● *soil* ● *2 plastic containers* ● *pen*
- *notepad* ● *tape*
- *ice pick* ● *scissors*

1 ASK AN ADULT to punch drainage holes with the ice pick in the bottom of one container. Fill it with soil, pressed gently in place.

2 PLACE THE SOIL CONTAINER on top of the empty container. Tape the two containers so water will not leak from between them.

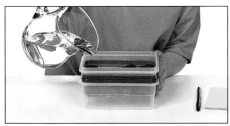

3 USE THE PITCHER to pour a known amount of water until there is water on the surface and in the lower container.

4 PLACE THE LAMP about 2 in (5 cm) above the soil. Leave it (possibly for several days) until the soil has dried out.

5 THE DIFFERENCE between the amount of water remaining in the bottom container and the amount you added is the evaporation during your "drought."

Climates of the past

CLIMATES ARE CONSTANTLY CHANGING. This is partly because continents are constantly moving —very slowly—and oceans gradually change shape and size. There are many different clues to show us the way climates have changed. Coal forms only where tropical swamps once existed, but it is found in many different parts of the world. There is coal in Antarctica, so we know it was once tropical. The Himalayan mountain range is growing higher because India is crashing into Asia, forcing rocks that were formed at the bottom of the sea high into the air. The Mediterranean is all that remains of an ancient ocean called Tethys; during ice ages, when sea levels fall, it has been reduced to a chain of lakes. Palaeoclimatologists are scientists who investigate the past climates. Their discoveries help us to understand the way the weather works and predict how it may change again in years to come.

■ DISCOVERY ■
Boxgrove man

Late in 1993, a human tibia (leg bone) was discovered in silt deposits at Boxgrove, in West Sussex, England. This leg bone is about 500,000 years old and its size indicates it is from a male. This picture shows a reconstruction by a scientist of what "Boxgrove man" may have looked like. He lived alongside now-extinct

species of rhinoceroses, bears, and smaller mammals during an interglacial period (a period between two ice ages). At that time England was joined to mainland Europe, and it may have had a climate much warmer than that of today.

EXPERIMENT
The moving earth

The earth's crust is made from pieces of rock, called plates, which move in relation to one another. There are seven large plates, including the North American, African, and Eurasian plates, and many smaller ones, such as the Caribbean and Arabian plates. Where plates move apart, new rock emerges from below the crust. Where they collide, one plate sinks below the other, back into the earth's mantle. Some plates move past one another along faults. You can demonstrate how this movement of plates both shifts continents and creates new crust material from beneath the surface.

YOU WILL NEED
● paper ● modeling clay
● scissors ● shoe box

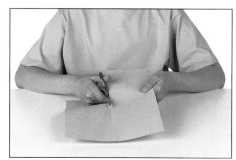

1 CUT A SHEET OF PAPER into two halves. These pieces of paper are "plates" pushing the "continents."

2 CUT A SLOT IN THE MIDDLE of the box, and cut away the two main sides so the box now looks like a table.

3 ROLL TWO LENGTHS of modeling clay out in your hands. These will be weights representing continents.

4 HOLD THE STRIPS (plates) beneath the box. As you push them up and down the continents will move.

EXPERIMENT
Soil clues

A sandy soil is one in which more than one-third of the mineral particles are sand grains. You can find out whether the soil near your home is sandy. If it is, the area may once have been a desert. Examine the sand with a magnifying glass; if tiny fragments of shell are mixed with it then you know your neighborhood may once have been a beach or part of the sea bed.

YOU WILL NEED
- soil ● notepad ● pen
- ruler ● water
- jar with lid

Ancient rivers
Special satellite photographs like this one reveal river courses beneath the sands of the Sahara. As the climate became drier thousands of years ago, the region was transformed into desert. The old features of the rivers were hidden as sand dunes were moved by the wind across them.

1 FIND SOME UNDISTURBED soil near your home. Half-fill a tall jar with this soil, but do not press it down. Fill the rest of the jar with water.

2 PLACE THE LID on the jar tightly and shake it vigorously until the water is muddy. Leave the jar standing upright to let the particles in the water settle.

3 THE SOIL WILL SETTLE in layers. Measure the sand thickness and multiply by 3. If the result is greater than the total thickness, the soil is sandy.

Ancient continents

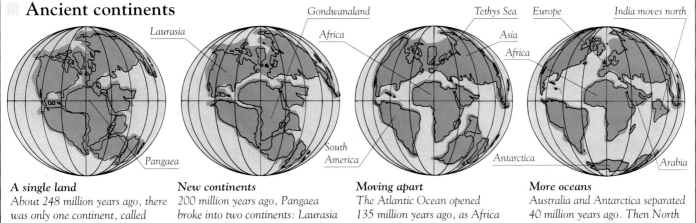

A single land
About 248 million years ago, there was only one continent, called Pangaea, surrounded by the world ocean, Panthalassa. The interior of Pangaea was very dry.

New continents
200 million years ago, Pangaea broke into two continents: Laurasia in the north and Gondwanaland in the south. For 100 million years, land bridges linked the continents.

Moving apart
The Atlantic Ocean opened 135 million years ago, as Africa and South America divided. The Tethys Sea separated Africa and South America from Asia.

More oceans
Australia and Antarctica separated 40 million years ago. Then North America separated from Europe. India reached the equator and Arabia broke from Africa.

The pollen, beetle, and ice core records

EVIDENCE THAT CLIMATES were different in the past is all around us, although it is not always easy to find. Coral reefs, for example, occur only in very clear seas 33–200 ft (10–60 m) deep, where the water temperature never falls below 68° F (20° C). Because it is hard, dead coral is often preserved—so if you find a fossil reef, you can be sure that once that place lay beneath a warm, shallow sea. Grains of plant pollen can survive for thousands of years. The discovery of pollen from alpine plants in regions that now have a mild climate indicates that their climates were once much cooler. Beetles also live in special conditions, and their hard wing cases are often preserved in the soil. To go back tens or hundreds of thousands of years, scientists analyze air bubbles preserved in the polar ice sheets.

■ Clues from a frozen past

In Greenland and Antarctica scientists drill deep for ice cores. The proportions of two forms of oxygen in water and of gases trapped in tiny bubbles are clues to past temperatures and to broad changes in local climates.

EXPERIMENT
Looking back in time

There are two important forms of oxygen, ^{16}O and ^{18}O. Cold conditions increase the proportion of ^{18}O in water, so analyzing the ^{18}O in layers of ancient ice allows scientists to tell summer from winter and to calculate past temperatures. By drilling down through thousands of years of layers scientists can find out about past climates. You can show how core drilling works.

YOU WILL NEED
● *baking tray* ● *scissors*
● *3 colors of modeling clay* ● *drinking straw* ● *rolling pin*

1 SOFTEN THE MODELING clay with your hands, and use a rolling pin to roll each color into a ⅓-in (1-cm) thick sheet.

2 STACK THE CLAY SHEETS one on top of another in the baking tray, making layers that represent the built-up layers of ice.

3 DRILL A CORE by carefully pushing and twisting the straw vertically all the way through the stack of colored modeling clay. Give the straw a final twist to separate it from the surrounding clay, and withdraw it gently.

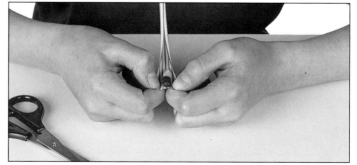

4 CUT THE STRAW OPEN WITH THE SCISSORS, then fold back the sides. Inside you will find your own core sample. Ice, peat, and other cores are collected in a metal cylinder which is opened to remove the sample.

THE POLLEN, BEETLE, AND ICE CORE RECORDS

EXPERIMENT
Plants from the past

Pollen grains are tiny, but their tough coats almost completely resist decay, so they can survive in peat and soil for thousands of years. Some regions which are now farmed and some areas of barren land are known to have been forested at one time. The tree pollen still found there allows scientists to identify the species of trees present in the ancient forests. All flowering plants produce pollen, so this recording of the climate continues. You can collect pollen quite easily and see the individual grains studied by scientists of past climates.

YOU WILL NEED
- white paper ● flowering plants
- strong magnifying glass or hand lens ● pen ● notebook ● small envelopes or plastic bags

The past from a tree trunk

The center of the tree shows different ring widths, indicating that some years had better growing periods than others

In spring, trees grow by producing new material in a band just beneath the bark. The last material to be produced in late summer looks darker. This forms a pattern of rings, one for each year of the tree's life. Rings provide a clue to climate, because in good weather there is more growth, so the bands are wider than those grown in poor years.

1 FIND SOME NATURALLY GROWING pollen-producing flowers in your area. If you do not know their names, identify the plants with a field guide. Place them in a labelled envelope.

2 FIND A FLOWER that is almost fully open. Tap it into an envelope. You will see pollen falling like fine powder. Use an envelope for each plant. Note how many species you see.

3 TO EXAMINE THE POLLEN, empty each envelope on to a clean sheet of white paper and study it with the magnifying glass. Notice how much pollen each plant has contributed and how many species of plants you have found.

4 LIST THE PLANT SPECIES in the order of the total amount of pollen you collected from each (as "little," "moderate," "a lot"). Briefly describe the climate that suits these plants. If the climate changes, so will the pollen record.

155

Ice ages

ABOUT 18,000 YEARS AGO, most of northern Europe, Asia, and North America lay beneath sheets of ice in places miles thick. The ice retreated about 10,000 years ago. Most scientists believe we live in an interglacial—a period of warmer weather between ice ages. Many scientists believe that ice ages occur when the amount of heat the planet receives from the sun is reduced, due in combination to the tilt of the earth's axis, changes in the way the earth rotates, and a slight lengthening and narrowing of the path of the earth's orbit. The earliest known ice age occurred about 290 million years ago, and there have been many since then. They appear to have grown more frequent over the last two million years, during which there were four major ice ages. Ice ages can begin and end rapidly, sometimes in a matter of decades.

■ DISCOVERY ■
Jean Louis Agassiz

Jean Louis Rodolphe Agassiz (1807–73) was a Swiss naturalist and expert on fossils. On a trip to the Alps he noticed that a hut built on a glacier had moved a mile (1.6 km) since he first saw it 12 years earlier. In 1836 he drove a line of stakes across the glacier and when he returned the following year he found they had moved. This proved that glaciers move, and helped him explain the position of rocks that had apparently been moved and scoured by glaciers, yet were far from any present glacier. He concluded that at one time much of northern Europe was covered by glaciers, and that there had been what he called a Great Ice Age.

EXPERIMENT
Frost shattering

Water seeps into tiny cracks in rocks. When the water freezes, it expands, and it does so with enough force to widen the cracks. This can shatter boulders. "Frost-shattering" helps produce the small fragments from which soil develops. You can demonstrate how simple it is for water to shatter a stone.

YOU WILL NEED
● *small stone*
● *plastic yogurt cup* ● *water*
● *paper*
● *plastic bag*

1 PLACE THE STONE in the yogurt cup and cover it with water. Leave it overnight to soak thoroughly.

2 REMOVE THE STONE and place it—still wet—in the plastic bag. Empty the cup, seal the bag, and place the bag containing the stone in the cup.

3 PUT THE CUP IN THE FREEZER, and leave it there for about two hours. Then remove it and let it defrost. Wait until the ice has melted and the stone is at room temperature. Empty the contents of the bag onto a sheet of paper, and see if the frost action has changed the stone in any way.

EXPERIMENT
Solifluction

At the edge of an ice sheet the ground is frozen for most of the year, but for a short time in summer the top layer may thaw. When this happens, water is released and the surface turns into a layer of slippery mud. If the ground is sloping, large boulders are loosened and slide slowly downhill. They stop when the ground refreezes, but each year they travel a little further. This is called solifluction. Scientists can recognize it by the pattern of rocks it produces on hillsides, which shows the rocks once lay close to an ice sheet. You can make this happen in your own home.

YOU WILL NEED
● a tray at least 20 in (50 cm) long ● dishwashing gloves ● rolling pin ● stones ● ice ● soil

1 COVER THE TRAY with a thin, even layer of soil and, wearing rubber gloves, pack the soil down as tightly as you can across the whole board.

2 CRUSH SOME ICE with a rolling pin and cover the soil with it. Then put a second layer of soil over the ice. This represents an Arctic permafrost soil with a thin upper level.

3 PUSH YOUR "BOULDERS," a few stones about 2 in (5 cm) across for a 20 in (50 cm) tray, into the soil near one end of the tray.

4 PUT THE TRAY in the freezer, and when it is thoroughly frozen, take it out of the freezer and prop it at an angle of about 30°, like a hillside, with the stones at the top end. See what happens to the stones as the ice melts.

The stones start at the top of the board

EXPERIMENT
Expanding ice

Because ice is less dense than liquid water (pp.128–129), water expands in volume when it freezes. You may not realize just how much more space ice occupies than water. This is very easy to measure, as you will see in this simple experiment.

YOU WILL NEED
● scissors
● tape
● 2 clear jars
● water

1 HALF FILL TWO JARS with water. Use some tape to mark the water level on the outside of the jars.

2 FREEZE ONE JAR. When the water is solid, remove it and compare its level with that on the unfrozen jar.

Volcanoes and asteroids

IN 1815 MOUNT TAMBORA, a volcano in what is now Indonesia, erupted with such violence that there was almost total darkness for three days in places up to 300 miles (about 500 km) away. Violent volcanic eruptions release vast quantities of particles. In the troposphere (p.18) these are removed quickly by rain, but if they reach the stratosphere they can remain for months or even years, blanketing large areas of the world and reflecting sunlight. The eruption of Krakatau in 1883 and Mount Katmai in 1912 caused 10 and 20 percent decreases in sunlight intensity lasting up to three years. More recently, the eruption of Mount Pinatubo in the Philippines reduced global temperatures. Asteroid and comet impacts can also throw huge amounts of material to great heights, but they are very rare.

A volcano erupts

Mount Pinatubo in the Philippines erupted on June 15, 1991, sending particles to a height of more than 49,000 ft (15 km) and burying land up to 8 miles (13 km) away beneath ash—in some places more than 10 ft (3 m) thick. The particles reaching the stratosphere consisted mainly of sulfuric acid. Within three weeks these covered 40 per cent of the earth's surface, in a belt circling the world. Scientists calculated they would reflect enough sunlight to reduce temperatures in the tropics by 3.6° F (2° C). The global temperature fell by 0.9° F (0.5° C).

EXPERIMENT
Asteroid strike

When an asteroid or comet, traveling at about 45,000 mph (72,000 km/h), collides with the earth, the energy of the impact may throw huge amounts of material high into the atmosphere. Particles that reach the stratosphere cause climatic cooling as the tiny particles of dust scatter the sun's radiation away from the earth and back into space. It is simple to demonstrate what happens, but do it outdoors because it is messy.

YOU WILL NEED
- *large tray*
- *modeling clay*
- *plain flour*

1 MAKE SEVERAL "asteroids" from clay, ranging from ½–4 in (1–10 cm) wide. Pour about 2 in (5 cm) of flour into the tray, and spread it evenly.

2 THROW THE ASTEROIDS into the flour. Notice how much dust each raises. The asteroids should raise more dust the harder you throw them.

EXPERIMENT
Scattering the light

Heat and light from the sun pass through the atmosphere to the surface but are absorbed, scattered, or reflected by small airborne particles. The amount that is scattered depends on how much of the sky the particles obscure, known as their column density. Imagine a column extending from the ground all the way to the top of the atmosphere. Radiation from the sun can reach the surface of the earth only if no particles interrupt it as it passes in a straight line through the column. Particles a few inches apart horizontally will affect radiation if they extend vertically through enough of the column. Radiation that is reflected back into space does not reach the Earth's surface, so the temperature is lowered. You can see for yourself how particles can reflect light.

YOU WILL NEED
- *tall jar with lid*
- *flashlight* ● *spoon*
- *talcum powder*

1 SPOON ENOUGH TALCUM POWDER into the jar to form a thin layer across the bottom, and then put on the lid. Allow the powder to settle.

2 TURN OUT THE LIGHT AND WAIT a few moments for your eyes to adjust to the darkness. Shine the flashlight into the jar and look from the other side. It should be completely clear, allowing all the light to pass through it, like clean air.

3 TURN THE JAR UPSIDE DOWN so the powder falls, and shine the flashlight on it again. The beam emerging from the other side will be dimmer, because the particles reflect much of the light, preventing it from passing freely through the jar.

■ Global dust

Small particles of ash from volcanoes—made mainly of sulfuric acid—may enter the stratosphere, where they are dispersed around the world by the high-level winds. This takes no more than a few weeks, but the effects may last for months or even years. These pictures trace the spread of particles from the Mexican volcano El Chichón, after it erupted on April 3, 1982.

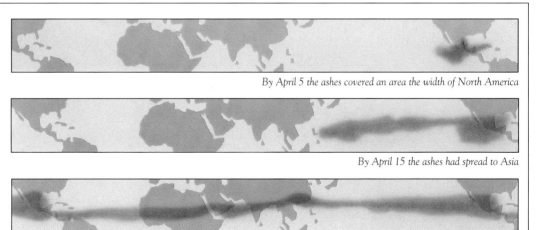

By April 5 the ashes covered an area the width of North America

By April 15 the ashes had spread to Asia

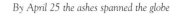

By April 25 the ashes spanned the globe

Local pollution

FOG FORMS when air at ground level becomes saturated. In early industrial cities coal smoke sometimes combined with natural fog. This produced choking, yellowish fogs so dense that city street lights had to be turned on during the day. Such smoke-fogs were nicknamed smog; they damaged health and buildings, and lowered temperatures. Smog has acquired a new meaning. Trapped beneath a temperature inversion (where warm air sits over cold air) nitrogen oxides and particles of unburned engine fuel react in strong sunlight to produce ozone and a range of chemical compounds that form an unpleasant, yellowish haze—smog. Large-scale burning of vegetation causes temporary cooling by shading the ground, and the removal of surface vegetation may change the color of the ground, which affects the way that it absorbs and reflects solar energy. Locally the climate becomes cooler and drier because plant transpiration decreases, and also windier, due to the loss of tree shelter.

EXPERIMENT
Air pollution

Over land, air always carries particles of dust, pollen grains, fungal spores, and other material. You can see for yourself how clean the air is where you live. If you find black specks, they are particles of soot from fires or vehicle exhausts.

EXPERIMENT
Everyday acid

Acid rain (see opposite) damages limestone, marble, and sandstone. Buildings such as the Taj Mahal in India and the Parthenon in Greece have suffered badly. The damage occurs because these stones contain carbonates that react with the acid. One product of the reaction is carbon dioxide, which is released as a gas. If you pour an acidic liquid on to a material containing carbonates, like some kinds of concrete, you will see the gas bubbling out.

YOU WILL NEED
● *vinegar* ● *baking tray* ● *small piece of concrete rubble*

Fizzy concrete
Place the lump of concrete rubble in the baking tray, and then pour a few drops of vinegar over it. Watch to see acid fizzing as the carbon dioxide gas is released.

YOU WILL NEED
● *rain gauge* ● *white coffee filter* ● *magnifying glass*

1 EMPTY THE RAIN GAUGE and place the filter paper in the funnel. Then reassemble the gauge, put it outside, and leave it until it has filled with rain.

2 REMOVE THE FILTER PAPER and lay it flat in a good light. Use the magnifying glass to search for particles on the paper. Is there anything on it that looks like pollution?

EXPERIMENT
Acid rain

Clean air contains a small amount of carbon dioxide, an even smaller amount of sulphate released from volcanoes and by bacteria, and nitrogen oxides produced when lightning supplies the energy to oxidize nitrogen. These dissolve in water droplets, making all precipitation slightly acid. Normally, rain has a pH of 5.6. If the pH is higher, the rain is alkaline. Precipitation is said to be acid rain if its pH falls below 5.0, the level at which fish and plants start to be hurt. You can demonstrate how neutral distilled water (pH 7.0) can become acid by making a little acid rain for yourself.

YOU WILL NEED
- knife ● saucer ● modeling clay
- candle ● saucepan ● matches
- water ● glass ● vinegar
- chopping board ● 2 coffee filters
- red cabbage

Adult supervision is advised for this experiment

EXPERIMENT
Testing the acidity of everyday things

The acidity of rain varies widely from place to place, but the industrial pollutants that cause it can travel a long distance—so even if you live far from any factories, your rain may be acid, with a pH lower than 5.0. It is not difficult to find out the acidity of rain, using your rain gauge to collect rain water and a pH kit into which you pour your sample. A pH kit works by mixing your sample with an indicator—a liquid that changes color to show whether something is acid or alkaline. A key on the packet shows you the pH of the substance you are measuring.

YOU WILL NEED
- pH kit ● eye dropper ● pen
- notepad
- rainwater
- vinegar
- distilled water

The test for acidity
Measure the pH of each liquid in turn, cleaning the equipment between samples. Write down each reading. How does the acidity of rain water compare with that of vinegar and distilled water?

1 ASK AN ADULT to chop some cabbage and boil it in a little water for a few minutes. The water, which is colored, is neutral and acts as an indicator.

2 ALLOW THE INDICATOR to cool. Pour a little on the saucer and add the acidic vinegar. Does the liquid change?

3 SOAK THE COFFEE filter in the indicator you have made. Squeeze it out gently, so it is damp but not soggy. Lay it flat on the chopping board.

4 STAND THE CANDLE in modeling clay on the coffee filter. Ask an adult to light it, and then cover it with the glass jar—making sure that it is air-tight.

5 REMOVE THE JAR about 2 minutes after the flame goes out. Has the carbon dioxide caused any change in the color of the indicator?

Global pollution

HEAT ENERGY RADIATED from the sun warms the earth's surface. The earth radiates heat back into the atmosphere and into space, but at much longer wavelengths. Some of this heat is absorbed by molecules of polluting gases such as water vapour, carbon dioxide, methane, CFC's, and nitrous oxide. This process warms the air and is called the greenhouse effect. Many scientists fear that by releasing more gases, we may change world climates. There are many uncertainties, and evidence of global warming is interpreted differently by scientists.

EXPERIMENT
Drowning in meltwater

If global climates become very much warmer because of pollution, the ice at the poles could begin to melt. It is unlikely that this will happen on a large scale, but if it did sea levels would rise as they did at the end of the ice ages. Here you will see what the result would be for low-lying islands and coasts.

YOU WILL NEED
● baking dish ● water ● ice
● modeling clay

2 POUR WATER INTO the dish to make a "sea." It should be high enough to leave only the top of the island above water. The continent remains dry, well above the water.

■ DISCOVERY ■
James Lovelock

James E. Lovelock (b. 1919) is a British chemist and inventor. In the 1960s, while working in California for the NASA space program, he and his colleagues wondered how we might detect the presence of living organisms on other planets without going there. They concluded that any organism must alter its environment in ways that can be detected. This led Lovelock to the Gaia hypothesis (*gaia* is a Greek word for "earth"), the idea that on any planet that supports life, living organisms maintain conditions, especially climates, favorable to life. If correct, this means living organisms will tend to undo any environmental damage caused by humans.

1 USE SOME MODELING CLAY to make a "continent" at one end of the dish, almost to the rim. Then make an "island" in the middle of the dish, about half as high as the dish.

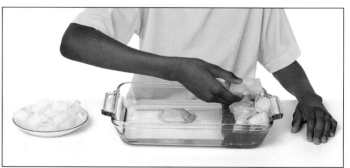

3 PACK AS MANY ICE CUBES as you can on top of the continent, out of the water. Leave them to melt. The ice represents landlocked ice sheets, such as those over Antarctica. What happens to the sea level when the ice melts? What happens to the island as the water level rises?

EXPERIMENT
Absorbing CO_2

Some of the carbon dioxide (CO_2) we add to the air by burning fuels dissolves in the oceans, and some is absorbed by green plants, which grow faster and bigger. Because plants use carbon dioxide to make food, this leaves less carbon dioxide in the air and thus decreases the chance of climatic warming. So far global warming is too slight to be measured easily, but planting crops of fast-growing trees on land not needed for farming has been suggested as a way to remove carbon dioxide from the air and help prevent global warming. With a simple experiment you can prove that plants absorb carbon dioxide and release oxygen, acting as natural air filters.

You Will Need
- 2 candles ● fresh leaves
- matches ● modeling
clay ● water ● 2 jars with lids

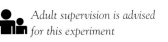 *Adult supervision is advised for this experiment*

1 Use blobs of modeling clay to stand one candle upright in the bottom of each jar. On a warm, sunny day place both jars outdoors, side by side in the open and in full sunshine.

2 Pour about 2 in (5 cm) of fresh water into one of the jars, and float enough freshly picked green leaves on the water to cover the surface. The more leaves you use, the better. Be careful not to bruise the leaves.

3 Ask an adult to light both candles. Fasten the lids on both jars. The flames will release carbon dioxide and consume oxygen until both candles are extinguished, but the leaves will absorb carbon dioxide and release oxygen. Which candle is the first to be extinguished?

Using available resources

In most green plants, photosynthesis (the process used by plants to make their own food) begins when the atoms of carbon dioxide are split apart and then joined in a compound with other atoms. Many plants use three carbon atoms in the first stage of photosynthesis. These plants, called C3 plants, are wasteful in their use of carbon dioxide, returning some of it to the air. C4 plants make a compound with four carbon atoms, and use almost all their carbon dioxide by the end of the photosynthesis. C4 plants use carbon dioxide much more efficiently; they may have evolved because the atmosphere contains very little carbon dioxide. C4 plants such as corn and sugarcane grow faster than C3 plants such as wheat. If more carbon dioxide is added by pollution to the air, C3 plants may make better use of it than C4 plants. C3 plants may then yield better harvests than C4 plants.

Green beans: a C3 plant

Corn: a C4 plant

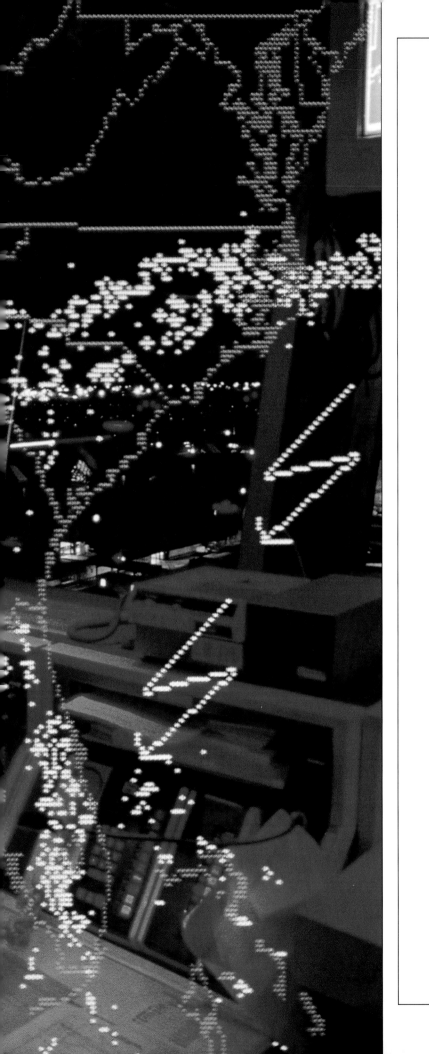

WEATHER FORECASTING

A world view
This image of the earth, taken by the weather
satellite Meteosat, shows cloud formations and
land temperatures (hot areas are red to yellow;
cooler areas are greens and blues). Earth-bound
offices (left) give a more local view. These air-
traffic controllers in Memphis are using
information from the Lightning Detection
Network. The green dots show lightning strikes.

PEOPLE HAVE ALWAYS
wanted to know what
the weather will bring, and
until fairly recently people
tried to use nature as a
forecasting system.
When flowers bloom, how
birds behave, or the color
of the sunset are all clues
to the weather. Today
forecasting uses up-to-the-
minute technology.
However, by keeping
accurate records, even an
amateur meteorologist can
contribute to the work of
international forecasters.

SEARCHING THE SKIES

People have always felt the wind and looked at the sky for signs of the weather to come. The Roman philosopher Pliny the Elder (AD 23–79) wrote: "A wind from the northwest will bring cold weather, perhaps with hailstorms. In winter a wind from the northeast may bring snow. Wind from the southwest is hot and will bring rain. The best wind for your health is from the north, the worst from the south."

Pliny was not the first person to write about the signs we can use to forecast the weather. Hesiod, a Greek poet who lived around 800 BC, advised sailors that when the first spray of leaves at the top of the fig tree was the size of a crow's footprint, it was safe to go to sea. Theophrastus, a Greek philosopher who lived around 300 BC, wrote down many of the weather signs that were relied upon in his day. He noted that thunder and lightning were accompanied by strong winds, and that when the sun's rays were split at dawn, some pointing to the north and some to the south, there was wind or rain later in the day. He also predicted a storm whenever a dolphin was seen close to shore.

Farmers and sailors, who needed to know what weather to expect and who spent much time outdoors, continued to watch the sky. Like the ancient Greeks, they noticed that some kinds of clouds and winds from certain directions were usually followed by fine or bad weather.

■ Folk signs

Most observers of the sky in ancient times believed the weather was caused by gods, spirits, or demons rather than by physical processes. They thought that plants and animals were more closely in touch with the spirit world and knew better than humans what weather was to come. It is true that some animals, such as dogs and cats, seem to sense the electrical disturbances associated with thunderstorms. They clearly show discomfort, but they are simply reacting to what they feel, not making a prediction. Their behaviour is a poor guide to the weather. The storm may miss you altogether, and if it does come your way, by the time the animals look uncomfortable the sky will probably be black and you may hear the thunder in the distance, so you do not need the animals to tell you what is about to happen.

Plants are not good predictors either. They burst into leaf, flower, and set seed according to weather conditions at the time. They do not know what will happen months or even minutes ahead. The facts that the winter is mild, the spring warm, and the plant growth begins a week or two earlier than it did last year tell us nothing about what the summer will be like. When fruit and nuts are abundant and animals that hoard food for the winter seem busier than usual, it does not mean they have foreseen a long winter. They take what they can find. If they seem to be hoarding more, it is probably because the same warm weather that helped the plants produce the nuts also allowed more of their young to survive, so there are more of them engaged in hoarding food.

Are the old weather signs reliable? Although many folk signs are based on the appearance of the sky, they are often not correct. This is because the people who worked them out centuries ago based them on an idea of the world's weather that was wrong. They thought that near the equator the weather was always hot and

Weather by numbers
Lewis Richardson tried forecasting weather numerically, using this calculator in the 1920's.

Admiral Robert Fitzroy
Fitzroy (1805–65) commanded HMS Beagle. *His* Weather Book, *published in 1863, helped sailors forecast the weather.*

Safety at sea
Radio broadcasts of weather forecasts help these sailors find the best wind and avoid dangerous storms.

Wet-bulb and dry-bulb
Simple predictions can be made by using a hygrometer to find the relative humidity.

dry, while near the poles it was always cold and wet. They believed winds from those directions would bring the same sort of weather.

Scientific methods

Modern methods of weather forecasting are more accurate and useful for our present needs. We have more information now about weather patterns than people had in the past, and we understand more about what causes the weather.

The first scientific attempts to forecast the weather began about 140 years ago in England, France, and the United States following the installation of the first telegraph services, which were used to transmit weather information. As telegraph lines were erected in other countries, they, too, introduced weather forecasts.

Forecasts improved steadily as the number of reporting stations increased. Some of the biggest advances were made soon after the first space satellites were launched, making it possible for meteorologists on the ground to receive constantly updated pictures of cloud formations over very large areas. Modern forecasting relies on advanced and very expensive technology, but observers on the surface are still needed. Meteorologists cannot have too much information. The sooner accurate data is sent to a weather station, the more accurate the weather forecast will be, especially if the

Nature's signs
In moist air, seaweed swells and becomes supple. In dry air it is dry and brittle. Home forecasters can use seaweed as a natural humidity tester.

forecast is for the immediate future. Accuracy declines as the period to be forecast moves farther from the time the observations were made. Constantly updated information allows forecasts to be updated and improved.

Professional forecasts cover a whole region, so they have to describe the average weather that can be expected. Conditions may be rather different around an individual home because it is in a sheltered place or in an exposed one. You can see in your own area if the changes that are forecast on television happen faster or more slowly than the forecaster has predicted. Accurate forecasts can be made only from accurate and detailed records of observations and measurements of present weather.

Measuring wind speed
The cups of this antique anemograph record the wind speed on graph paper on the cylinder. Wind speed information is essential to pilots and sailors. Rapid shifts of wind direction can be caused by fronts passing overhead.

Home forecasts

To make your own forecasts, you need to practice observing the weather and carefully recording what you observe. To start, you need a notebook, a pencil, and a little time each day. To take measurements, however, you need

some instruments. You want your measurements to be accurate, expecially if you intend to send them off for use by professional meteorologists. So you need good instruments. Some can be homemade, but certain instruments, such as a barometer, should be bought.

Reasonable forecasts for personal use can be made with basic instruments if you improvise. The Beaufort wind scale (pp.58–59), for example, allows you to estimate the strength of the wind without actually measuring its speed. Without a wind vane or sock of your own, the best guide to wind direction is a wind vane on top of a nearby tall building.

Weather forecasting begins with observation. By following the techniques in this book you can start preparing weather forecasts for the area around your own home. Like a detective, you are looking for clues. You may find some signs in the sky or among the plants and animals in your area, although not all these clues are reliable. Gather as much information as possible to help you decide which clues to use and which to ignore.

Taking air pressure
A barometer measures air pressure as the height of a column of mercury the air will support. Differences in air pressure can tell forecasters a lot about the weather. This antique French instrument is a barometer with a thermometer below.

Weather information
A modern meteorologist uses information from weather stations and satellites. The data is processed by computers to produce both general forecasts and specialized ones for farmers, sailors, and pilots.

Plant folklore

BEFORE PEOPLE HAD barometers, hygrometers, and satellite photographs, weather forecasts were based on the appearance of the sky and the behavior of living things. Plants cannot foretell the weather, but some are sensitive to temperature, humidity, or electrical changes and can thus indicate atmospheric conditions. For instance, many trees show the undersides of their leaves when the air is humid, because the moisture softens their leafstalks, which then bend. Many different beliefs about the weather are based on plants and their appearance in different weather and climatic conditions.

EXPERIMENT
Nature's hygrometer

Pine trees produce their seeds inside cones, which are the female parts of their reproductive systems. The seeds are dispersed by the wind. As the cone dries, it opens to release the seeds, but it closes when the air is moist. When the seeds are gone, a pinecone will continue to open and close with changes in humidity, so you can use it as a natural hygrometer. Pick a large, mature cone from a pine or larch tree.

YOU WILL NEED
● wet- and dry -bulb hygrometer ● warm water ● pine cone ● string ● scissors ● pen ● notepad

■ DISCOVERY ■
Theophrastus

Theophrastus (c.372–287 BC), a Greek philosopher, compiled a book of weather signs. He claimed that if the sun looked dim there would be rain or wind, that it would rain if the sun rose out of clouds, that the south wind brought hot weather, and that thunder and lightning came with strong winds.
Often called the father of botany because of his very detailed plant descriptions, he studied under the philosopher Plato and was a close friend of Aristotle, another philosopher. His real name was Tyrtamus, but Aristotle called him *Theophrastus*, which means "divine speech."

1 IN A SHELTERED PLACE OUTSIDE and well above the ground, hang the biggest pine cone you can find. After two hours note the relative humidity by using a wet- and dry-bulb hygrometer. Check the cone to see if it is open or closed.

2 ON A DRY DAY, when the cone is open, place a bowl of warm water beneath it, as close as possible without touching. After about two hours, check the hygrometer for any change in humidity. Has the cone changed?

▉ Plant clues

Many plants react to changes in humidity. Some rely on wind and convection currents to disperse their seeds and pollen. In wet weather these particles will not travel far before being washed to the ground, so the plants open to release them only in fine weather. Insects also prefer dry air, so insect-pollinated flowers may close in moist air to avoid wasting pollen.

Onions

Onion skin story

Some people believe there will be a hard winter if onions grow thick outer skins, but in fact there is no way a plant can predict weather months ahead. The thickness of the skin is more likely to be related to the weather during the time the bulb forms.

Weed warning

Dandelions and pimpernels open their flowers only when the air is dry. In moist air they remain closed. Dry air means fine weather, so by responding to relative humidity these plants give an indication of the weather to expect over the next few hours.

Dandelion

Bog pimpernel

Cultivated hawthorn

Wild hawthorn

Hawthorn

It used to be thought that wild plants, such as the hawthorn, would produce more berries than usual in the summer before a harsh winter, but the number of berries depends on the number of flowers produced in the spring.

Sea changes

Seaweeds that grow near the tide line must survive the dry conditions at low tide. They become dry and brittle. But as soon as even a little water covers them, they absorb it and become moist and supple. You can use those that have tough, flat fronds, such as kelps or rockweed, to detect changes in humidity. If they look shriveled the air is dry; if they are soft, the air is moist.

Bladderwrack

Kelp

Animal folklore and sky signs

THE BEHAVIOR of large and small animals can change because of changes in the weather. Hot weather can make large animals uncomfortable, and static electricity makes some small animals restless. In hot weather, convection currents often carry insects to a great height. You cannot see them, but you can see the birds that chase after them for food. Sky signs are often more accurate than animal behavior in terms of weather prediction. Observing the weather that is happening at the moment can give you a good idea of the weather to come.

Spinning a web
Spiders that spin webs make bigger webs in dry than in moist air. If the weather is very wet, they may make no webs at all. Perhaps the spiders are saving energy by not building when few insects are flying. Spiders can live a long time without food, so they can wait for better weather.

Animals and insects
Animals and insects may respond to changing atmospheric conditions, but they cannot foretell the weather. They are simply reacting to the feel of the air around them. This may indicate the weather to come, of course. When the air becomes drier or moister a front may be approaching or passing, and finer or wetter weather may follow, but it is we humans who turn these observations into forecasts. Not all predictions based on animal behavior are useful. Behavior may change for reasons that have nothing at all to do with the weather.

Restless pigs
When pigs become restless, rushing around their sties and tossing their bedding, some people believe gales are approaching. Pigs are supposed to be able to see the wind.

A mouse in the house
Field mice are supposed to enter houses for shelter when rain threatens. House mice are supposed to be able to warn of changing weather. They can be heard running about and squeaking.

Meadow madness
If cows feed lying down it will rain, according to folklore. Before a storm they run about, tails held high—probably to avoid biting insects, which are more active in warm, humid air.

Bee behavior
Bees navigate by the sun and stay in the hive on days that are likely to be cloudy. They do not fly in wind stronger than 15 mph (25 km/h). They readily acquire static electrical charges, and take shelter when thunderstorms approach.

Chirping crickets
House crickets are said to chirp only when rain is approaching. This may be because cricket chirping is affected by temperature. People can tell the temperature by counting the chirping rate of the "thermometer cricket."

Sky signs

Sayings about the sky are probably the best-known clues to the weather and are among the most accurate. Some are even mentioned in the Bible: "When it is evening, it will be fair weather: for the sky is red. And in the morning, it will be foul weather today: for the sky is red" (Matthew 16, 2–3). This forecast is often true, as are "rain before seven, fine before eleven" and a pale yellow sunset as a rain warning. By studying the way events in the sky follow one another, observers can work out what might normally happen, without knowing why.

Sailor's delight
Weather usually moves from west to east, so a red sky at sunset means dry air is approaching and will arrive tomorrow. A red dawn means the dry air has already passed. One of the best known sky sayings is "Red sky at night—sailor's delight, red sky in the morning—sailor take warning."

Rain on its way
A ring, or halo, around the moon is often followed by rain. The halo is caused by the refraction of light by ice crystals in high-level clouds. These clouds often arrive ahead of a vigorous depression. The bigger the halo, the sooner it will rain.

Corona
A corona is caused by diffraction of light by water droplets. If it rapidly becomes smaller, rain is likely. In foggy weather a corona means the fog is starting to clear.

Rainbows
A morning rainbow in the west means that a shower is approaching. A rainbow at sunset in the east means that the shower is moving away, bringing fair weather.

171

Making a Stevenson screen

WHEN YOU RECORD temperature, humidity, and pressure and use the readings to make weather forecasts, your measurements must be accurate and be made under similar conditions. The best way to standardize conditions is to place your instruments inside a Stevenson screen.

How it fits together

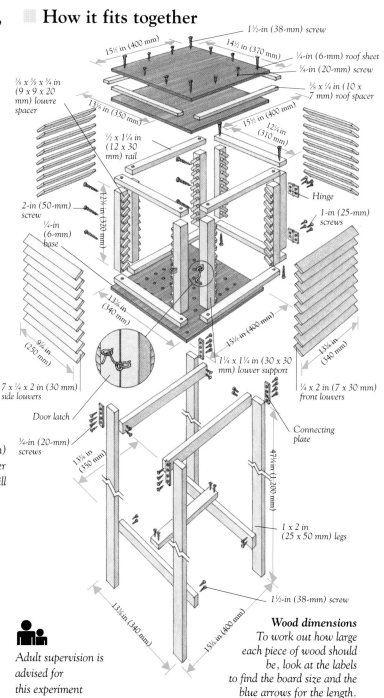

1½-in (38-mm) screw
15½ in (400 mm)
14½ in (370 mm)
¼-in (6-mm) roof sheet
¾-in (20-mm) screw
⅜ x ¼ in (10 x 7 mm) roof spacer
⅜ x ⅜ x ¾ in (9 x 9 x 20 mm) louvre spacer
13¾ in (350 mm)
15½ in (400 mm)
12¼ in (310 mm)
½ x 1¼ in (12 x 30 mm) rail
Hinge
2-in (50-mm) screw
12¾ in (320 mm)
¼-in (6-mm) base
1-in (25-mm) screws
13½ in (340 mm)
9¾ in (250 mm)
15¾ in (400 mm)
1¼ x 1¼ in (30 x 30 mm) louver support
13¾ in (340 mm)
7 x ¼ x 2 in (30 mm) side louvers
Door latch
¾-in (20-mm) screws
¼ x 2 in (7 x 30 mm) front louvers
Connecting plate
13⅜ in (350 mm)
47¼ in (1,200 mm)
1 x 2 in (25 x 50 mm) legs
13¾ in (340 mm)
15½ in (400 mm)
1½-in (38-mm) screw

Wood dimensions
To work out how large each piece of wood should be, look at the labels to find the board size and the blue arrows for the length.

EXPERIMENT
Constructing the screen

A Stevenson screen is a ventilated box on legs. You can make one to use at home. The total lengths of each size of wood have been given below, rounded up a bit to allow for mistakes.

YOU WILL NEED

● *23 ft (7 m) of 1 x 2 in (25 x 50 mm) pine (for the legs)* ● *10 ft (3 m) of 1¼ x 1¼ in (30 x 30 mm) pine (for the louver supports)* ● *5 ft (1.5 m) of ⅜ x ⅜ in (9 x 9 mm) pine (for the louver spacers)* ● *10½ ft (3 m) of ½ x 1¼ in (12 x 30 mm) pine (for the rails)* ● *41 ft (12.5 m) of ¼ x 2 in (7 x 30 mm) pine (for the louvers and roof spacers)* ● *clamp* ● *pencil* ● *bradawl* ● *screwdriver* ● *24 1½-in (38-mm) screws* ● *8 1-in (25-mm) screws* ● *6 2-in (50-mm) screws* ● *30 ¾-in (20-mm) screws* ● *set square* ● *ruler* ● *saw* ● *⅛-in (3-mm) drill bit* ● *hand drill* ● *50 in (1.27 m) of ¼ x 15¾ in (6 x 400 mm) exterior-grade plywood sheet (for the roof and base)* ● *2-in (50-mm) door latch* ● *2 1½-in (38-mm) hinges* ● *4 3-in (76-mm) steel connection plates* ● *scrap wood board* ● *wood glue* ● *paintbrush* ● *white exterior gloss paint*

Adult supervision is advised for this experiment

1 ASK AN ADULT to cut all the wood to size, as shown in the diagram above right, using a saw and clamp. Keep the wood for each part of the screen separate.

2 MARK EACH louver support with nine evenly spaced diagonal marks. Glue nine louver spacers in position on the marks on each louver support.

3 MAKE SIDE FRAMES by screwing two louver supports to each small rail. Make door and back frames by screwing four louver supports to the large rails.

4 GLUE NINE small louvers onto the louver spacers of each side frame. Then glue the remaining louvers onto the door and back frames. When you assemble the box, be sure that all the louvers point down.

5 MAKE A THREE-SIDED BOX with two side frames and a back frame. Secure the frames with 6 2-in (50-mm) screws through the back frame.

6 ASK AN ADULT to drill about 40 evenly spaced $1/8$-in holes in the small plywood sheet for the base. Drill on top of scrap wood. Screw the base to the bottom of the frame.

7 MAKE THE DOUBLE-SKIN ROOF from the two remaining plywood sheets. Glue the roof spacers around the edges of one sheet, then glue the other to the spacers and clamp until dry.

8 SCREW THE ROOF onto the frame, so that it slightly overhangs the open area where the door will hang.

9 ATTACH the remaining louvered frame (the door) using screws and hinges. Then screw in the door latch.

10 TO SUPPORT the box, fasten top and middle crossbars to the legs. Use the diagram (left) for measurements.

11 ASK AN ADULT to place the box on top of the legs. Screw on four connection plates to fasten the box.

12 FINALLY, paint the box with several coats of exterior-grade white gloss paint. When it has dried, your Stevenson screen is ready to use.

Making a weather station

ONCE YOU MAKE your Stevenson screen, you can set up your own weather station so that you can take accurate meteorological measurements. As soon as the station is established you can start keeping a record of the observations you make every day. Apart from taking regular readings, the instruments should require little attention or maintenance. If you can put a low fence around the site, this will help protect your equipment and discourage household pets. Keep the site neat and tidy so that your readings are not affected by dirt or litter.

Inside your Stevenson screen

Set up the Stevenson screen in the site you have chosen. Make sure it is standing securely and that it is level. Install your maximum-minimum thermometer and wet- and dry-bulb hygrometer inside. Hang them on the rear wall where you can read them easily without moving them. The hygrometer reservoir should rest on the floor. Finally, place a barometer inside the screen. Keep the paint clean so that heat radiation is reflected away.

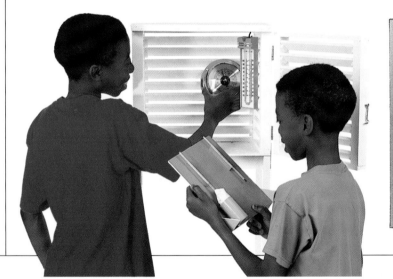

The weather station

To find a site for your station, look for an open space, away from trees and buildings, where it can remain permanently without being disturbed.

The Stevenson screen

Temperature range
A maximum-minimum thermometer is a U-shaped thermometer with two scales and small pins that are moved by the columns of liquid. It shows the highest and lowest temperatures of any time period. To get the daily maximum and minimum temperature, reset it at the same time every day using the operating instructions.

Temperature and humidity
To read the humidity you should use a wet- and dry-bulb hygrometer. The hygrometer you have made (pp.42–43) will work best if you use distilled water. Make sure the wet-bulb has a constant water supply.

Pressure
A proper barometer is essential for accurate record keeping. A mercury barometer is best, but aneroid barometers can be used. You must adjust the barometer to allow for the altitude difference between your site and sea level. Follow the maker's instructions and get the sea-level pressure from a weather center.

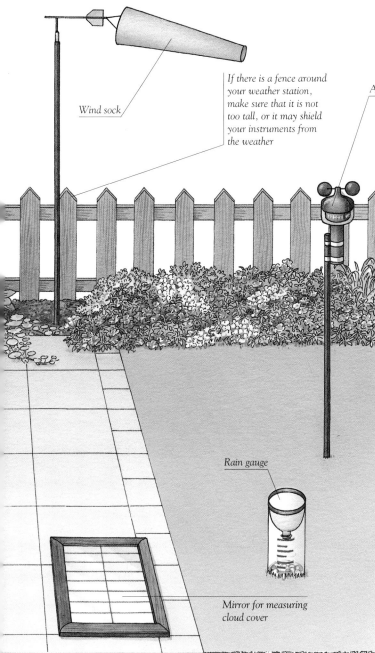

Wind sock

If there is a fence around your weather station, make sure that it is not too tall, or it may shield your instruments from the weather

Anemometer

Rain gauge

Mirror for measuring cloud cover

▪ Wind vane

To measure the wind direction accurately, your wind sock or vane should be well above the ground and as far as possible from trees or buildings. A wind sock, like those at airports, works well. You can buy one with a lightweight pole and ties or make one from weatherproof cloth and wire hoops. Use a compass to read the wind direction.

▪ Anemometer

An anemometer measures wind speed. The most common type uses spinning cups. You read the speed in knots or km/h from a dial. If you cannot obtain an anemometer, use the Beaufort scale (p.58) to estimate wind force.

▪ Cloud cover

Take the mirror used to measure cloud cover (pp.180–181) outside with you each time you go to take your readings. If you leave it out all the time it may get broken, and rain carrying dust may make it dirty.

▪ Rain gauge

You can use the rain gauge on page 46–47. Install it in the open, not far from the Stevenson screen but away from overhanging plants and walls. If you set it in a small hole, with the bottom of the gauge below ground level, it will be more stable. It must not blow down in the wind. Clean it from time to time, or a sediment will form from dust in the rain.

Recording the weather

PEOPLE HAVE always kept track of the weather. But the accuracy of a forecast depends on the accuracy of the records used to make it. Professional meteorologists keep meticulous records of weather conditions. If you have made a Stevenson screen (pp.172–173) and set up a weather station (pp.174–175), you can begin to measure a wide range of weather conditions for yourself. These are useful for forecasting only if you keep a careful record of them, so it is a good idea to get into the habit of keeping a weather diary. If your records are extremely accurate, you can even help the professional forecasters by sending your information to a weather center.

Cherry blossom time in Japan

For centuries, cherry trees have been grown in Japan for the beauty of their spring blossoms. As with many plants, the time when the flowers open depends on the air temperature. Records have been kept of the date of flowering in Japan for centuries. These can be used as a kind of reverse forecast—to give a hint of future weather based on what past weather was like.

Identify the air mass

One quick way to make a forecast is to find out the type of air mass (pp.70–71) you are in. If you know the air mass, you can more easily predict the weather, and vice-versa. For instance, if the weather is hot and fairly dry, you will know that you are experiencing an air mass that brings those characteristics—probably a continental tropical air mass.
Keep simple records of the temperature and relative humidity (use the wet- and dry-bulb hygrometer on pp.42–43) over a month or so, and then use the table on the right to find the air mass.

TEMPERATURE	RELATIVE HUMIDITY	AIR MASS
Cold	Low (dry)	Continental polar (cP)
Warm	Low (dry)	Continental tropical (cT)
Cold	High (wet)	Maritime polar (mP)
Warm	High (wet)	Maritime tropical (mT)

Air mass characteristics
If you know the temperature and relative humidity, you can find out which air mass you are in. This table summarizes how the three are related. The region you live in may not experience all of these air masses.

Record keeper
Keep a note of the temperature and relative humidity on a piece of paper, or keep these records as part of your weather diary (see opposite).

The big picture
To find out how your records can be used to help professional forecasters, contact your nearest weather center. They will tell you how to take your readings and where to send them. If you have access to a computer, you may be able to do this on Internet.

Keeping a weather diary

It is best to keep your weather diary in a special notebook. Copy the one-week chart below on paper, or make photocopies of this page. You will need a column for each day of the week, with an entry for each of the following categories: the date, the time, the actual temperature (°F or °C), the maximum and minimum temperatures (in °F or °C), the dewpoint temperature (°F or °C), the pressure (mb), the pressure change since the last reading (+/– mb), the pressure tendency (rising or falling), the wind direction to the nearest 10° on a compass, the wind speed (mph or km/h—use the Beaufort scale as a guide), the cloud cover in oktas (p.180), the cloud type and estimated height (low, medium, or high), the present weather (fair, rainy), the weather over the past six hours, and the visibility (miles or km). When you have established a routine, take your readings at the same two times every day. Use the green columns for morning readings and the white columns for afternoon readings.

Logging your weather data
You can ask a friend to help you write down the readings from the instruments in your weather station. Copy them into your weather diary when you come inside.

Day of the week	MONDAY		TUESDAY		WEDNESDAY		THURSDAY		FRIDAY		SATURDAY		SUNDAY	
Date														
Time (a.m. and p.m.)														
Actual temperature														
Max/min temperature														
Dew-point temperature														
Pressure														
Pressure change														
Pressure tendency														
Wind direction														
Wind speed														
Cloud cover														
Cloud type and height														
Present weather														
Past weather														
Visibility														

Weather stations

WEATHER INFORMATION is required in all kinds of situations. Millions of people fly every day in commercial airliners, and for their safety the pilots must have adequate warning of dangerous weather. In regions that experience hurricanes, forecasts can save many lives. Predictions of the weather depend on the knowledge and experience of the forecaster and on the quality of the data received. The best forecaster is almost useless without good data, so a worldwide network of information gathering has built up. Satellites, aircraft, weather ships, balloons, and ground stations send in the raw data, which meteorologists then interpret.

■ Balloons

Helium-filled balloons called radiosondes are released at standard times from about 1,000 weather stations around the world. They take readings of temperature, humidity, and pressure in the upper atmosphere. Some balloons called rawinsondes are tracked to measure wind speed and direction. Instruments hang beneath the balloon, and readings are sent by radio to the weather station. Eventually the equipment parachutes down.

Satellites
Some meteorological satellites are in fixed orbits 22,000 miles (35,400 km) above the equator. They send photographs of cloud formations back to the earth.

Ground-based weather stations
Thousands of ground-based weather stations around the world collect local data. They are essential to the network.

Balloons
Balloons collect data from high in the atmosphere and automatically radio the data back to earth.

Aircraft
Aircraft with instruments in pods beneath the wings, or attached to the nose cone, fly through storm clouds to measure temperatures, pressures, winds, and turbulence—even in hurricanes.

Weather ships
Weather ships are permanently stationed at in specific positions at sea and send data to shore stations.

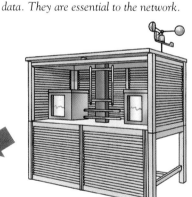

■ The global weather network

Satellites in orbit transmit measurements about every half hour; balloons send measurements from the upper atmosphere; and ships, aircraft, and ground stations send information from lower levels. All this data is fed into computers, from which the forecasts are compiled.

Forecasting
The forecaster you see on television is usually a professional meteorologist who prepares the forecast from information in the computer, gathered from all the different sources.

Weather radar

Ships and aircraft carry radar to detect the weather conditions ahead of them. Radio waves, emitted constantly from a rotating transmitter, are reflected by clouds and rain and return to a receiver. The time the waves take to return reveals the distance to the next band of bad weather.

Radar at home

To see how radar works, stand in a darkened room surrounded by friends holding mirrors facing you at waist level. Turn slowly, pointing a lit flashlight at waist level. A flash of light means the rays have been reflected, like the radar waves from a cloud or rain.

Light spot

Mirror

Flashlight

Recording dangerous weather conditions

A thunderstorm is one of the most violent of all atmospheric events. It is also complex, and scientists still have much to learn about what is happening inside storm clouds. Radiosondes (instrument-laden balloons) cannot be used because the intense electrical activity inside the cloud would drown their radio transmissions from the receiving station. The only effective way to explore the cloud is to send special aircraft through it. The inside of such a cloud is a dangerous place. Other planes, such as commercial airliners, avoid storm clouds.

In the control room

This is the control room at a meteorological station specializing in research into lightning and the processes that take place inside storm clouds. The radio controllers are in radio contact with a pilot, who describes what is visible and what the aircraft instruments read as the plane flies right through the cloud. The station has aircraft equipped to measure temperatures, pressures, wind speeds and directions, and vertical air movements inside the clouds.

The airplane

This special airplane is used to explore storm clouds. Its wings and body are reinforced to make it strong enough to withstand the battering by hail and the buffeting it will experience as currents lift it to the top of the cloud, then drop it to the bottom of the cloud. The wings must also tolerate the weight of ice forming on them. The plane will try to fly straight through the cloud and out the other side.

Weather maps

THE WEATHER MAP you see on television is a simplified version of the one the forecasters use to plot weather systems and calculate the way they are moving. It begins as an ordinary map showing only the most important features, such as coastlines, large rivers, big cities, national or state borders, and the positions of all the weather stations. Isobars, which are labeled lines joining stations reporting the same air pressure, reveal highs and lows, so that fronts can be added. Station reports are also plotted. They tell of their local weather and how it is changing. Forecasters relate this information to patterns of air pressure and work out the direction of the weather system.

Test your weather skills

The weather map in your local newspaper can be used to make a forecast. Ask a friend to cut out the weather map, report, and forecast from a newspaper, choosing a paper that publishes a fairly full report. Then ask the friend to remove the forecast. Use the map and the report, which will show the position of highs, lows, and fronts—and the pressures associated with them—to produce your own forecast. The closer together the isobars, the stronger the winds will be, blowing counterclockwise around low-pressure centers. The report will describe the weather situation and the way it is moving. When you have made your forecast, compare it with the map in the following day's paper to see how you did.

Estimating visibility

When you report the weather you will need to include the visibility in miles. Find a hilltop or upstairs window where you have an uninterrupted view into the far distance. Look for several prominent features, such as buildings, hills, or trees at different distances. You will find binoculars useful. Use a large-scale map (1:25,000, which is 21 in to 1 mile, or 4 cm to 1 km) to locate the features and measure their distance. Every day, about the time you take your instrument readings, go to your vantage point and see which is the most distant feature you can see that day.

EXPERIMENT
Cloud cover

Weather reports include information on the cloud type and amount. Use the cloud atlas (pp.88–119) to help you identify the cloud type. Unless the cloud base is low enough to cover tall landscape features, it is very difficult to measure its height (meteorologists use lasers for this), but it is not difficult to measure the amount of sky the cloud covers. This is measured in eighths or oktas.

YOU WILL NEED
● *notebook* ● *pen* ● *large mirror* ● *crayon* ● *ruler*

1 USE THE RULER and crayon to divide the mirror into a grid with 16 equal squares. Draw the grid on the mirror with a colored crayon darker than the sky.

2 ON DAYS WHEN the clouds cover part of the sky, take the mirror to where you can see the whole sky. Lay the mirror on the ground and look at the reflection of the sky. Count the number of grid squares, or fractions of squares, with cloud in them. Divide that number by two to convert sixteenths into oktas.

Station circle

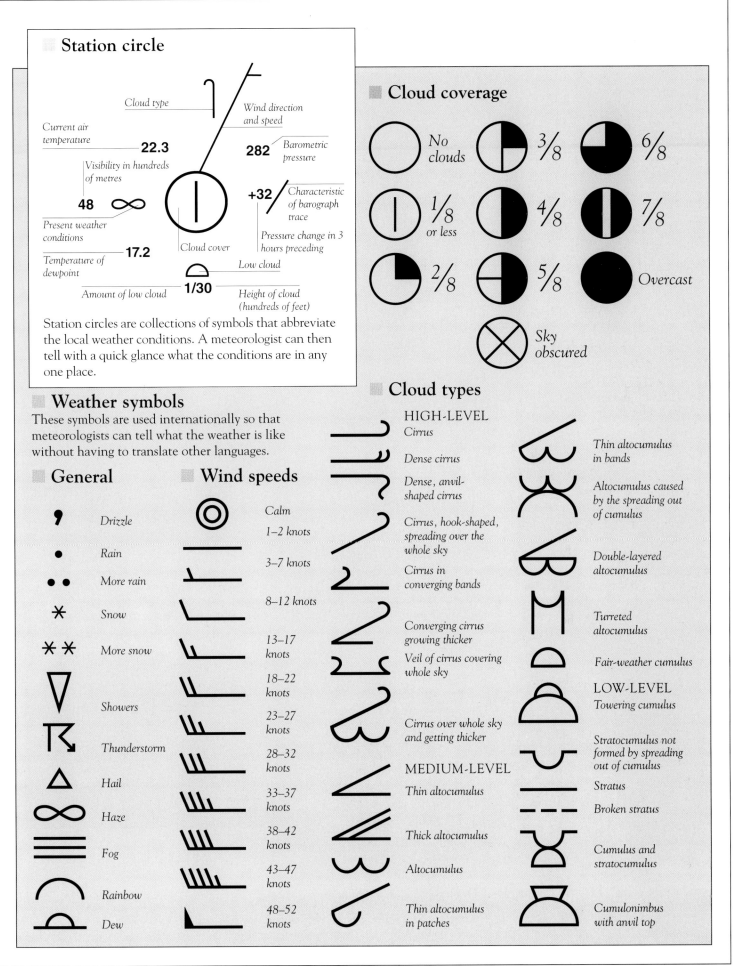

Cloud type

Wind direction and speed

Current air temperature

22.3

282 Barometric pressure

Visibility in hundreds of metres

+32 Characteristic of barograph trace

48 ∞

Present weather conditions

Pressure change in 3 hours preceding

17.2

Cloud cover

Temperature of dewpoint

Low cloud

1/30

Amount of low cloud

Height of cloud (hundreds of feet)

Station circles are collections of symbols that abbreviate the local weather conditions. A meteorologist can then tell with a quick glance what the conditions are in any one place.

Cloud coverage

No clouds	3/8	6/8
1/8 or less	4/8	7/8
2/8	5/8	Overcast

Sky obscured

Weather symbols

These symbols are used internationally so that meteorologists can tell what the weather is like without having to translate other languages.

General

𝄃	Drizzle
•	Rain
••	More rain
✳	Snow
✳✳	More snow
▽	Showers
⌐∇	Thunderstorm
△	Hail
∞	Haze
☰	Fog
⌒	Rainbow
⌒	Dew

Wind speeds

Symbol	Speed
◎	Calm
	1–2 knots
	3–7 knots
	8–12 knots
	13–17 knots
	18–22 knots
	23–27 knots
	28–32 knots
	33–37 knots
	38–42 knots
	43–47 knots
	48–52 knots

Cloud types

HIGH-LEVEL
Cirrus

Dense cirrus

Dense, anvil-shaped cirrus

Cirrus, hook-shaped, spreading over the whole sky

Cirrus in converging bands

Converging cirrus growing thicker

Veil of cirrus covering whole sky

Cirrus over whole sky and getting thicker

MEDIUM-LEVEL
Thin altocumulus

Thick altocumulus

Altocumulus

Thin altocumulus in patches

Thin altocumulus in bands

Altocumulus caused by the spreading out of cumulus

Double-layered altocumulus

Turreted altocumulus

Fair-weather cumulus

LOW-LEVEL
Towering cumulus

Stratocumulus not formed by spreading out of cumulus

Stratus

Broken stratus

Cumulus and stratocumulus

Cumulonimbus with anvil top

How forecasts are made

PROFESSIONAL WEATHER forecasters need large computers because their work involves literally millions of calculations. Using information from weather stations, the computers plot the temperature, pressure, wind, humidity, and other information for thousands of points on a grid covering the whole planet—at sea level and at up to 25 levels above the ground. Information from satellites and radar helps to fill the gaps. All these go together to form "ground truth." The computers calculate how temperature, pressure, and humidity will change in half an hour at each of these points. The calculations are then repeated over and over again to produce forecasts at regular intervals for up to 10 days ahead.

■ Forecasting rain

To predict whether or not it will rain, you will need a barometer and thermometer. Start the evening before. Note the air pressure in the evening and the following morning. Is it rising, steady, or falling? Rising pressure usually means fine weather. Now look at the sky. If upper clouds are thickening toward the west and pressure is falling, expect rain. If cumulus cloud (pp.92–93) is growing, there may be heavy showers, perhaps with thunder. If there is stratiform cloud (pp.92–93) but pressure is steady, rain is unlikely. Next, measure the air temperature. Temperatures below 37° F (3° C) mean precipitation could fall as snow or sleet.

EXPERIMENT
Predicting temperatures

If there is a clear sky and a light wind you can predict the minimum night temperature. The time of the first reading varies. In the Northern Hemisphere take it 1 hour after sunset in December and January; 1½ hours in October, November, and February; and 2 hours in the other months. In the Southern Hemisphere wait 1 hour in June and July; 1½ hours in April, May, and August; and 2 hours in the rest of the year.

YOU WILL NEED
● *flashlight* ● *thermometer* ● *pen* ● *notepad*

1 LOOK UP THE TIME of sunset in a newspaper. Depending on the month, wait until 1, 1½, or 2 hours after the sun has gone down, then go outside and measure the air temperature away from any warm air from that may be close to the house. Write this temperature down.

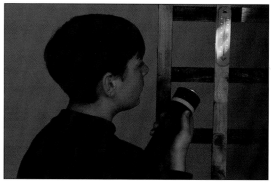

2 TAKE THE TEMPERATURE again after one hour. Subtract this reading from the first to find the hourly drop. Now count the hours until one hour before dawn. Multiply this by the rate of temperature fall. Subtract this from the second reading, to predict the minimum temperature.

Will it be warm or cold?

The chart below will help you find out whether the day will be warm or cold for the time of year. You need to know if the air mass controlling the weather is tropical or polar (p.176), and if the weather is fair, overcast, or windy or not. Then you need to know the average temperature for the time of year in your region. This information can be found at your local public library or weather center. Measure the air temperature and subtract the average from it. This will tell you whether the air is warmer or cooler than usual.

Air mass	Tropical air				Polar air			
Fair or overcast	☀	☁			☀	☁		
Wind speed								
If the temperature is 18° F (10° C) higher than normal	Very hot	Hot	Warm	Warm	Warm	Normal	Normal	Cool
If the temperature is 9° F (5° C) higher than normal	Hot	Warm	Warm	Normal	Warm	Normal	Cool	Cold
If the temperature is normal	Hot	Warm	Normal	Normal	Normal	Cool	Cold	Cold
If the temperature is 9° F (5° C) lower than normal	Warm	Warm	Normal	Cool	Cool	Cool	Cold	Cold
If the temperature is 18° F (10° C) lower than normal	Warm	Normal	Normal	Cool	Cool	Cold	Cold	Very cold

What the forecasters see

Short-range forecasts for a few days ahead are usually reliable, but small-scale events, such as the precise location and timing of showers in unstable air, are impossible to predict. Below you can see some of the working documents that professional meteorologists use and produce so that they can make forecasts.

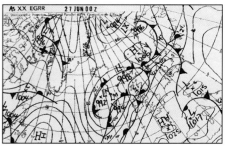

Weather report
This is what an official weather report looks like. Sheets like this are sent to television and radio stations so that weather broadcasts can be made.

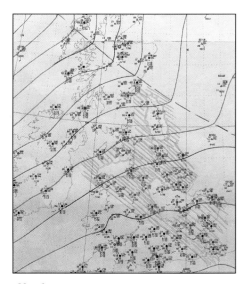

Clouds at 7:00 a.m.
This map is covered with tiny station circles (p.181) from local weather stations. A meteorologist has drawn over it in orange to show cloud-covered areas. The pencil lines are isobars.

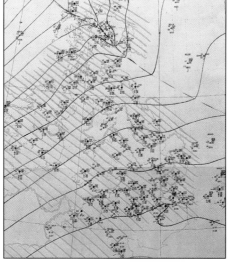

Clouds at 8:00 p.m.
One hour later, the meteorologist has updated a new map to show the progression of cloud cover and changes to the isobars. This information is now combined with other data to produce a forecast.

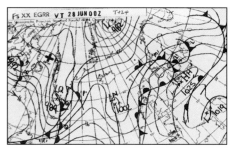

24-hour forecast
When the current report is made, a series of forecasts are made to accompany it. This is the forecast for one day ahead of the report shown above. Some forecasts are for two or three days.

Glossary

ACID RAIN Rain that is more acidic than normal precipitation because water vapor has condensed onto particles of sulfate or nitrogen oxide.

ADIABATIC Changes in temperature caused by the expansion (cooling) or compression (warming) of a body of air as it rises or descends in the atmosphere. There is no exchange of heat with the surrounding air.

ADVECTION The transfer of heat by the horizontal movement of air or water, such as a warm wind or ocean current.

ADVECTION FOG Fog caused by the condensation of water vapor when warm, moist air crosses cold land or sea.

AIR MASS A large body of air, covering much of a continent or an ocean, throughout which the temperature, surface pressure, and humidity are fairly constant.

ALBEDO The reflectiveness of a surface. Albedo values are written either as a percentage (90 percent) or a decimal (0.9).

ANABATIC Rising, as when air moves up a hillside.

ANEMOMETER An instrument for measuring wind speed.

ANGULAR MOMENTUM The energy of motion of a spinning body or mass of air or water. Its value depends on the mass of the body, its radius of spin, and its rate of spin.

ANGULAR VELOCITY The rate at which a spinning body, such as a planet, rotates. The earth rotates at 15° per hour, which is its angular velocity.

ANTICYCLONE A body of air in which the atmospheric pressure is higher than the pressure in the surrounding air. Air is sinking and spilling outwards from its center. Winds blow counterclockwise around anticyclones in the Southern Hemisphere and clockwise in the Northern Hemisphere.

ATOMS The basic units of an element, such as hydrogen or oxygen.

BAROMETER An instrument for measuring atmospheric pressure. The most accurate type is the mercury barometer, which measures the height of a column of mercury forced by pressure up a glass tube containing no air. The most common type is the aneroid barometer, which measures changes in the volume of a corrugated metal box.

BEAUFORT SCALE A scale that indicates wind speed by the effect wind has on familiar objects.

BLACK ICE Transparent ice that forms when liquid water on the ground freezes—for instance when the temperature falls sharply after rain.

BLIZZARD A wind storm in which large amounts of snow are blown into the air from the surface and carried at high speed.

CHINOOK A warm, dry wind on the eastern side of the Rocky Mountains in North America. See föhn wind (p.185).

CIRRIFORM A cloud of the cirrus type that is fibrous or wispy, like hair blowing in the wind.

CLIMATOLOGY The scientific study of climate, which is the weather typical of a region or the entire earth over a long period.

CLOUD CONDENSATION NUCLEI Small airborne particles on which water vapor condenses to form cloud droplets.

CONDENSATION The change from gas to liquid.

CONDUCTION The transfer of heat between bodies that are in contact. The air is mainly warmed by conduction from the surface of land or water.

CONVECTION The transfer of heat within a gas or liquid by the movement of the gas or liquid. The warm fluid expands— becoming less dense—and rises, with cooler, denser fluid sinking to replace it.

CONVECTION CELL A region within a body of liquid or gas in which convection is taking place, with warm fluid rising, cooling, and descending again. Large-scale convection cells produce tropical climates.

CORIOLIS EFFECT The apparent deflection of a body moving in a straight line toward or away from the equator. It is caused by the rotation of the earth. It deflects air masses and ocean currents moving away from the equator to the right in the Northern Hemisphere and to the left in the Southern Hemisphere.

CORONA A disk of light surrounding the sun or the moon that is caused by the diffraction of light by small water droplets. Coronas are often colored, with red on the outside of the disk and violet on the inside.

CUMULIFORM Heaped clouds, especially cumulus and cumulonimbus. They may reach a height of 8 miles (13 km).

CYCLONE A body of air in which the pressure is lower than that of the surrounding air; another name for a depression or low. Cyclonic winds blow

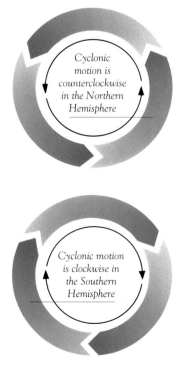

Cyclonic motion is counterclockwise in the Northern Hemisphere

Cyclonic motion is clockwise in the Southern Hemisphere

Air movement
Air moves in different directions in either hemisphere. This movement is called cyclonic motion.

counterclockwise around cyclones in the Northern Hemisphere and they blow clockwise in the Southern Hemisphere. The name cyclone is also given to hurricanes near India and Australia.

DEPRESSION A region of low atmospheric pressure (also called a low or cyclone). Depressions usually bring low clouds and precipitation.

DEW POINT The temperature at which water vapor will condense if air is cooled.

DOLDRUMS The regions on either side of the equator where air pressure is low and winds are light.

DRIZZLE Rain composed entirely of droplets less than $\frac{1}{50}$ in (0.5 mm) in diameter. The droplets are so small they make no visible splash in puddles of water.

DUST DEVIL A small, local wind storm. Dust devils are very common in deserts, where several may occur at the same time. Dry, unstable air rises, twisting as it does so and carrying dust and sometimes other loose material to a height of up to 6,500 ft (2 km).

EL NIÑO A warm current, occurring every few years, that flows eastward across the Pacific, just south of the equator. El Niño is associated with a weakening of the trade winds.

ENSO The name for the combined El Niño and Southern Oscillation.

EQUINOX Either of two days in each year when the day and night are the same length. On these days the earth is tilted on its axis so that the sun is directly overhead at the equator.

EVAPORATION The change from liquid to gas.

FALLSTREAKS Lines sometimes seen beneath a cloud. Fallstreaks are caused by precipitation falling from the cloud and evaporating before it reaches the surface. They are also known as virgas.

FOG Water that has condensed close to ground level, producing a cloud of very small droplets that reduces visibility to less than 3,300 ft (1 km).

FOGBOW A rainbow formed in fog. Because of the small size of water droplets in fog, the reflected and refracted light rays overlap and the rainbow colors merge together into a very bright white bow.

FÖHN WIND A warm, dry wind that occurs when air sinks down a mountainside and is warmed by compression as it does so. The name was first used for winds in the Swiss Alps.

FREEZING FOG Fog in which the water droplets are cooled to below freezing temperature and form ice immediately on contact with a surface.

FREEZING RAIN Rain at close to freezing temperature that falls through a shallow layer of air at below freezing temperature before striking the ground. The drops have time to spread into a film of water before they freeze into a "glaze" of ice.

FRONT The boundary between two masses of air of different temperatures and humidities. As they move, fronts are named by the relative temperature of the air behind them. A front followed by warm air is a warm front, and one followed by cool air is a cold front.

FUNNELING The passage of wind through a confined space, such as a narrow valley. This increases the wind speed.

GLORY A circle of bright light, often colored, that is seen around the shadow of a person's head when cast on a bank of fog. It is caused by light passing through very small droplets of water.

The main cloud varieties
These three clouds are the main types at their levels of the atmosphere. The bottom picture shows stratiform (low-level) the middle shows cumuliform (medium-level) and the top is cirriform (high-level).

GREENHOUSE EFFECT The retention and buildup of heat in the lower atmosphere due to the absorption of long-wave radiation from the earth's surface by molecules of such gases as water vapor, carbon dioxide, nitrous oxide, and ozone.

HADLEY CELL A large-scale convection cell in which warm air rises at the equator, moves away from the equator at high altitude, and then descends as dry air in the subtropics—warming by compression as it does so—and returns at low level to the equator. The Coriolis effect deflects the returning air, forming the trade winds on each side of the equator.

HALO A bright circle sometimes seen around the sun or moon. It is white, with a touch of red on the inside and violet on the outside when it appears around the sun. It is caused by the refraction of light through ice crystals at high altitude and may be followed by rain as part of a depression or low.

HARMATTAN A hot, dry, dusty, northeasterly or easterly wind that occurs in West Africa north of the equator. It is caused by the outflow of air from subtropical high-pressure regions.

HAZE A reduction in visibility or whiteness of the sky produced when light is scattered by small dust particles.

HEAT CAPACITY The ratio of the amount of heat supplied to a body and the change in the temperature of the body. The higher the heat capacity, the more heat must be applied to raise the temperature.

HORSE LATITUDES Subtropical regions where anticyclones produce settled weather.

HUMIDITY The amount of water vapor present in a volume of air. Relative humidity is the amount of water vapor as a percentage of the maximum amount a given parcel of air can contain.

HURRICANE A severe tropical storm in which winds with speeds in excess of 73 mph (116 km/h) blow around an area of intensely low pressure. Towering clouds bring torrential rain.

HYGROMETER An instrument used to measure humidity. Two types are the wet- and dry-bulb, which measures the rate of evaporation by its chilling effect on the wet

Water particles
These are the comparative sizes of the different water-based particles found in the water cycle. All these droplets are based around microscopic condensation nuclei, far too small to be seen. They are measured in "microns".

A large cloud drop has a diameter of 100 microns

A typical cloud drop has a diameter of 10 microns

A drop on the border between a cloud drop and a raindrop

A normal raindrop has a diameter of 200 microns

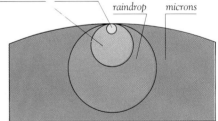

bulb which—compared with the dry-bulb temperature—can be used to calculate humidity; and the hair hygrometer, which measures the expansion and contraction of human hair in response to changing humidity.

ICE AGE A period during which a substantial part of the earth's surface is covered by ice sheets and glaciers that have

grown out from the polar and mountainous regions.

INVERSION An atmospheric layer in which temperature increases with height.

IRIDESCENCE Brilliant patches of green or pink sometimes seen near the edges of high- or medium-level clouds.

ISOBAR A line drawn on a map to connect places that are of equal atmospheric pressure.

JET STREAM A band of extremely strong, generally westerly winds in the upper atmosphere, occasionally blowing at over 200 mph (320 km/h).

KATABATIC Flowing down a slope—normally refers to wind.

LAND BREEZE A coastal breeze flowing from land to sea on summer mornings and evenings, due to the land being cooler than the sea surface.

LATENT HEAT The heat energy that must be absorbed when a substance changes from solid to liquid and liquid to gas, and which is released when a gas condenses and a liquid solidifies.

METEOROLOGY The study of all the processes that take place in the atmosphere and their relationships with processes at the surface of the earth—in particular, the study of weather.

MICROCLIMATE A very local climate that differs from the main climate around it. A narrow valley or the ground under a growing crop has a microclimate.

MILLIBAR The scientific unit usually used in measuring and reporting atmospheric pressure.

MIST Very fine water droplets at ground level that occur in air with a relative humidity of more than 95 percent. It does not reduce visibility to less than 3,300 ft (1 km).

MISTRAL A seasonal, strong, cold, north to northwesterly wind blowing down the Rhône valley and affecting the Mediterranean coast of France.

MOCK SUN A bright patch of light that is sometimes seen to one or both sides of the sun and is produced in the same way as a halo. It is also known as a sun dog or parhelion.

MOLECULE A chemical combination of two or more atoms. Some molecules are composed of thousands of atoms.

MONSOON A seasonal change in wind direction bringing dry air or heavy rain. Monsoons affect much of southern Asia, northern Australia, and western Africa.

OCCLUSION A frontal system in the atmosphere in which the warm-sector air has been lifted clear of the ground by cooler air below it.

OCEAN GYRE The approximately circular current present in all the main oceans.

OZONE A form of oxygen in which the molecule is made of three atoms (O_3) rather than the usual two (O_2). In the lower atmosphere ozone is a pollutant, but its absorption of ultraviolet radiation makes its presence valuable in the upper atmosphere.

OZONE LAYER A layer in the stratosphere, about 9–19 miles (15–30 km) above the surface, where ozone accumulates in concentrations of 1 to 10 parts per million.

PERMAFROST A soil layer below the surface of tundra regions that remains permanently frozen throughout the year.

RADAR A method for detecting the distance, size, and movement of objects, including rain, by their reflection of radio waves.

RADIOSONDE A balloon carrying instruments for measuring conditions in the upper atmosphere.

RAWINSONDE A balloon that is tracked by radar to measure wind speeds and directions in the atmosphere.

RIDGE A tongue of high air pressure in the atmosphere that lies between two areas of low pressure.

ROSSBY WAVES Long waves that form in air or water flowing approximately parallel to the equator, caused by the effect of the earth's rotation.

SEA BREEZE A coastal breeze blowing from sea to land during daytime in summer, caused by the rising of warm air over land and its replacement by cooler air from over the sea.

SLEET A mixture of rain and snow that falls when the temperature is around the freezing point.

SMOG A mixture of smoke and fog. Photochemical smog is a haze formed by reactions between chemicals in the presence of strong sunlight.

SOLSTICES Either of the two days each year when the sun is farthest north or south of the equator and the difference between the hours of daylight and of darkness is greatest.

SOUTHERN OSCILLATION A change in the circulation of air between the tropics caused by temperature differences in the Pacific and Indian Oceans. It is closely linked to El Niño.

SPECTRUM The range of wavelengths of electromagnetic radiation. The sun radiates across the full electromagnetic spectrum, from gamma rays (short waves) to radio waves (long waves). The visible parts of the solar spectrum are revealed when white light is separated by a prism into its constituent colors (violet, indigo, blue, green, yellow, orange, red). These colors are seen in rainbows, and iridescence patches on the edges of clouds.

Troughs and ridges
Troughs are arms of low pressure extending between two areas of higher pressure, similar to a valley between two hills. Ridges are extensions of high-pressure regions sitting between low-pressure regions.

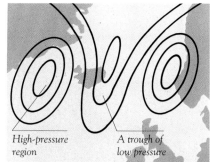

High-pressure region   A trough of low pressure

STORM SURGE A buildup of water levels along a coastline caused by long-lasting strong winds. A storm surge coinciding with a natural high tide can cause widespread flooding.

STRATIFORM Sheetlike; the stratiform clouds are stratus, nimbostratus, stratocumulus, altostratus, and cirrostratus.

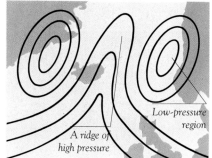

A ridge of high pressure   Low-pressure region

SUPERCOOLED WATER Water that has been cooled to a temperature below its normal freezing point but that stays in liquid form if it remains undisturbed. Supercooled water is common in clouds.

THREE-CELL MODEL A general description of the circulation of air between the equator and poles. The Hadley cell operates between the equator and subtropics; a second cell is formed by air descending at and flowing away from the poles; and these two drive a third cell in mid-latitudes.

TORNADO A violently rotating column of air, usually less than 330 ft (100 m) in diameter, surrounding a core of extremely low air pressure. Wind speeds may exceed 200 mph (320 km/h).

TRADE WINDS The prevailing easterly-blowing winds that are found on either side of the equator. The trade winds blow northeasterly in the Northern Hemisphere and southeasterly in the Southern Hemisphere. They were named trade winds when ships used sail and relied on the winds for propulsion.

TRANSPIRATION The loss of water by evaporation from plant leaves through holes in the leaves called stomata.

TROUGH A tongue of low air pressure between two areas of high pressure.

TYPHOON A hurricane that occurs in eastern Asia.

VELOCITY Speed and direction reported together.

VORTICITY The tendency of a moving gas or liquid to rotate around an axis, forming a vortex.

WATERSPOUT A column of rapidly spiraling air that forms over warm, usually shallow, water in seas or large lakes.

WET-BULB DEPRESSION The difference between the dry- and wet-bulb temperatures measured by a hygrometer. It is used to calculate relative humidity and dew point.

DEW-POINT TEMPERATURE

Current Temperature	Wet-bulb depression				
	1.8 °F (1.0 °C)	3.6 °F (2.0 °C)	5.4 °F (3.0 °C)	7.2 °F (4.0 °C)	9.0 °F (5.0 °C)
14.0° F (–10.0° C)	5.9° F (–14.5° C)	–6.3° F (–21.3° C)	–33.3° F (–36.3° C)		
18.5° F (–7.5° C)	11.5° F (–11.4° C)	1.9° F (–16.7° C)	–13.9° F (–25.5° C)		
23.0° F (–5.0° C)	16.9° F (–8.4° C)	9.0° F (–12.8° C)	–2.2° F (–19.0° C)	–24.3° F (–31.3° C)	
27.5° F (–2.5° C)	22.1° F (–5.5° C)	15.4° F (–9.2° C)	6.6° F (–14.1° C)	–6.7° F (–21.5° C)	–42.3° F (–41.3° C)
32.0° F (0.0° C)	27.1° F (–2.7° C)	21.4° F (–5.9° C)	14.4° F (–9.8° C)	4.6° F (–15.2° C)	–11.0° F (–23.9° C)
36.5° F (2.5° C)	32.2° F (0.1° C)	27.1° F (–2.7° C)	21.0° F (–6.1° C)	13.5° F (–10.3° C)	3.0° F (–16.1° C)
41.0° F (5.0° C)	37.0° F (2.8° C)	32.5° F (0.3° C)	27.3° F (–2.6° C)	21.0° F (–6.1° C)	13.3° F (–10.4° C)
45.5° F (7.5° C)	41.9° F (5.5° C)	37.8° F (3.2° C)	33.3° F (0.7° C)	27.9° F (–2.3° C)	21.6° F (–5.8° C)
50.0° F (10.0° C)	46.6° F (8.1° C)	42.8° F (6.0° C)	38.8° F (3.8° C)	34.2° F (1.2° C)	28.8° F (–1.8° C)
54.5° F (12.5° C)	51.3° F (10.7° C)	47.8° F (8.8° C)	44.1° F (6.7° C)	40.1° F (4.5° C)	35.4° F (1.9° C)
59.0° F (15.0° C)	55.9° F (13.3° C)	52.9° F (11.6° C)	49.2° F (9.6° C)	45.7° F (7.6° C)	41.5° F (5.3° C)
63.5° F (17.5° C)	60.6° F (15.9° C)	57.7° F (14.3° C)	54.5° F (12.5° C)	51.1° F (10.6° C)	47.3° F (8.5° C)
68.0° F (20.0° C)	65.3° F (18.5° C)	62.4° F (16.9° C)	59.5° F (15.3° C)	56.3° F (13.5° C)	52.9° F (11.6° C)
72.5° F (22.5° C)	70.0° F (21.1° C)	67.3° F (19.6° C)	64.4° F (18.0° C)	61.3° F (16.4° C)	58.3° F (14.6° C)
77.0° F (25.0° C)	75.7° F (24.3° C)	72.0° F (22.2° C)	69.3° F (20.7° C)	66.3° F (19.1° C)	63.5° F (17.5° C)
81.5° F (27.5° C)	79.2° F (26.2° C)	76.6° F (24.8° C)	73.9° F (23.3° C)	71.4° F (21.9° C)	68.5° F (20.3° C)
86.0° F (30.0° C)	83.7° F (28.7° C)	81.3° F (27.4° C)	78.8° F (26.0° C)	76.3° F (24.6° C)	73.6° F (23.1° C)
90.5° F (32.5° C)	88.2° F (31.2° C)	85.8° F (29.9° C)	83.5° F (28.6° C)	81.0° F (27.2° C)	78.4° F (25.8° C)
95.0° F (35.0° C)	92.8° F (33.8° C)	90.5° F (32.5° C)	88.2° F (31.2° C)	85.8° F (29.9° C)	83.3° F (28.5° C)
99.5° F (37.5° C)	97.3° F (36.3° C)	95.2° F (35.1° C)	92.8° F (33.8° C)	90.5° F (32.5° C)	88.2° F (31.2° C)
104.0° F (40.0° C)	101.8° F (38.8° C)	99.7° F (37.6° C)	97.5° F (36.4° C)	95.2° F (35.1° C)	93.0° F (33.9° C)

RELATIVE HUMIDITY (%)

Current Temperature	Wet-bulb depression				
	2.0 °F (1 °C)	3.6 °F (2 °C)	5.4 °F (3 °C)	7.2 °F (4 °C)	9.0 °F (5 °C)
14.0° F (–10.0° C)	69%	39%	10%		
18.5° F (–7.5° C)	73%	48%	22%		
23.0° F (–5.0° C)	77%	54%	32%	11%	
27.5° F (–2.5° C)	80%	60%	41%	22%	3%
32.0° F (0.0° C)	82%	65%	47%	31%	15%
36.5° F (2.5° C)	84%	68%	53%	38%	24%
41.0° F (5.0° C)	86%	71%	58%	45%	32%
45.5° F (7.5° C)	87%	74%	62%	50%	38%
50.0° F (10.0° C)	88%	76%	65%	54%	44%
54.5° F (12.5° C)	89%	78%	68%	58%	48%
59.0° F (15.0° C)	90%	80%	70%	61%	52%
63.5° F (17.5° C)	90%	81%	72%	64%	55%
68.0° F (20.0° C)	91%	82%	74%	66%	58%
72.5° F (22.5° C)	92%	83%	76%	68%	61%
77.0° F (25.0° C)	92%	84%	77%	70%	63%
81.5° F (27.5° C)	92%	85%	78%	71%	65%
86.0° F (30.0° C)	93%	86%	79%	73%	67%
90.5° F (32.5° C)	93%	86%	80%	74%	68%
95.0° F (35.0° C)	93%	87%	81%	75%	69%
99.5° F (37.5° C)	94%	87%	82%	76%	70%
104.0° F (40.0° C)	94%	88%	82%	77%	72%

How to find the dew-point temperature
To find the dew-point temperature, check the current temperature and the wet-bulb temperature on a hygrometer. The difference between the two is the wet-bulb depression. Find these numbers in the row containing the current temperature and the column under the wet-bulb depression. For example, if the temperature is 59° F (15° C) and the wet-bulb depression is 3.6° F (2° C), the dew-point temperature is 52.9° F (11.6° C).

How to find the relative humidity
To find the relative humidity, check the current temperature and the wet-bulb depression. The relative humidity is the number in the row for the current temperature and the column under the wet-bulb depression. For example, if the current temperature is 59° F (15° C) and the wet-bulb depression is 3.6° F (2.0° C), then the relative humidity is 80 per cent.

Index

Acknowledgments

MICHAEL ALLABY would like to thank Peter Meredith, Richard Jenkin, and Peter Roddis, teachers at Wadebridge School, Cornwall, UK, and the pupils of Peter Roddis' science class who tested many of the experiments in this book.

DORLING KINDERSLEY would like to thank David Burnie for consultancy; Charlotte Bush and Christine Rista for picture research; Colette Connolly for editorial assistance; Chris Walker for design assistance; the U.K Meteorological Office for the use of the four weather charts on p.183; Patricia Coward for the index; the Hampstead Garden Centre for the outdoor props; Times books, Scientific American, Guinness Publishing, Methuen, Dr M. Matson, and Dr A. Roberts for artwork reference.

PHOTOGRAPHY BY Tim Ridley, Andy Crawford, and Steve Gorton. Photographic assistance from Nick Goodall, Sarah Ashun, and Gary Ombler. Additional photography by Paul Bricknell, Jane Burton, Peter Chadwick, Gordon Clayton, Philip Dowell, Neil Fletcher, Frank Greenaway, Dave King, Roger Philips, Steve Shott, and Bill Ung.

PICTURE CREDITS
The publishers are grateful to the following individuals, companies, and picture libraries for permission to reproduce their photographs: t top; c center; b below; r right; l left; a above

Brian & Cherry Alexander: 29tl.
Associated Press: 83tl.
Bilderdienst Suddeutscher Verlag: 28cr.
Bridgeman Art Library: Museum of Mankind, London 34tr.
Richard Brooks: 111tl.
Bruce Coleman: Thomas Buchholz 166tr; Inigo Everson 163br; Frithfoto 142tr; Carol Hughes 120–121; Charlie Ott 147tr; Dr Eckart Pott 32tr; John Shaw 144tr; Norbert Schwirtz 121r; Uwe Walz GDT 38bl.
Brian Cosgrove: 45tr, 45ctr, 45cbr, 45br, 90t, 90br, 93tcl, 93ccl, 93bcl, 93tcc, 93ccc, 93bcc, 93tcr, 93ccr, 93bcr, 94cl, 94br, 95bc, 96 tr, 97tr, 98tr, 100tc, 101bl, 101bc, 104tr, 106tl, 106bl,106br, 107tr, 107bl, 109br, 111br, 112cl, 113cr, 113bl, 114br, 115tr, 115c, 116br, 117tl.
English Heritage: Peter Dunn 152tr.

Environmental Picture Library: John Arnould 154tr.
Mary Evans Picture Library: 14bl, 33br, 40tr, 51tr, 82tr.
Martyn Foote: 109tl.
Robert Harding Picture Library: 69b, 91bl, 175tr; Nedra Westwater 147tc;
Adam Woolfitt 123tr.
Hulton Deutsch Collection: 58tr.
Hutchison Library: 176tr; Bernard Régert: 171t.
Image Bank: Ian Carmichael 40bl; David W Hamilton 146tc; Nino Mascardi 163bc; Peter M Miller 146tr; Steve Satushek 171br.
Image Select: Ann Ronan Collection 25tr, 156tr.
Frank Lane Picture Agency: Australian Information Service 85br; R Bird 80br; C Carvalho 117cl; D Hoadley 67r; R Jennings 81cr; D Kinzler 81cc, 83tr, 83ctr, 83ccr, 83cbr, 83br; S McCutcheon 60tr; M Nimmo 96–97b, 97cc, 98cc, 98–99b, 108br, 116cl; Silvestris 117cr.
Sandy Lovelock: 162tr.
Mansell Collection: 91cl.
Mountain Camera: John Cleare 24tr.
National Maritime Museum, Greenwich: 69t, 69c, 122cr, 167tr.
National Metereological Office: 72tr, 79tr, 111tr, 114cr; J Atherwech 119tl; S D Burt 100–101t; S Cornford 56tr, 94bl; D Cross 111cr; Crown: 166cc; M Digby 110tl; PT Eerskine 98cl; JFP Galvin 95t; G Giles 116bl; Brian Goddard 65cb; Dr LA Hissott 118tl; CG Holmes 113cl; Richard Howes 110bc; RN Hughes 99tr; R Long 110tr; Jeronimo Lorente 100tl, 111bl; J Newberry 104tr; M Nimmo 103cr; PJB Nye 116cr; Mrs E Oatey 119tr; Ken Pilsbury 5bl, 113tr, 114l; Kevin Richardson 95cl; T Rigg 118bl; RF Saunders 103cl; JR Stapleton 118tr; Julian H Williams 98bl, 100cc; KE Woodley 92tl; JRC Young 118cr, 170tr.
Natural History Photographic Agency: A Bannister 42tr.
Oxford Scientific Films Ltd.: 170bl.
RK Pilsbury: 14t, 44tr, 50tr, 91tr, 91cr, 93bl, 95br, 97tl, 102tr, 102bc, 103br, 104bc, 107br, 109cr, 112bl, 113tl, 114tr, 115br, 117tr, 117bl, 171bl, 171bc.
Planet Earth: Tony Bennett 53tc; Richard Coomber 38cl; J MacKinnon 47tr; Mark Mattock 13r; David A Ponton 48tr.
Popperfoto: AFP/NAEG 158tr.
Science Museum, London: 28tr, 123tl.

Science Photo Library: 14br, 77tr, 86tr, 90bl, 168tr; Edward d'Arms 54tr; Dr Jeremy Burgess 16tr; Tony Craddock 35tr; European Space Agency, coloured by John Wells 165r; Simon Fraser 22tr, 54cr, 112br; Gordon Garradd 105tr; John Mead 88–89, 99tl; Peter Menzel 164–165, 179cr, 179bl; NASA 15b, 68t, 89r, 97br, 105br, 122tr, 153tr; NRSC Ltd 66–67, 74tr; David Parker 167br; Pekka Parviainen 119br; Philippe Plailly 178tr; George Post 119bl; Science Source 31tr. Sporting Pictures: 55bl.
Tony Stone Images: Kim Blaxland 129bc; Paul Chesley 59tr; Tony Craddock 12–13; Jake Evans 63tl; Ralph Wetmore 81b. Zefa: 20tr, 30–31, 46tr.

Every effort has been made to trace the copyright holders, and we apologize in advance for any unintentional omissions. We would be pleased to insert the appropriate acknowledgements in any subsequent edition of this publication.

ILLUSTRATIONS
Mark Franklin: 136–137, 140, 141, 143, 178. Janos Marfy: 15, 17, 18, 23, 33, 41, 46, 58, 64, 68, 72, 74, 76, 78, 79, 80, 84, 123, 124, 126, 127, 130, 131, 133, 134, 135, 147, 150, 153, 159, 183, 184, 186, 187.
Additional illusrations by Eugene Fleury, Anne Winterbotham, John Woodcock, Martin Woodward, and Nicholas Hall.
All models by Peter Griffiths.

MODELS
Bissy Adejare, Wole Adejare, Sarah Ashun, Sabina Awan, Helen Benfield, Catherine Boys Jee, Rebekah Boys Jee, Jack Challoner, Jonathan Chen, Amy Davies, Georgina Davies, Jack Davies, Thomas Davies, Laura Douglas, Jake Emms, Lia Foa, Mia Foa, Nick Goodall, Georgina Grant, Abigail Haward, Arthur Hewlings, Maud Hewlings, Sophie Holbrook, Spencer Holbrook, George Hull, Stephanie Jackson, Sadie Jenkyn, Grace Jones, Ella Kaye, Maddy Kaye, Aedan Lake, Eleanor Lake, Paul Lamb, Amanda Lunn, Essie Marks, Jaejarel Mitchell, Michaela Mitchell, Ben Morris, Jean Morris, Humerah Mughal, Jay Orsborn, Anita Parsons, Elizabeth Parsons, Alastair Raitt, Duncan Raitt, Octavia Raitt, Samantha Schneider, Samuel Schneider, Henrietta Short, Nicholas Turpin, Ailsa Williams, Andy Williams.